P9-DIY-261

THE END OF FAITH

Religion, Terror,

and the Future of Reason

SAM HARRIS

W · W · NORTON & COMPANY

NEW YORK   LONDON

Copyright © 2004 by Sam Harris

All rights reserved
Printed in the United States of America
First Edition

For information about permission to reproduce selections from this book, write to
Permissions, W. W. Norton & Company, Inc., 500 Fifth Avenue, New York, NY 10110

Manufacturing by The Courier Companies, Inc.
Book design by Margaret M. Wagner
Production manager: Amanda Morrison

Library of Congress Cataloging-in-Publication Data

Harris, Sam, date.
The end of faith : religion, terror, and the future of reason / Sam Harris.— 1st ed.
p. cm.
Includes bibliographical references and index.
ISBN 0-393-03515-8 (hardcover)
ISBN 0-393-32765-5 (paperback)
ISBN 978-0-393-32765-6 (paperback)
1. Religion—Controversial literature. 2. Terrorism—Religious aspects.
3. Psychology, Religious. 4. Secular humanism. I. Title.
BL2775.3.H37 2004
200—dc22

2004007874

W. W. Norton & Company, Inc., 500 Fifth Avenue, New York, N.Y. 10110
www.wwnorton.com

W. W. Norton & Company Ltd., Castle House, 75/76 Wells Street, London W1T 3QT

5 6 7 8 9 0

Further Praise for *The End of Faith*

"A radical attack on the most sacred of liberal precepts—the notion of tolerance. . . . [*The End of Faith*] is an eminently sensible rallying cry for a more ruthless secularisation of society."
—Stephanie Merritt, *The Observer*

"Harris's tour de force demonstrates how faith—blind, deaf, dumb, and unreasoned—threatens our very existence. His exposé of faith-based unreason—from the religious fanaticism of Islamic suicide bombers to the secular fanaticism of Noam Chomsky—is a clarion call for reasoned debate in this age of terrorism. *The End of Faith* shows how the perfect tyranny of religious and secular totalitarianism demonizes imperfect democracies such as the United States and Israel. A must read for all rational people."
—Alan Dershowitz, professor of law at Harvard University and author of *America on Trial*

"[Harris] writes with such verve and frequent insight that even skeptical readers will find it hard to put down."
—Daniel Blue, *San Francisco Chronicle*

"At last we have a book that focuses on the common thread that links Islamic terrorism with the irrationality of all religious faith. *The End of Faith* will challenge not only Muslims but Hindus, Jews, and Christians as well."   —Peter Singer, author of
*The President of Good and Evil:
The Ethics of George W. Bush*

"[Harris's] brief accounts of intuition, and of the notion of a 'moral community,' are as good as anything I have read on these topics."
—John Derbyshire, *New York Sun*

"Here is a ringing challenge to all Americans who recognize the danger to American democracy posed by the political alliance of right-wing religion and politics and the failure of the tepid and tentative responses by liberal persons of faith. While one might dispute some of the claims and arguments presented by Harris, the need for a wake-up call to religious liberals is right on the mark."

—Joseph C. Hough Jr., president of
Union Theological Seminary, New York

For my mother

Contents

●

THE END OF FAITH

1

Reason in Exile

●

THE young man boards the bus as it leaves the terminal. He wears an overcoat. Beneath his overcoat, he is wearing a bomb. His pockets are filled with nails, ball bearings, and rat poison.

The bus is crowded and headed for the heart of the city. The young man takes his seat beside a middle-aged couple. He will wait for the bus to reach its next stop. The couple at his side appears to be shopping for a new refrigerator. The woman has decided on a model, but her husband worries that it will be too expensive. He indicates another one in a brochure that lies open on her lap. The next stop comes into view. The bus doors swing. The woman observes that the model her husband has selected will not fit in the space underneath their cabinets. New passengers have taken the last remaining seats and begun gathering in the aisle. The bus is now full. The young man smiles. With the press of a button he destroys himself, the couple at his side, and twenty others on the bus. The nails, ball bearings, and rat poison ensure further casualties on the street and in the surrounding cars. All has gone according to plan.

The young man's parents soon learn of his fate. Although saddened to have lost a son, they feel tremendous pride at his accomplishment. They know that he has gone to heaven and prepared the way for them to follow. He has also sent his victims to hell for eternity. It is a double victory. The neighbors find the event a great cause for celebration and honor the young man's parents by giving them gifts of food and money.

These are the facts. This is all we know for certain about the young man. Is there anything else that we can infer about him on the basis of his behavior? Was he popular in school? Was he rich or was he poor? Was he of low or high intelligence? His actions leave no clue at all. Did he have a college education? Did he have a bright future as a mechanical engineer? His behavior is simply mute on questions of this sort, and hundreds like them.[1] Why is it so easy, then, so trivially easy—you-could-almost-bet-your-life-on-it easy—to guess the young man's religion?[2]

A BELIEF is a lever that, once pulled, moves almost everything else in a person's life. Are you a scientist? A liberal? A racist? These are merely species of belief in action. Your beliefs define your vision of the world; they dictate your behavior; they determine your emotional responses to other human beings. If you doubt this, consider how your experience would suddenly change if you came to believe one of the following propositions:

1. You have only two weeks to live.
2. You've just won a lottery prize of one hundred million dollars.
3. Aliens have implanted a receiver in your skull and are manipulating your thoughts.

These are mere words—until you believe them. Once believed, they become part of the very apparatus of your mind, determining your desires, fears, expectations, and subsequent behavior.

There seems, however, to be a problem with some of our most cherished beliefs about the world: they are leading us, inexorably, to kill one another. A glance at history, or at the pages of any newspaper, reveals that ideas which divide one group of human beings from another, only to unite them in slaughter, generally have their roots in religion. It seems that if our species ever eradicates itself through war, it will not be because it was written in the stars but because it was written in our books; it is what we do with words like "God" and "paradise" and "sin" in the present that will determine our future.

Our situation is this: most of the people in this world believe that the Creator of the universe has written a book. We have the misfortune of having many such books on hand, each making an exclusive claim as to its infallibility. People tend to organize themselves into factions according to which of these incompatible claims they accept—rather than on the basis of language, skin color, location of birth, or any other criterion of tribalism. Each of these texts urges its readers to adopt a variety of beliefs and practices, some of which are benign, many of which are not. All are in perverse agreement on one point of fundamental importance, however: "respect" for other faiths, or for the views of unbelievers, is not an attitude that God endorses. While all faiths have been touched, here and there, by the spirit of ecumenicalism, the central tenet of every religious tradition is that all others are mere repositories of error or, at best, dangerously incomplete. Intolerance is thus intrinsic to every creed. Once a person believes—*really* believes—that certain ideas can lead to eternal happiness, or to its antithesis, he cannot tolerate the possibility that the people he loves might be led astray by the blandishments of unbelievers. Certainty about the next life is simply incompatible with tolerance in this one.

Observations of this sort pose an immediate problem for us, however, because criticizing a person's faith is currently taboo in every corner of our culture. On this subject, liberals and conservatives have reached a rare consensus: religious beliefs are simply beyond the scope of rational discourse. Criticizing a person's ideas about God and the afterlife is thought to be impolitic in a way that criticizing his ideas about physics or history is not. And so it is that when a Muslim suicide bomber obliterates himself along with a score of innocents on a Jerusalem street, the role that faith played in his actions is invariably discounted. His motives must have been political, economic, or entirely personal. Without faith, desperate people would still do terrible things. Faith itself is always, and everywhere, exonerated.

But technology has a way of creating fresh moral imperatives. Our technical advances in the art of war have finally rendered our religious differences—and hence our religious *beliefs*—antithetical to our survival. We can no longer ignore the fact that billions of our neighbors believe in the metaphysics of martyrdom, or in the literal truth of the book of Revelation, or any of the other fantastical notions that have lurked in the minds of the faithful for millennia— because our neighbors are now armed with chemical, biological, and nuclear weapons. There is no doubt that these developments mark the terminal phase of our credulity. Words like "God" and "Allah" must go the way of "Apollo" and "Baal," or they will unmake our world.

A few minutes spent wandering the graveyard of bad ideas suggests that such conceptual revolutions are possible. Consider the case of alchemy: it fascinated human beings for over a thousand years, and yet anyone who seriously claims to be a practicing alchemist today will have disqualified himself for most positions of responsibility in our society. Faith-based religion must suffer the same slide into obsolescence.

What is the alternative to religion as we know it? As it turns out, this is the wrong question to ask. Chemistry was not an "alternative" to alchemy; it was a wholesale exchange of ignorance at its most rococo for genuine knowledge.[3] We will find that, as with alchemy, to speak of "alternatives" to religious faith is to miss the point.

OF COURSE, people of faith fall on a continuum: some draw solace and inspiration from a specific spiritual tradition, and yet remain fully committed to tolerance and diversity, while others would burn the earth to cinders if it would put an end to heresy. There are, in other words, religious *moderates* and religious *extremists,* and their various passions and projects should not be confused. One of the central themes of this book, however, is that religious moderates are themselves the bearers of a terrible dogma: they imagine that the path to peace will be paved once each of us has learned to respect the unjustified beliefs of others. I hope to show that the very ideal of religious tolerance—born of the notion that every human being should be free to believe whatever he wants about God—is one of the principal forces driving us toward the abyss.

We have been slow to recognize the degree to which religious faith perpetuates man's inhumanity to man. This is not surprising, since many of us still believe that faith is an essential component of human life. Two myths now keep faith beyond the fray of rational criticism, and they seem to foster religious extremism and religious moderation equally: (1) most of us believe that there are good things that people get from religious faith (e.g., strong communities, ethical behavior, spiritual experience) that cannot be had elsewhere; (2) many of us also believe that the terrible things that are sometimes done in the name of religion are the products not of *faith* per se but of our baser natures—forces like greed, hatred, and fear—for which religious beliefs are themselves the best (or even the only) remedy. Taken together, these myths seem to have granted us perfect immunity to outbreaks of reasonableness in our public discourse.

Many religious moderates have taken the apparent high road of pluralism, asserting the equal validity of all faiths, but in doing so they neglect to notice the irredeemably sectarian truth claims of each. As long as a Christian believes that only his baptized brethren will be saved on the Day of Judgment, he cannot possibly "respect" the beliefs of others, for he knows that the flames of hell have been stoked by these very ideas and await their adherents even now. Muslims and Jews generally take the same arrogant view of their own enterprises and have spent millennia passionately reiterating the errors of other faiths. It should go without saying that these rival belief systems are all equally uncontaminated by evidence.

And yet, intellectuals as diverse as H. G. Wells, Albert Einstein, Carl Jung, Max Planck, Freeman Dyson, and Stephen Jay Gould have declared the war between reason and faith to be long over. On this view, there is no need to have all of our beliefs about the universe cohere. A person can be a God-fearing Christian on Sunday and a working scientist come Monday morning, without ever having to account for the partition that seems to have erected itself in his head while he slept. He can, as it were, have his reason and eat it too. As the early chapters of this book will illustrate, it is only because the church has been politically hobbled in the West that anyone can afford to think this way. In places where scholars can still be stoned to death for doubting the veracity of the Koran, Gould's notion of a "loving concordat" between faith and reason would be perfectly delusional.[4]

This is not to say that the deepest concerns of the faithful, whether moderate or extreme, are trivial or even misguided. There is no denying that most of us have emotional and spiritual needs that are now addressed—however obliquely and at a terrible price—by mainstream religion. And these are needs that a mere *understanding* of our world, scientific or otherwise, will never fulfill. There is clearly a sacred dimension to our existence, and coming to terms with it could well be the highest purpose of human life. But we will find that it requires no faith in untestable propositions—Jesus was born of a virgin; the Koran is the word of God—for us to do this.

The Myth of "Moderation" in Religion

The idea that any one of our religions represents the infallible word of the One True God requires an encyclopedic ignorance of history, mythology, and art even to be entertained—as the beliefs, rituals, and iconography of each of our religions attest to centuries of cross-pollination among them. Whatever their imagined source, the doctrines of modern religions are no more tenable than those which, for lack of adherents, were cast upon the scrap heap of mythology millennia ago; for there is no more evidence to justify a belief in the literal existence of Yahweh and Satan than there was to keep Zeus perched upon his mountain throne or Poseidon churning the seas.

According to Gallup, 35 percent of Americans believe that the Bible is the literal and inerrant word of the Creator of the universe.[5] Another 48 percent believe that it is the "inspired" word of the same—still inerrant, though certain of its passages must be interpreted symbolically before their truth can be brought to light. Only 17 percent of us remain to doubt that a personal God, in his infinite wisdom, is likely to have authored this text—or, for that matter, to have created the earth with its 250,000 species of beetles. Some 46 percent of Americans take a literalist view of creation (40 percent believe that God has guided creation over the course of millions of years). This means that 120 million of us place the big bang 2,500 years *after* the Babylonians and Sumerians learned to brew beer. If our polls are to be trusted, nearly 230 million Americans believe that a book showing neither unity of style nor internal consistency was authored by an omniscient, omnipotent, and omnipresent deity. A survey of Hindus, Muslims, and Jews around the world would surely yield similar results, revealing that we, as a species, have grown almost perfectly intoxicated by our myths. How is it that, in this one area of our lives, we have convinced ourselves that our beliefs about the world can float entirely free of reason and evidence?

It is with respect to this rather surprising cognitive scenery that we must decide what it means to be a religious "moderate" in the twenty-first century. Moderates in every faith are obliged to loosely interpret (or simply ignore) much of their canons in the interests of living in the modern world. No doubt an obscure truth of economics is at work here: societies appear to become considerably less productive whenever large numbers of people stop making widgets and begin killing their customers and creditors for heresy. The first thing to observe about the moderate's retreat from scriptural literalism is that it draws its inspiration not from scripture but from cultural developments that have rendered many of God's utterances difficult to accept as written. In America, religious moderation is further enforced by the fact that most Christians and Jews do not read the Bible in its entirety and consequently have no idea just how vigorously the God of Abraham wants heresy expunged. One look at the book of Deuteronomy reveals that he has something very specific in mind should your son or daughter return from yoga class advocating the worship of Krishna:

> If your brother, the son of your father or of your mother, or your son or daughter, or the spouse whom you embrace, or your most intimate friend, tries to secretly seduce you, saying, "Let us go and serve other gods," unknown to you or your ancestors before you, gods of the peoples surrounding you, whether near you or far away, anywhere throughout the world, you must not consent, you must not listen to him; you must show him no pity, you must not spare him or conceal his guilt. No, you must kill him, your hand must strike the first blow in putting him to death and the hands of the rest of the people following. You must stone him to death, since he has tried to divert you from Yahweh your God. . . . (Deuteronomy 13:7–11)

While the stoning of children for heresy has fallen out of fashion in our country, you will not hear a moderate Christian or Jew arguing for a "symbolic" reading of passages of this sort. (In fact, one seems to be explicitly blocked by God himself in Deuteronomy 13:1— "Whatever I am now commanding you, you must keep and observe, adding nothing to it, taking nothing away.") The above passage is as canonical as any in the Bible, and it is only by ignoring such barbarisms that the Good Book can be reconciled with life in the modern world. This is a problem for "moderation" in religion: it has nothing underwriting it other than the unacknowledged neglect of the letter of the divine law.

The only reason anyone is "moderate" in matters of faith these days is that he has assimilated some of the fruits of the last two thousand years of human thought (democratic politics,[6] scientific advancement on every front, concern for human rights, an end to cultural and geographic isolation, etc.). The doors leading out of scriptural literalism do not open from the *inside*. The moderation we see among nonfundamentalists is not some sign that faith itself has evolved; it is, rather, the product of the many hammer blows of modernity that have exposed certain tenets of faith to doubt. Not the least among these developments has been the emergence of our tendency to value evidence and to be convinced by a proposition to the degree that there is evidence for it. Even most fundamentalists live by the lights of reason in this regard; it is just that their minds seem to have been partitioned to accommodate the profligate truth claims of their faith. Tell a devout Christian that his wife is cheating on him, or that frozen yogurt can make a man invisible, and he is likely to require as much evidence as anyone else, and to be persuaded only to the extent that you give it. Tell him that the book he keeps by his bed was written by an invisible deity who will punish him with fire for eternity if he fails to accept its every incredible claim about the universe, and he seems to require no evidence whatsoever.

Religious moderation springs from the fact that even the least educated person among us simply *knows* more about certain matters than anyone did two thousand years ago—and much of this knowledge is incompatible with scripture. Having heard something about the medical discoveries of the last hundred years, most of us no longer equate disease processes with sin or demonic possession. Having learned about the known distances between objects in our universe, most of us (about half of us, actually) find the idea that the whole works was created six thousand years ago (with light from distant stars already in transit toward the earth) impossible to take seriously. Such concessions to modernity do not in the least suggest that faith is compatible with reason, or that our religious traditions are in principle open to new learning: it is just that the utility of ignoring (or "reinterpreting") certain articles of faith is now overwhelming. Anyone being flown to a distant city for heart-bypass surgery has conceded, tacitly at least, that we have learned a few things about physics, geography, engineering, and medicine since the time of Moses.

So it is not that these texts have maintained their integrity over time (they haven't); it is just that they have been effectively edited by our neglect of certain of their passages. Most of what remains—the "good parts"—has been spared the same winnowing because we do not yet have a truly modern understanding of our ethical intuitions and our capacity for spiritual experience. If we better understood the workings of the human brain, we would undoubtedly discover lawful connections between our states of consciousness, our modes of conduct, and the various ways we use our attention. What makes one person happier than another? Why is love more conducive to happiness than hate? Why do we generally prefer beauty to ugliness and order to chaos? Why does it feel so good to smile and laugh, and why do these shared experiences generally bring people closer together? Is the ego an illusion, and, if so, what implications does this have for human life? Is there life after death? These are ultimately questions for a mature science of the mind. If we ever develop such a science, most of our religious texts will be no more useful to mystics than they now are to astronomers.

While moderation in religion may seem a reasonable position to stake out, in light of all that we have (and have not) learned about the universe, it offers no bulwark against religious extremism and religious violence. From the perspective of those seeking to live by the letter of the texts, the religious moderate is nothing more than a failed fundamentalist. He is, in all likelihood, going to wind up in hell with the rest of the unbelievers. The problem that religious moderation poses for all of us is that it does not permit anything very critical to be said about religious literalism. We cannot say that fundamentalists are crazy, because they are merely practicing their freedom of belief; we cannot even say that they are mistaken in *religious* terms, because their knowledge of scripture is generally unrivaled. All we can say, as religious moderates, is that we don't like the personal and social costs that a full embrace of scripture imposes on us. This is not a new form of faith, or even a new species of scriptural exegesis; it is simply a capitulation to a variety of all-too-human interests that have nothing, in principle, to do with God. Religious moderation is the product of *secular* knowledge and scriptural *ignorance*—and it has no bona fides, in religious terms, to put it on a par with fundamentalism.[7] The texts themselves are unequivocal: they are perfect in all their parts. By their light, religious moderation appears to be nothing more than an unwillingness to fully submit to God's law. By failing to live by the letter of the texts, while tolerating the irrationality of those who do, religious moderates betray faith and reason equally. Unless the core dogmas of faith are called into question—i.e., that we know there is a God, and that we know what he wants from us—religious moderation will do nothing to lead us out of the wilderness.

The benignity of most religious moderates does not suggest that religious faith is anything more than a desperate marriage of hope and ignorance, nor does it guarantee that there is not a terrible price to be paid for limiting the scope of reason in our dealings with other human beings. Religious moderation, insofar as it represents an attempt to hold on to what is still serviceable in orthodox religion, closes the door to more sophisticated approaches to spirituality, ethics, and the building of strong communities. Religious moderates seem to believe that what we need is not radical insight and innovation in these areas but a mere dilution of Iron Age philosophy. Rather than bring the full force of our creativity and rationality to bear on the problems of ethics, social cohesion, and even spiritual experience, moderates merely ask that we relax our standards of adherence to ancient superstitions and taboos, while otherwise maintaining a belief system that was passed down to us from men and women whose lives were simply ravaged by their basic ignorance about the world. In what other sphere of life is such subservience to tradition acceptable? Medicine? Engineering? Not even politics suffers the anachronism that still dominates our thinking about ethical values and spiritual experience.

Imagine that we could revive a well-educated Christian of the fourteenth century. The man would prove to be a total ignoramus, except on matters of faith. His beliefs about geography, astronomy, and medicine would embarrass even a child, but he would know more or less everything there is to know about God. Though he would be considered a fool to think that the earth is the center of the cosmos, or that trepanning* constitutes a wise medical intervention, his religious ideas would still be beyond reproach. There are two explanations for this: either we perfected our religious understanding of the world a millennium ago—while our knowledge on all other fronts was still hopelessly inchoate—or religion, being the mere maintenance of dogma, is one area of discourse that does not admit of progress. We will see that there is much to recommend the latter view.

With each passing year, do our religious beliefs conserve more and more of the data of human experience? If religion addresses a genuine sphere of understanding and human necessity, then it should be susceptible to *progress*; its doctrines should become more useful, rather than less. Progress in religion, as in other fields, would have to be a matter of *present* inquiry, not the mere reiteration of past doctrine. Whatever is true now should be *discoverable* now, and describable in terms that are not an outright affront to the rest of what we know about the world. By this measure, the entire project of religion seems perfectly backward. It cannot survive the changes that have come over us—culturally, technologically, and even ethically. Otherwise, there are few reasons to believe that we will survive *it*.

Moderates do not want to kill anyone in the name of God, but they want us to keep using the word "God" as though we knew what we were talking about. And they do not want anything too critical said about people who *really* believe in the God of their fathers, because tolerance, perhaps above all else, is sacred. To speak plainly

---

*Trepanning (or trephining) is the practice of boring holes in the human skull. Archaeological evidence suggests that it is one of the oldest surgical procedures. It was presumably performed on epileptics and the mentally ill as an attempt at exorcism. While there are still many reasons to open a person's skull nowadays, the hope that an evil spirit will use the hole as a point of egress is not among them.

and truthfully about the state of our world—to say, for instance, that the Bible and the Koran both contain mountains of life-destroying gibberish—is antithetical to tolerance as moderates currently conceive it. But we can no longer afford the luxury of such political correctness. We must finally recognize the price we are paying to maintain the iconography of our ignorance.

The Shadow of the Past

Finding ourselves in a universe that seems bent upon destroying us, we quickly discover, both as individuals and as societies, that it is a good thing to understand the forces arrayed against us. And so it is that every human being comes to desire genuine knowledge about the world. This has always posed a special problem for religion, because every religion preaches the truth of propositions for which it has no evidence. In fact, every religion preaches the truth of propositions for which no evidence is even *conceivable*. This put the "leap" in Kierkegaard's leap of faith.

What if all our knowledge about the world were suddenly to disappear? Imagine that six billion of us wake up tomorrow morning in a state of utter ignorance and confusion. Our books and computers are still here, but we can't make heads or tails of their contents. We have even forgotten how to drive our cars and brush our teeth. What knowledge would we want to reclaim first? Well, there's that business about growing food and building shelter that we would want to get reacquainted with. We would want to relearn how to use and repair many of our machines. Learning to understand spoken and written language would also be a top priority, given that these skills are necessary for acquiring most others. When in this process of reclaiming our humanity will it be important to know that Jesus was born of a virgin? Or that he was resurrected? And how would we relearn these truths, if they are indeed *true*? By reading the Bible? Our tour of the shelves will deliver similar pearls from antiquity—

like the "fact" that Isis, the goddess of fertility, sports an impressive pair of cow horns. Reading further, we will learn that Thor carries a hammer and that Marduk's sacred animals are horses, dogs, and a dragon with a forked tongue. Whom shall we give top billing in our resurrected world? Yaweh or Shiva? And when will we want to relearn that premarital sex is a sin? Or that adulteresses should be stoned to death? Or that the soul enters the zygote at the moment of conception? And what will we think of those curious people who begin proclaiming that one of our books is distinct from all others in that it was actually written by the Creator of the universe?

There are undoubtedly spiritual truths that we would want to relearn—once we manage to feed and clothe ourselves—and these are truths that we have learned imperfectly in our present state. How is it possible, for instance, to overcome one's fear and inwardness and simply love other human beings? Assume, for the moment, that such a process of personal transformation exists and that there is something worth knowing about it; there is, in other words, some skill, or discipline, or conceptual understanding, or dietary supplement that allows for the reliable transformation of fearful, hateful, or indifferent persons into loving ones. If so, we should be positively desperate to know about it. There may even be a few biblical passages that would be useful in this regard—but as for whole rafts of untestable doctrines, clearly there would be no reasonable basis to take them up again. The Bible and Koran, it seems certain, would find themselves respectfully shelved next to Ovid's *Metamorphoses* and the *Egyptian Book of the Dead*.

The point is that most of what we currently hold sacred is not sacred for any reason other than that it was thought sacred *yesterday*. Surely, if we could create the world anew, the practice of organizing our lives around untestable propositions found in ancient literature—to say nothing of killing and dying for them—would be impossible to justify. What stops us from finding it impossible *now*?

Many have observed that religion, by lending meaning to human life, permits communities (at least those united under a single faith) to cohere. Historically this is true, and on this score religion is to be credited as much for wars of conquest as for feast days and brotherly love. But in its effect upon the *modern* world—a world already united, at least potentially, by economic, environmental, political, and epidemiological necessity—religious ideology is dangerously retrograde. Our past is not sacred for being *past*, and there is much that is behind us that we are struggling to *keep* behind us, and to which, it is to be hoped, we could never return with a clear conscience: the divine right of kings, feudalism, the caste system, slavery, political executions, forced castration, vivisection, bearbaiting, honorable duels, chastity belts, trial by ordeal, child labor, human and animal sacrifice, the stoning of heretics, cannibalism, sodomy laws, taboos against contraception, human radiation experiments—the list is nearly endless, and if it were extended indefinitely, the proportion of abuses for which religion could be found directly responsible is likely to remain undiminished. In fact, almost every indignity just mentioned can be attributed to an insufficient taste for evidence, to an uncritical faith in one dogma or another. The idea, therefore, that religious faith is somehow a *sacred* human convention—distinguished, as it is, both by the extravagance of its claims and by the paucity of its evidence—is really too great a monstrosity to be appreciated in all its glory. Religious faith represents so uncompromising a misuse of the power of our minds that it forms a kind of perverse, cultural singularity—a vanishing point beyond which rational discourse proves impossible. When foisted upon each generation anew, it renders us incapable of realizing just how much of our world has been unnecessarily ceded to a dark and barbarous past.

The Burden of Paradise

Our world is fast succumbing to the activities of men and women who would stake the future of our species on beliefs that should not survive an elementary school education. That so many of us are still dying on account of ancient myths is as bewildering as it is horrible, and our own attachment to these myths, whether moderate or extreme, has kept us silent in the face of developments that could ultimately destroy us. Indeed, religion is as much a living spring of violence today as it was at any time in the past. The recent conflicts in Palestine (Jews v. Muslims), the Balkans (Orthodox Serbians v. Catholic Croatians; Orthodox Serbians v. Bosnian and Albanian Muslims), Northern Ireland (Protestants v. Catholics), Kashmir (Muslims v. Hindus), Sudan (Muslims v. Christians and animists), Nigeria (Muslims v. Christians), Ethiopia and Eritrea (Muslims v. Christians), Sri Lanka (Sinhalese Buddhists v. Tamil Hindus), Indonesia (Muslims v. Timorese Christians), and the Caucasus (Orthodox Russians v. Chechen Muslims; Muslim Azerbaijanis v. Catholic and Orthodox Armenians) are merely a few cases in point. In these places religion has been the *explicit* cause of literally millions of deaths in the last ten years. These events should strike us like psychological experiments run amok, for that is what they are. Give people divergent, irreconcilable, and untestable notions about what happens after death, and then oblige them to live together with limited resources. The result is just what we see: an unending cycle of murder and cease-fire. If history reveals any categorical truth, it is that an insufficient taste for evidence regularly brings out the worst in us. Add weapons of mass destruction to this diabolical clockwork, and you have found a recipe for the fall of civilization.

What can be said of the nuclear brinkmanship between India and Pakistan if their divergent religious beliefs are to be "respected"? There is nothing for religious pluralists to criticize but each country's poor diplomacy—while, in truth, the entire conflict is born of an irrational embrace of myth. Over one million people died in the orgy of religious killing that attended the partitioning of India and Pakistan. The two countries have since fought three official wars, suffered a continuous bloodletting at their shared border, and are now poised to exterminate one another with nuclear weapons simply because they disagree about "facts" that are every bit as fanciful

as the names of Santa's reindeer. And their discourse is such that
they are capable of mustering a suicidal level of enthusiasm for
these subjects *without* evidence. Their conflict is only nominally
about land, because their incompatible claims upon the territory of
Kashmir are a direct consequence of their religious differences.
Indeed, the only reason India and Pakistan are different countries is
that the beliefs of Islam cannot be reconciled with those of Hinduism. From the point of view of Islam, it would be scarcely possible to conceive a way of scandalizing Allah that is not perpetrated,
each morning, by some observant Hindu. The "land" these people
are actually fighting over is not to be found in this world. When will
we realize that the concessions we have made to faith in our political discourse have prevented us from even speaking about, much less
uprooting, the most prolific source of violence in our history?

> Mothers were skewered on swords as their children watched.
> Young women were stripped and raped in broad daylight, then . . .
> set on fire. A pregnant woman's belly was slit open, her fetus
> raised skyward on the tip of sword and then tossed onto one of
> the fires that blazed across the city.[8]

This is not an account of the Middle Ages, nor is it a tale from Middle Earth. This is *our* world. The cause of this behavior was not economic, it was not racial, and it was not political. The above passage
describes the violence that erupted between Hindus and Muslims in
India in the winter of 2002. The only difference between these
groups consists in what they believe about God. Over one thousand
people died in this monthlong series of riots—nearly half as many
as have died in the Israeli-Palestinian conflict in more than a decade.
And these are tiny numbers, considering the possibilities. A nuclear
war between India and Pakistan seems almost inevitable, given what
most Indians and Pakistanis believe about the afterlife. Arundhati
Roy has said that Western concern over this situation is just a matter of white imperialists believing that "blacks cannot be trusted

with the Bomb."[9] This is a grotesque charge. One might argue that no group of people can quite be "trusted" with the bomb, but to ignore the destabilizing role that religion plays on the subcontinent is both reckless and disingenuous. We can only hope that the forces of secularism and rationality will keep the missiles in their silos for a while yet, until the deeper reasons for this conflict can be finally addressed.

While I do not mean to single out the doctrine of Islam for special abuse, there is no question that, at this point in history, it represents a unique danger to all of us, Muslim and non-Muslim alike. Needless to say, many Muslims are basically rational and tolerant of others. As we will see, however, these modern virtues are not likely to be products of their faith. In chapter 4, I will argue that insofar as a person is *observant* of the doctrine of Islam—that is, insofar as he *really* believes it—he will pose a problem for us. Indeed, it has grown rather obvious that the liabilities of the Muslim faith are by no means confined to the beliefs of Muslim "extremists." The response of the Muslim world to the events of September 11, 2001, leaves no doubt that a significant number of human beings in the twenty-first century believe in the possibility of martyrdom. We have, in response to this improbable fact, declared a war on "terrorism." This is rather like declaring war on "murder"; it is a category error that obscures the true cause of our troubles. Terrorism is not a *source* of human violence, but merely one its inflections. If Osama bin Laden were the leader of a nation, and the World Trade Center had been brought down with missiles, the atrocities of September 11 would have been acts of war. It should go without saying that we would have resisted the temptation to declare a war on "war" in response.

To see that our problem is with Islam itself, and not merely with "terrorism," we need only ask ourselves *why* Muslim terrorists do what they do. Why would someone as conspicuously devoid of personal grievances or psychological dysfunction as Osama bin Laden—who is neither poor, uneducated, delusional, nor a prior victim of

Western aggression—devote himself to cave-dwelling machinations with the intention of killing innumerable men, women, and children he has never met? The answer to this question is obvious—if only because it has been patiently articulated ad nauseam by bin Laden himself. The answer is that men like bin Laden *actually* believe what they say they believe. They believe in the literal truth of the Koran. Why did nineteen well-educated, middle-class men trade their lives in this world for the privilege of killing thousands of our neighbors? Because they believed that they would go straight to paradise for doing so. It is rare to find the behavior of human beings so fully and satisfactorily explained. Why have we been reluctant to accept this explanation?

As we have seen, there is something that most Americans share with Osama bin Laden, the nineteen hijackers, and much of the Muslim world. We, too, cherish the idea that certain fantastic propositions can be believed without evidence. Such heroic acts of credulity are thought not only acceptable but redeeming—even *necessary*. This is a problem that is considerably deeper and more troubling than the problem of anthrax in the mail. The concessions we have made to religious faith—to the idea that belief can be sanctified by something other than *evidence*—have rendered us unable to name, much less address, one of the most pervasive causes of conflict in our world.

Muslim Extremism

It is important to specify the dimension in which Muslim "extremists" are actually extreme. They are extreme in their *faith*. They are extreme in their devotion to the literal word of the Koran and the hadith (the literature recounting the sayings and actions of the Prophet), and *this* leads them to be extreme in the degree to which they believe that modernity and secular culture are incompatible with moral and spiritual health. Muslim extremists are certain that the exports of Western culture are leading their wives and children away from God. They also consider our unbelief to be a sin so grave that it merits death whenever it becomes an impediment to the spread of Islam. These sundry passions are not reducible to "hatred" in any ordinary sense. Most Muslim extremists have never been to America or even met an American. And they have far fewer grievances with Western imperialism than is the norm around the globe.[10] Above all, they appear to be suffering from a fear of contamination. As has been widely noted, they are also consumed by feelings of "humiliation"—humiliation over the fact that while their civilization has foundered, they have watched a godless, sin-loving people become the masters of everything they touch. This feeling is also a product of their faith. Muslims do not merely feel the outrage of the poor who are deprived of the necessities of life. They feel the outrage of a chosen people who have been subjugated by barbarians. Osama bin Laden wants for nothing. What, then, does he want? He has not called for the equal distribution of wealth around the globe. Even his demand for Palestinian statehood seems an afterthought, stemming as much from his anti-Semitism as from any solidarity he feels with the Palestinians (needless to say, such anti-Semitism and solidarity are also products of his faith). He seems most exercised over the presence of unbelievers (American troops and Jews) in the Muslim holy land and over what he imagines to be the territorial ambitions of Zionists. These are purely theological grievances. It would be much better, for all concerned, if he merely hated us.

To be sure, hatred is an eminently human emotion, and it is obvious that many Muslim extremists feel it. But faith is still the mother of hatred here, as it is wherever people define their moral identities in religious terms. The only salient difference between Muslims and non-Muslims is that the latter have not proclaimed their faith in Allah, and in Mohammed as his prophet. Islam is a missionary religion: there is not likely to be an underlying doctrine of racism, or even nationalism, animating the militant Muslim world. Muslims can be both racist and nationalistic, of course, but it seems all but certain that if the West underwent a massive conversion to Islam—and, perforce, repudiated all Jewish interests in the Holy Land—the basis for Muslim "hatred" would simply disappear.[11]

Most Muslims who commit atrocities are explicit about their desire to get to paradise. One failed Palestinian suicide bomber described being "pushed" to attack Israelis by "the love of martyrdom." He added, "I didn't want revenge for anything. I just wanted to be a martyr." Mr. Zaydan, the would-be martyr, conceded that his Jewish captors were "better than many, many Arabs." With regard to the suffering that his death would have inflicted upon his family, he reminded his interviewer that a martyr gets to pick seventy people to join him in paradise. He would have been sure to invite his family along.[12]

As I HAVE SAID, people of faith tend to argue that it is not faith itself but man's baser nature that inspires such violence. But I take it to be self-evident that ordinary people cannot be moved to burn genial old scholars alive for blaspheming the Koran,[13] or celebrate the violent deaths of their children, unless they believe some improbable things about the nature of the universe. Because most religions offer no valid mechanism by which their core beliefs can be tested and revised, each new generation of believers is condemned to inherit the superstitions and tribal hatreds of its predecessors. If we would speak of the baseness of our natures, our willingness to live, kill, and die on account of propositions for which we have no evidence should be among the first topics of discussion.

Most people in positions of leadership in our country will say that there is no direct link between the Muslim faith and "terrorism." It is clear, however, that Muslims hate the West in the very terms of their faith and that the Koran mandates such hatred. It is widely claimed by "moderate" Muslims that the Koran mandates nothing of the kind and that Islam is a "religion of peace." But one need only read the Koran itself to see that this is untrue:

Prophet, make war on the unbelievers and the hypocrites and deal rigorously with them. Hell shall be their home: an evil fate. (Koran 9:73)

Believers, make war on the infidels who dwell around you. Deal firmly with them. Know that God is with the righteous. (Koran 9:123)

Religious Muslims cannot help but disdain a culture that, to the degree that it is secular, is a culture of infidels; to the degree that it is religious, our culture is the product of a partial revelation (that of Christians and Jews), inferior in every respect to the revelation of Islam. The reality that the West currently enjoys far more wealth and temporal power than any nation under Islam is viewed by devout Muslims as a diabolical perversity, and this situation will always stand as an open invitation for jihad. Insofar as a person is Muslim—that is, insofar as he believes that Islam constitutes the only viable path to God and that the Koran enunciates it perfectly— he will feel contempt for any man or woman who doubts the truth of his beliefs. What is more, he will feel that the eternal happiness of his children is put in peril by the mere presence of such unbelievers in the world. If such people happen to be making the policies under which he and his children must live, the potential for violence imposed by his beliefs seems unlikely to dissipate. This is why economic advantages and education, in and of themselves, are insufficient remedies for the causes of religious violence. There is no doubt that many well-educated, middle-class fundamentalists are ready to kill and die for God. As Samuel Huntington[14] and others have observed, religious fundamentalism in the developing world is not, principally, a movement of the poor and uneducated.

To see the role that faith plays in propagating Muslim violence, we need only ask why so many Muslims are eager to turn themselves into bombs these days. The answer: because the Koran makes this activity seem like a career opportunity. Nothing in the history of Western colonialism explains this behavior (though we can certainly concede that this history offers us much to atone for). Subtract the Muslim belief in martyrdom and jihad, and the actions of suicide bombers become completely unintelligible, as does the spectacle of public jubilation that invariably follows their deaths; insert these peculiar beliefs, and one can only marvel that suicide bombing is not more widespread. Anyone who says that the doctrines of Islam have "nothing to do with terrorism"—and our airways have been filled with apologists for Islam making this claim—is just playing a game with words.

> The believers who stay at home—apart from those that suffer from a grave impediment—are not the equal of those who fight for the cause of God with their goods and their persons. God has given those that fight with their goods and their persons a higher rank than those who stay at home. God has promised all a good reward; but far richer is the recompense of those who fight for Him. . . . He that leaves his dwelling to fight for God and His apostle and is then overtaken by death, shall be rewarded by God. . . . The unbelievers are your inveterate enemies. (Koran 4:95–101)

Outright prestidigitation with the articles of faith regularly produces utterances of this sort: "Islam is a religion of peace. The very word 'Islam,' after all, means 'peace.' And suicide is forbidden in the Koran. So there is no scriptural basis whatsoever for the actions of these terrorists." To such magician's patter, we might add that the phrase "dirty bomb" does not appear anywhere in the text of the Koran. Yes, the Koran seems to say something that can be construed as a prohibition against suicide—"Do not destroy yourselves" (4:29)—but it leaves many loopholes large enough to fly a 767 through:

> Let those who would exchange the life of this world for the hereafter, fight for the cause of God; whoever fights for the cause of

God, whether he dies or triumphs, We shall richly reward him. . . . The true believers fight for the cause of God, but the infidels fight for the devil. Fight then against the friends of Satan. . . . Say: "Trifling are the pleasures of this life. The hereafter is better for those who would keep from evil. . . ." (Koran 4:74–78)

When the above invitations to martyrdom are considered in light of the fact that Islam does not distinguish between religious and civil authority,[15] the twin terrors of Koranic literalism spring into view: on the level of the state, a Muslim aspiration for world domination is explicitly enjoined by God; on the level of the individual, the metaphysics of martyrdom provides a rationale for ultimate self-sacrifice toward this end. As Bernard Lewis observes, since the time of the Prophet, Islam has been "associated in the minds and memories of Muslims with the exercise of political and military power."[16] The metaphysics of Islam are particularly inauspicious where tolerance and religious diversity are concerned, for martyrdom is the only way that a Muslim can bypass the painful litigation that awaits us all on the Day of Judgment and proceed directly to paradise. Rather than spend centuries moldering in the earth in anticipation of being resurrected and subsequently interrogated by wrathful angels, the martyr is immediately transported to Allah's Garden, where a flock of "dark-eyed" virgins awaits him.

Because they are believed to be nothing less than verbatim transcripts of God's utterances, texts like the Koran and the Bible must be appreciated, and criticized, for any *possible* interpretations to which they are susceptible—and to which they will be subjected, with varying emphases and elisions, throughout the religious world. The problem is not that some Muslims neglect to notice the few references to nonaggression that can be found in the Koran, and that this leads them to do terrible things to innocent unbelievers; the problem is that most Muslims believe that the Koran is the *literal word of God*. The corrective to the worldview of Osama bin Laden is not to point out the single line in the Koran that condemns suicide, because this ambiguous statement is set in a thicket of other passages that can be read only as direct summons to war against the "friends of Satan." The appropriate response to the bin Ladens of the world is to correct everyone's reading of these texts by making the same evidentiary demands in religious matters that we make in all others. If we cannot find our way to a time when most of us are willing to admit that, at the very least, *we are not sure* whether or not God wrote some of our books, then we need only count the days to Armageddon—because God has given us far many more reasons to kill one another than to turn the other cheek.

We live in an age in which most people believe that mere words— "Jesus," "Allah," "Ram"—can mean the difference between eternal torment and bliss everlasting. Considering the stakes here, it is not surprising that many of us occasionally find it necessary to murder other human beings for using the wrong magic words, or the right ones for the wrong reasons. How can any person presume to know that this is the way the universe works? Because it says so in our holy books. How do we know that our holy books are free from error? Because the books *themselves* say so. Epistemological black holes of this sort are fast draining the light from our world.

There is, of course, much that is wise and consoling and beautiful in our religious books. But words of wisdom and consolation and beauty abound in the pages of Shakespeare, Virgil, and Homer as well, and no one ever murdered strangers by the thousands because of the inspiration he found there. The belief that certain books were written by God (who, for reasons difficult to fathom, made Shakespeare a far better writer than himself) leaves us powerless to address the most potent source of human conflict, past and present.[17] How is it that the absurdity of this idea does not bring us, hourly, to our knees? It is safe to say that few of us would have thought so many people could believe such a thing, if they did not *actually* believe it. Imagine a world in which generations of human beings come to believe that certain *films* were made by God or that specific software was coded by him. Imagine a future in which millions of our descendants murder each other over rival interpretations of *Star Wars* or Windows 98. Could anything—*anything*—be more ridiculous? And yet, this would be no more ridiculous than the world we are living in.

Death: The Fount of Illusions

We live in a world where all things, good and bad, are finally destroyed by change. The world sustains us, it would seem, only to devour us at its leisure. Parents lose their children and children their parents. Husbands and wives are separated in an instant, never to meet again. Friends part company in haste, without knowing that it will be for the last time. This life, when surveyed with a broad glance, presents little more than a vast spectacle of loss.

But it seems that there is a cure for all this. If we live rightly—not necessarily ethically, but within the framework of certain ancient beliefs and stereotyped behaviors—we will get everything we want *after* we die. When our bodies finally fail us, we just shed our corporeal ballast and travel to a land where we are reunited with everyone we loved while alive. Of course, overly rational people and other rabble will be kept out of this happy place, and those who suspended their disbelief while alive will be free to enjoy themselves for all eternity.

We live in a world of unimaginable surprises—from the fusion energy that lights the sun to the genetic and evolutionary consequences of this light's dancing for eons upon the earth—and yet paradise conforms to our most superficial concerns with all the fidelity of a Caribbean cruise. This is wondrously strange. If one didn't know better, one would think that man, in his fear of losing all that he loves, had created heaven, along with its gatekeeper God, in his own image.

IMAGINE that you have gone to your doctor for a routine checkup, and he gives you terrible news: you have contracted a virus that kills

100 percent of those it infects. The virus mutates so often that its course is totally unpredictable. It can lie dormant for many years, even decades, or it can kill you outright in an hour. It can lead to heart attack, stroke, myriad forms of cancer, dementia, even suicide; in fact, there seems to be no constraints upon what its terminal stages might be. As for strategies of avoidance—diet and health regimes, sequestration to one's bed—nothing avails. You can be certain that even if you live with no other purpose than to keep the progress of this virus in check, you will die, for there is no cure for it in sight, and the corruption of your body has already begun.

Surely, most people would consider this report to be terrible news indeed—but would it be *news*, in fact? Isn't the inevitability of death just such a prognosis? Doesn't life itself have all the properties of our hypothetical virus?

You could die at any moment. You might not even live to see the end of this paragraph. Not only that, you will *definitely* die at some moment in the future. If being prepared for death entails knowing when and where it will happen, the odds are you will not be prepared. Not only are you bound to die and leave this world; you are bound to leave it in such a precipitate fashion that the present significance of anything—your relationships, your plans for the future, your hobbies, your possessions—will appear to have been totally illusory. While all such things, when projected across an indefinite future, seem to be acquisitions of a kind, death proves that they are nothing of the sort. When the stopper on this life is pulled by an unseen hand, there will have been, in the final reckoning, no acquisition of anything at all.

And as if this were not insult enough, most of us suffer the quiet discomposure, if not frank unhappiness, of our neuroses in the meantime. We love our family and friends, are terrified of losing them, and yet are not in the least free *merely* to love them while our short lives coincide. We have, after all, our *selves* to worry about. As Freud and his descendants never tired of pointing out, each of us is dragged and sundered by diametrical urges: to merge with the world

and disappear, or to retreat within the citadel of our apparent separateness. Either impulse, taken to its extreme, seems to condemn us
to unhappiness. We are terrified of our creaturely insignificance, and
much of what we do with our lives is a rather transparent attempt to
keep this fear at bay. While we try not to think about it, nearly the
only thing we can be certain of in this life is that we will one day die
and leave everything behind; and yet, paradoxically, it seems almost
impossible to believe that this is so. Our felt sense of what is real
seems not to include our own death. We doubt the one thing that is
not open to any doubt at all.

What one believes happens after death dictates much of what one
believes about life, and this is why faith-based religion, in presuming to fill in the blanks in our knowledge of the hereafter, does such
heavy lifting for those who fall under its power. A single proposition—*you will not die*—once believed, determines a response to life
that would be otherwise unthinkable.

Imagine how you would feel if your only child suddenly died of
pneumonia. Your reaction to this tragedy will be largely determined
by what you think happens to human beings after they die. It would
undoubtedly be comforting to believe something like: "He was
God's little angel, and God took him back early because he wanted
him close to Jesus. He'll be waiting for us when we get to heaven."
If your beliefs are those of a Christian Scientist, obliging you to
forgo all medical interventions, you may even have collaborated
with God by refusing to give your child antibiotics.

Or consider how you would feel if you learned that a nuclear war
had erupted between Israel and its neighbors over the ownership of
the Temple Mount. If you were a millennium-minded Christian,
you would undoubtedly view this as a sign of Christ's imminent
return to earth. This would be nothing if not good news, no matter
what the death toll. There's no denying that a person's conception of
the afterlife has direct consequences for his view of the world.

Of course, religious moderation consists in not being too sure
about what happens after death. This is a reasonable attitude, given

the paucity of evidence on the subject. But religious moderation still represents a failure to criticize the unreasonable (and dangerous) certainty of others. As a consequence of our silence on these matters, we live in a country in which a person cannot get elected president if he openly doubts the existence of heaven and hell. This is truly remarkable, given that there is no other body of "knowledge" that we require our political leaders to master. Even a hairstylist must pass a licensing exam before plying his trade in the United States, and yet those given the power to make war and national policy—those whose decisions will inevitably affect human life for generations—are not expected to know anything in particular before setting to work. They do not have to be political scientists, economists, or even lawyers; they need not have studied international relations, military history, resource management, civil engineering, or any other field of knowledge that might be brought to bear in the governance of a modern superpower; they need only be expert fund-raisers, comport themselves well on television, and be indulgent of certain *myths*. In our next presidential election, an actor who reads his Bible would almost certainly defeat a rocket scientist who does not. Could there be any clearer indication that we are allowing unreason and otherworldliness to govern our affairs?

Without death, the influence of faith-based religion would be unthinkable. Clearly, the fact of death is intolerable to us, and faith is little more than the shadow cast by our hope for a better life beyond the grave.

The World beyond Reason

As we will see in the last chapter of this book, there is little doubt that a certain range of human experience can be appropriately described as "spiritual" or "mystical"—experiences of meaningfulness, selflessness, and heightened emotion that surpass our narrow identities as "selves" and escape our current understanding of the mind and brain. But nothing about these experiences justifies arrogant and exclusionary claims about the unique sanctity of any text. There is no reason that our ability to sustain ourselves emotionally and spiritually cannot evolve with technology, politics, and the rest of culture. Indeed, it *must* evolve, if we are to have any future at all.

The basis of our spirituality surely consists in this: the range of possible human experience far exceeds the ordinary limits of our subjectivity. Clearly, some experiences can utterly transform a person's vision of the world. Every spiritual tradition rests on the insight that how we use our attention, from moment to moment, largely determines the quality of our lives. Many of the results of spiritual practice are genuinely desirable, and we owe it to ourselves to seek them out. It is important to note that these changes are not merely emotional but cognitive and conceptual as well. Just as it is possible for us to have insights in fields like mathematics or biology, it is possible for us to have insights about the very nature of our own subjectivity. A variety of techniques, ranging from the practice of meditation to the use of psychedelic drugs, attest to the scope and plasticity of human experience. For millennia, contemplatives have known that ordinary people can divest themselves of the feeling that they call "I" and thereby relinquish the sense that they are separate from the rest of the universe. This phenomenon, which has been reported by practitioners in many spiritual traditions, is supported by a wealth of evidence—neuroscientific, philosophical, and introspective. Such experiences are "spiritual" or "mystical," for want of better words, in that they are relatively rare (unnecessarily so), significant (in that they uncover genuine facts about the world), and personally transformative. They also reveal a far deeper connection between ourselves and the rest of the universe than is suggested by the ordinary confines of our subjectivity. There is no doubt that experiences of this sort are worth seeking, just as there is no doubt that the popular religious ideas that have grown up around them, especially in the West, are as dangerous as they are incredible. A truly rational approach to this dimension of our lives would allow us to explore the heights of our subjectivity with an open mind, while shedding the provincialism and dogmatism of our religious traditions in favor of free and rigorous inquiry.

There also seems to be a body of data attesting to the reality of psychic phenomena, much of which has been ignored by mainstream science.[18] The dictum that "extraordinary claims require extraordinary evidence" remains a reasonable guide in these areas, but this does not mean that the universe isn't far stranger than many of us suppose. It is important to realize that a healthy, scientific skepticism is compatible with a fundamental openness of mind.

The claims of mystics are neurologically quite astute. No human being has ever experienced an objective world, or even a *world* at all. You are, at this moment, having a visionary experience. The world that you see and hear is nothing more than a modification of your consciousness, the physical status of which remains a mystery. Your nervous system sections the undifferentiated buzz of the universe into separate channels of sight, sound, smell, taste, and touch, as well as other senses of lesser renown—proprioception, kinesthesia, enteroreception, and even echolocation.[19] The sights and sounds and pulsings that you experience at this moment are like different spectra of light thrown forth by the prism of the brain. We really are such stuff as dreams are made of. Our waking and dreaming brains are engaged in substantially the same activity; it is just that while dreaming, our brains are far less constrained by sensory information or by the fact-checkers who appear to live somewhere in our frontal lobes. This is not to say that sensory experience offers us no indication of reality at large; it is merely that, as a matter of experience, nothing arises in consciousness that has not first been structured, edited, or amplified by the nervous system. While this gives rise to a few philosophical problems concerning the foundations of our knowledge, it also offers us a remarkable opportunity to deliberately transform the character of our experience.

For every neuron that receives its input from the outside world, there are ten to a hundred others that do not. The brain is therefore talking mostly to itself, and no information from the world (with the exception of olfaction) runs directly from a sensory receptor to the cortex, where the contents of consciousness appear to be sequestered. There are always one or two breaks in the circuit— *synapses*—giving the neurons in question the opportunity to integrate feedback information, or information from other regions of the brain. This sort of integration/contamination of signal explains how certain drugs, emotional states, or even conceptual insights can radically alter the character of our experience. Your brain is tuned to deliver the vision of the world that you are having at this moment. At the heart of most spiritual traditions lurks the entirely valid claim that it can be tuned differently.

It is also true, however, that people occasionally have experiences that are rightly characterized as psychotic. As it turns out, there are many ways to deconstruct a self, to extract (apparent) meaningfulness from the deliverances of one's senses, and to believe that one knows how the world is. Not all visionary experiences are created equal, to say nothing of the worldviews derived from them. As in all things, some differences here make all the difference; these differences, moreover, can be rationally discussed.

As we will see, there is an intimate connection between spirituality, ethics, and positive emotions. Although a scientific approach to these subjects is still struggling to be born, it is probably no more mysterious that most of us prefer love to fear, or regard cruelty as wrong, than that we agree in our judgments about the relative size of objects or about the gender of faces. At the level of the brain, the laws that underwrite human happiness are unlikely to vary widely from person to person. In the later chapters of this book, we will see that much can be made of this fact, long before the scientific details ever become available to us.

ONCE we have examined the problems inherent to faith, and the threat that even "moderate" religious faith, however inadvertently, now poses to our survival, we can begin to situate our ethical intuitions and our capacity for spiritual experience within the context of a rational worldview. This will require that we marshal insights from our growing understanding of the human brain, our genetic continuity with the rest of life, and the history of our religious ideas. In the chapters that follow, I will try to reconcile the bewildering juxtaposition of two facts: (1) our religious traditions attest to a range of spiritual experiences that are real and significant and entirely worthy of our investigation, both personally and scientifically; (2) many of the beliefs that have grown up around these experiences now threaten to destroy us.

We cannot live by reason alone. This is why no quantity of reason, applied as antiseptic, can compete with the balm of faith, once the terrors of this world begin to intrude upon our lives.[20] Your child has died, or your wife has acquired a horrible illness that no doctor can cure, or your own body has suddenly begun striding toward the grave—and reason, no matter how broad its compass, will begin to smell distinctly of formaldehyde. This has led many of us to conclude, wrongly, that human beings have needs that only faith in certain fantastical ideas can fulfill. It is nowhere written, however, that human beings must be irrational, or live in a perpetual state of siege, to enjoy an abiding sense of the sacred. On the contrary, I hope to show that spirituality can be—indeed, *must* be—deeply rational, even as it elucidates the limits of reason. Seeing this, we can begin to divest ourselves of many of the reasons we currently have to kill one another.

Science will not remain mute on spiritual and ethical questions for long. Even now, we can see the first stirrings among psychologists and neuroscientists of what may one day become a genuinely rational approach to these matters—one that will bring even the most rarefied mystical experience within the purview of open, scientific inquiry. It is time we realized that we need not be unreasonable to suffuse our lives with love, compassion, ecstasy, and awe; nor must we renounce all forms of spirituality or mysticism to be on good terms with reason.

In the chapters that follow, I will attempt to make both the conceptual and the experiential bases for these claims explicit.

Coming to Terms with Belief

It is time we recognized that belief is not a private matter; it has never been merely private. In fact, beliefs are scarcely more private than actions are, for every belief is a fount of action *in potentia*. The belief that it will rain puts an umbrella in the hand of every man or woman who owns one. It should be easy enough to see that belief in the full efficacy of prayer, for instance, becomes an emphatically *public* concern the moment it is actually put into practice: the moment a surgeon lays aside his worldly instruments and attempts to suture his patients with prayer, or a pilot tries to land a passenger jet with nothing but repetitions of the word "Hallelujah" applied to the controls, we are swiftly delivered from the provinces of private faith to those of a criminal court.

As a man believes, so he will act. Believe that you are the member of a chosen people, awash in the salacious exports of an evil culture that is turning your children away from God, believe that you will be rewarded with an eternity of unimaginable delights by dealing death to these infidels—and flying a plane into a building is scarcely more than a matter of being asked to do it. It follows, then, that certain beliefs are *intrinsically* dangerous. We all know that human beings are capable of incredible brutality, but we would do well to ask, What sort of ideology will make us *most* capable of it? And how can we place these beliefs beyond the fray of normal discourse, so that they might endure for thousands of years, unperturbed by the course of history or the conquests of reason? These are problems of both cultural and psychological engineering. It has long been obvious that the dogma of faith—particularly in a scheme in which the faithful are promised eternal salvation and doubters are damned—is nothing less than their perfect solution.

It is time we admitted, from kings and presidents on down, that there is no evidence that any of our books was authored by the Creator of the universe. The Bible, it seems certain, was the work of sand-strewn men and women who thought the earth was flat and for whom a wheelbarrow would have been a breathtaking example of emerging technology. To rely on such a document as the basis for our worldview—however heroic the efforts of redactors—is to repudiate two thousand years of civilizing insights that the human mind has only just begun to inscribe upon itself through secular politics and scientific culture. We will see that the greatest problem confronting civilization is not merely religious extremism: rather, it is the larger set of cultural and intellectual accommodations we have made to faith itself. Religious moderates are, in large part, responsible for the religious conflict in our world, because their beliefs provide the context in which scriptural literalism and religious violence can never be adequately opposed.

EVERY sphere of genuine discourse must, at a minimum, admit of *discourse*—and hence the possibility that those standing on its fringe can come to understand the truths that it strives to articulate. This is why any sustained exercise of reason must necessarily transcend national, religious, and ethnic boundaries. There is, after all, no such thing as an inherently American (or Christian, or Caucasian) *physics*.[21] Even spirituality and ethics meet this criterion of universality because human beings, whatever their background, seem to converge on similar spiritual experiences and ethical insights when given the same methods of inquiry. Such is not the case with the "truths" of religion, however. Nothing that a Christian and a Muslim can say to each other will render their beliefs mutually vulnerable to discourse, because the very tenets of their faith have immunized them against the power of conversation. Believing strongly, without evidence, they have kicked themselves loose of the world. It is therefore in the very nature of faith to serve as an impediment to further inquiry. And yet, the fact that we are no longer killing people for heresy in the West suggests that bad ideas, however sacred, cannot survive the company of good ones forever.

Given the link between belief and action, it is clear that we can no more tolerate a diversity of religious beliefs than a diversity of beliefs about epidemiology and basic hygiene. There are still a number of cultures in which the germ theory of disease has yet to put in an appearance, where people suffer from a debilitating ignorance on most matters relevant to their physical health. Do we "tolerate" these beliefs? Not if they put our own health in jeopardy.[22]

Even apparently innocuous beliefs, when unjustified, can lead to intolerable consequences. Many Muslims, for instance, are convinced that God takes an active interest in women's clothing. While it may seem harmless enough, the amount of suffering that this incredible idea has caused is astonishing. The rioting in Nigeria over the 2002 Miss World Pageant claimed over two hundred lives; innocent men and women were butchered with machetes or burned alive simply to keep that troubled place free of women in bikinis. Earlier in the year, the religious police in Mecca prevented paramedics and firefighters from rescuing scores of teenage girls trapped in a burning building.[23] Why? Because the girls were not wearing the traditional head covering that Koranic law requires. Fourteen girls died in the fire; fifty were injured. Should Muslims really be free to believe that the Creator of the universe is concerned about hemlines?

Gathering Our Wits

Recent events have done more than expose our vulnerability to the militant discontents of the world: they have uncovered a dark current of unreason in our national discourse. To see how much our culture currently partakes of the irrationality of our enemies, just substitute the name of your favorite Olympian for "God" wherever this word appears in public discourse. Imagine President Bush addressing the National Prayer Breakfast in these terms: "Behind all of life and all history there is a dedication and a purpose, set by the hand of a just and faithful *Zeus*." Imagine his speech to Congress (September 20, 2001) containing the sentence "Freedom and fear, justice and cruelty have always been at war, and we know that *Apollo* is not neutral between them." Clearly, the commonplaces of language conceal the vacuity and strangeness of many of our beliefs. Our president regularly speaks in phrases appropriate to the fourteenth century, and no one seems inclined to find out what words like "God" and "crusade" and "wonder-working power" mean to him. Not only do we still eat the offal of the ancient world; we are positively smug about it. Garry Wills has noted that the Bush White House "is currently honeycombed with prayer groups and Bible study cells, like a whited monastery."[24] This should trouble us as much as it troubles the fanatics of the Muslim world. We should be humbled, perhaps to the point of spontaneous genuflection, by the knowledge that the ancient Greeks began to lay their Olympian myths to rest several hundred years before the birth of Christ, whereas we have the likes of Bill Moyers convening earnest gatherings of scholars for the high purpose of determining just how the book of Genesis can be reconciled with life in the modern world. As we stride boldly into the Middle Ages, it does not seem out of place to wonder whether the myths that now saturate our discourse will wind up killing many of us, as the myths of others already have.

Two hundred years from now, when we are a thriving global civilization beginning to colonize space, *something* about us will have changed: it must have; otherwise, we would have killed ourselves ten times over before this day ever dawned. We are fast approaching a time when the manufacture of weapons of mass destruction will be a trivial undertaking; the requisite information and technology are now seeping into every corner of our world. As the physicist Martin Rees points out, "We are entering an era where a single person can, by one clandestine act, cause millions of deaths or render a city uninhabitable for years. . . ."[25] Given the power of our technology, we can see at a glance that aspiring martyrs will not make good neighbors in the future. We have simply lost the right to our myths, and to our mythic identities.

It is time we recognized that the only thing that permits human beings to collaborate with one another in a truly open-ended way is their willingness to have their beliefs modified by new facts. Only openness to evidence and argument will secure a common world for us. Nothing guarantees that reasonable people will agree about everything, of course, but the unreasonable are certain to be divided by their dogmas. This spirit of mutual inquiry is the very antithesis of religious faith.

While we may never achieve closure in our view of the world, it seems extraordinarily likely that our descendants will look upon many of our beliefs as both impossibly quaint and suicidally stupid. Our primary task in our discourse with one another should be to identify those beliefs that seem least likely to survive another thousand years of human inquiry, or most likely to prevent it, and subject them to sustained criticism. Which of our present practices will appear most ridiculous from the point of view of those future generations that might yet survive the folly of the present? It is hard to imagine that our religious preoccupations will not top the list.[26] It is natural to hope that our descendants will look upon us with gratitude. But we should also hope that they look upon us with pity and disgust, just as we view the slaveholders of our all-too-recent past. Rather than congratulate ourselves for the state of our civilization, we should consider how, in the fullness of time, we will seem hopelessly backward, and work to lay a foundation for such refinements in the present. We must find our way to a time when faith, without evidence, disgraces anyone who would claim it. Given the present state of our world, there appears to be no other future worth wanting.

It is imperative that we begin speaking plainly about the absurdity of most of our religious beliefs. I fear, however, that the time has not yet arrived. In this sense, what follows is written very much in the spirit of a prayer. I pray that we may one day think clearly enough about these matters to render our children incapable of killing themselves over their books. If not our children, then I suspect it could well be too late for us, because while it has never been difficult to meet your maker, in fifty years it will simply be too easy to drag everyone else along to meet him with you.[27]

2

The Nature of Belief

IT IS OFTEN argued that religious beliefs are somehow distinct from other claims to knowledge about the world. There is no doubt that we *treat* them differently—particularly in the degree to which we demand, in ordinary discourse, that people justify their beliefs—but this does not indicate that religious beliefs are special in any important sense. What do we mean when we say that a person *believes* a given proposition about the world? As with all questions about familiar mental events, we must be careful that the familiarity of our terms does not lead us astray. The fact that we have one word for "belief" does not guarantee that believing is itself a unitary phenomenon. An analogy can be drawn to the case of memory: while people commonly refer to their failures of "memory," decades of experiment have shown that human memory comes in many forms. Not only are our *long-term* and *short-term* memories the products of distinct and dissimilar neural circuits; they have themselves been divided into multiple subsystems.[1] To speak simply of "memory," therefore, is now rather like speaking of "experience." Clearly, we must be more precise about what our mental terms mean before we attempt to understand them at the level of the brain.[2]

Even dogs and cats, insofar as they form associations between people, places, and events, can be said to "believe" many things about the world. But this is not the sort of believing we are after. When we talk about the beliefs to which people consciously subscribe—"The house is infested with termites," "Tofu is not a dessert," "Muhammad ascended to heaven on a winged horse"—we are talking about beliefs that are communicated, and acquired, linguistically. Believing a given proposition is a matter of believing that it faithfully represents some state of the world, and this fact yields some immediate insights into the standards by which our beliefs should function.[3] In particular, it reveals why we cannot help but value evidence and demand that propositions about the world logically cohere. These constraints apply equally to matters of religion. "Freedom of belief" (in anything but the legal sense) is a myth. We will see that we are no more free to believe whatever we want about God than we are free to adopt unjustified beliefs about science or history, or free to *mean* whatever we want when using words like "poison" or "north" or "zero." Anyone who would lay claim to such entitlements should not be surprised when the rest of us stop listening to him.

Beliefs as Principles of Action

The human brain is a prolific generator of beliefs about the world. In fact, the very *humanness* of any brain consists largely in its capacity to evaluate new statements of propositional truth in light of innumerable others that it already accepts. By recourse to intuitions of truth and falsity, logical necessity and contradiction, human beings are able to knit together private visions of the world that largely cohere. What neural events underlie this process? What must a brain do in order to believe that a given statement is *true* or *false*? We currently have no idea. Language processing must play a large role, of course, but the challenge will be to discover how the brain brings the products of perception, memory, and reasoning to bear on individual propositions and magically transforms them into the very substance of our living.

It was probably the capacity for movement, enjoyed by certain primitive organisms, that drove the evolution of our sensory and cognitive faculties. This follows from the fact that if no creature could *do* anything with the information it acquired from the world, nature could not have selected for improvements in the physical structures that gather, store, and process such information. Even a sense as primitive as vision, therefore, seems predicated on the existence of a motor system. If you cannot catch food, avoid becoming food yourself, or wander off a cliff, there does not seem to be much reason to see the world in the first place—and certainly refinements in vision, of the sort found everywhere in the animal kingdom, would never have come about at all.

For this reason, it seems uncontroversial to say that all higher-order cognitive states (of which beliefs are an example) are in some way an outgrowth of our capacity for action. In adaptive terms, belief has been extraordinarily useful. It is, after all, by *believing* various propositions about the world that we predict events and consider the likely consequences of our actions. Beliefs are *principles of action*: whatever they may be at the level of the brain, they are processes by which our understanding (and *mis*understanding) of the world is represented and made available to guide our behavior.[4]

THE power that belief has over our emotional lives appears to be total. For every emotion that you are capable of feeling, there is surely a belief that could invoke it in a matter of moments. Consider the following proposition:

Your daughter is being slowly tortured in an English jail.

What is it that stands between you and the absolute panic that such a proposition would loose in the mind and body of a person who believed it? Perhaps you do not have a daughter, or you know her to be safely at home, or you believe that English jailors are renowned for their congeniality. Whatever the reason, the door to belief has not yet swung upon its hinges.

The link between belief and behavior raises the stakes considerably. Some propositions are so dangerous that it may even be ethical to kill people for believing them. This may seem an extraordinary claim, but it merely enunciates an ordinary fact about the world in which we live. Certain beliefs place their adherents beyond the reach of every peaceful means of persuasion, while inspiring them to commit acts of extraordinary violence against others. There is, in fact, no talking to some people. If they cannot be captured, and they often cannot, otherwise tolerant people may be justified in killing them in self-defense. This is what the United States attempted in Afghanistan, and it is what we and other Western powers are bound to attempt, at an even greater cost to ourselves and to innocents abroad, elsewhere in the Muslim world. We will continue to spill blood in what is, at bottom, a war of ideas.[5]

The Necessity for Logical Coherence

The first thing to notice about beliefs is that they must suffer the company of their neighbors. Beliefs are both logically and semantically related. Each constrains, and is in turn constrained by, many others. A belief like *the Boeing 747 is the world's best airplane* logically entails many other beliefs that are both more basic (e.g., *airplanes exist*) and more derivative (e.g., *747s are better than 757s*). The belief that *some men are husbands* demands that the proposition *some women are wives* also be endorsed, because the very terms "husband" and "wife" mutually define one another.[6] In fact, logical and semantic constraints appear to be two sides of the same coin, because our need to understand what words mean in each new context requires that our beliefs be free from contradiction (at least locally). If I am to mean the same thing by the word "mother" from one instance to the next, I cannot both believe *my mother was born in Rome* and believe *my mother was born in Nevada*. Even if my mother were born on an airplane flying at supersonic speeds, these propositions cannot both be true. There are tricks to be played here—perhaps there is a town called "Rome" somewhere in the state of Nevada; or perhaps "mother" means "biological mother" in one sentence and "adoptive mother" in another—but these are not truly exceptions to the rule. To know what a given belief is *about*, I must know what my words mean; to know what my words mean, my beliefs must be generally consistent.[7] There is just no escaping the fact that there is a tight relationship between the words we use, the type of thoughts we can think, and what we can believe to be true about the world.

And behavioral constraints are just as pressing. When going to a friend's home for dinner, I cannot both believe that he lives *north of Main Street* and *south of Main Street* and then act on the basis of what I believe. A normal degree of psychological and bodily integration precludes my being motivated to head in two opposing directions at once.

Personal identity itself requires such consistency: unless a person's beliefs are highly coherent, he will have as many identities as there are mutually incompatible sets of beliefs careening around his brain. If you doubt this, just try to imagine the subjectivity of a man who believes that he spent the entire day in bed with the flu, but also played a round of golf; that his name is Jim, and that his name is Tom; that he has a young son, and that he is childless. Multiply these incompatible beliefs indefinitely, and any sense that their owner is a single subject entirely disappears. There is a degree of logical inconsistency that is incompatible with our notion of personhood.

So it seems that the value we put on logical consistency is neither misplaced nor mysterious. In order for my speech to be intelligible to others—and, indeed, to *myself*—my beliefs about the world must largely cohere. In order for my behavior to be informed by what I believe, I must believe things that admit of behavior that is, at a minimum, *possible*. Certain logical relations, after all, seem etched into the very structure of our world.[8] The telephone rings . . . either it is my brother on the line, or it isn't. I may believe one proposition or the other—or I may believe that I do not know—but under no circumstances is it acceptable for me to believe *both*.

Departures from normativity, in particular with respect to the rules of inference that lead us to construct new beliefs on the basis of old ones, have been the subject of much research and much debate.[9] Whatever construal of these matters one adopts, no one believes that human beings are perfect engines of coherence. Our inevitable failures of rationality can take many forms, ranging from mere logical inconsistencies to radical discontinuities in subjectivity itself. Most of the literature on "self-deception," for instance, suggests that a person can tacitly believe one proposition, while successfully convincing himself of its antithesis (e.g., *my wife is having an affair; my wife is faithful*), though considerable controversy still surrounds the question of how (or whether) such cognitive contortions actually occur.[10] Other failures of psychological integration— ranging from "split-brain" patients to cases of "multiple-personality"—are at least partially explicable in terms of areas of belief processing in the brain that have become structurally and/or functionally partitioned from one another.

The American Embassy

A case in point: While traveling in France, my fiancée and I experienced a bizarre partitioning of our beliefs about the American embassy in Paris:

> *Belief system 1:* As the events of September 11 still cast a shadow over the world, we had decided to avoid obvious terrorist targets while traveling. First on our list of such places was the American embassy in Paris. Paris is home to the largest Muslim population in the Western world, and this embassy had already been the target of a foiled suicide plot. The American embassy would have been the last place we would have willingly visited while in France.

> *Belief system 2:* Prior to our arrival in Paris, we had great difficulty finding a hotel room. Every hotel we checked was full,

except for one on the Right Bank, which had abundant vacancies. The woman at reservations even offered us a complimentary upgrade to a suite. She also gave us a choice of views—we could face the inner courtyard, or outward, overlooking the American embassy. "Which view would you choose?" I asked. "The view of the embassy," she replied. "It's much more peaceful." I envisioned a large, embassy garden. "Great," I said. "We'll take it."

The next day, we arrived at the hotel and found that we had been given a room with a courtyard view. Both my fiancée and I were disappointed. We had, after all, been promised a view of the American embassy.

We called a friend living in Paris to inform her of our whereabouts. Our friend, who is wise in the ways of the world, had this to say: "That hotel is directly next to the American embassy. That's why they're offering you an upgrade. Have you guys lost your minds? Do you know what day it is? It's the Fourth of July."

The appearance of this degree of inconsistency in our lives was astounding. We had spent the better part of the day simultaneously trying to *avoid* and *gain proximity to* the very same point in space. Realizing this, we could scarcely have been more surprised had we both grown antlers.

But what seems psychologically so mysterious may be quite trivial in neurological terms. It appears that the phrase "American embassy," spoken in two different contexts, merely activated distinct networks of association within our brains. Consequently, the phrase had acquired two distinct *meanings*. In the first case, it signified a prime terrorist target; in the second, it promised a desirable view from a hotel window. The significance of the phrase in the *world*, however, is single and indivisible, since only one building answers to this name in Paris. The communication between these networks of neurons appeared to be negligible; our brains were effectively partitioned. The flimsiness of this partition was revealed by just how easily it came down. All it took for me to unify my fiancée's outlook on this subject was to turn to her—she who was still silently coveting a view of the American embassy—and say, with obvious alarm, "This hotel is ten feet from the American embassy!" The partition came down, and she was as flabbergasted as I was.

And yet, the psychologically irreconcilable facts are these: on the day in question, never was there a time when we would have willingly placed ourselves near the American embassy, and never was there a time when we were not eager to move to a room with a view of it.

While behavioral and linguistic necessity demands that we seek coherence among our beliefs wherever we can, we know that *total* coherence, even in a maximally integrated brain, would be impossible to achieve. This becomes apparent the moment we imagine a person's beliefs recorded as a list of assertions like *I am walking in the park; Parks generally have animals; Lions are animals*; and so on—each being a belief unto itself, as well as a possible basis upon which to form further inferences (both good ones: *I may soon see an animal*; and bad ones: *I may soon see a lion*), and hence new beliefs, about the world. If perfect coherence is to be had, each new belief must be checked against all others, and every combination thereof, for logical contradictions.[11] But here we encounter a minor computational difficulty: the number of necessary comparisons grows exponentially as each new proposition is added to the list. How many beliefs could a *perfect* brain check for logical contradictions? The answer is surprising. Even if a computer were as large as the known universe, built of components no larger than protons, with switching speeds as fast as the speed of light, all laboring in parallel from the moment of the big bang up to the present, it would still be fighting to add a 300th belief to its list.[12] What does this say about the possibility of our ever guaranteeing that our worldview is perfectly free from contradiction? It is not even a dream within a dream.[13] And yet, given the demands of language and behavior, it remains true that we must strive for coherence wherever it is in doubt, because failure here is synonymous with a failure either of linguistic sense or of behavioral possibility.[14]

Beliefs as Representations of the World

For even the most basic knowledge of the world to be possible, regularities in a nervous system must consistently mirror regularities in the environment. If a different assemblage of neurons in my brain fired whenever I saw a person's face, I would have no way to form a memory of him. His face could look like a face one moment and a toaster the next, and I would have no reason to be surprised by the inconsistency, for there would be nothing for a given pattern of neural activation to be consistent *with*. As Steven Pinker points out, it is only the orderly mirroring between a system that processes information (a brain or a computer) and the laws of logic or probability that explains "how rationality can emerge from mindless physical process" in the first place.[15] Words are arranged in a systematic and rule-based way (syntax), and beliefs are likewise (in that they must logically cohere), because both body and world are so arranged. Consider the statement *There is an apple and an orange in Jack's lunch box*. The syntactical (and hence logical) significance of the word "and" guarantees that anyone who believes this statement will also believe the following propositions: *There is an apple in Jack's lunch box* and *There is an orange in Jack's lunch box*. This is not due to some magical property that syntax holds over the world; rather, it is a simple consequence of the fact that we use words like "and" to mirror the orderly behavior of objects. Someone who will endorse the conjunction of two statements, while denying them individually, either does not understand the use of the word "and" or does not understand things like apples, oranges, and lunch boxes.[16] It just so happens that we live in a universe in which, if you put an apple and an orange in Jack's lunch box, you will be able to pull out an apple, an orange, or both. There is a point at which the meanings of words, their syntactical relations, and rationality itself can no longer be divorced from the orderly behavior of objects in the world.[17]

WHATEVER beliefs are, none of us harbors an infinite number of them.[18] While philosophers may doubt whether beliefs are the sort of thing that can be counted, it is clear that we have a finite amount of storage in our brains,[19] a finite number of discrete memories, and a finite vocabulary that waxes and wanes somewhere well shy of 100,000 words. There is a distinction to be made, therefore, between beliefs that are *causally active*[20]—i.e., those that we already have in our heads—and those that can be constructed on demand. If believing is anything like perceiving, it is obvious that our intuitions about how many of our beliefs are present within us at any given moment might be unreliable. Studies of "change blindness," for instance, have revealed that we do not perceive nearly as much of the world as we think we do, since a large percentage of the visual scene can be suddenly altered without our noticing.[21] An analogy with computer gaming also seems apropos: current generations of computer games do not compute parts of their virtual world until a player makes a move that demands their existence.[22] Perhaps many of our cognitive commitments are just like this.[23]

Whether most of what we believe is always present within our minds or whether it must be continually reconstructed, it seems that many beliefs must be freshly vetted before they can guide our behavior. This is demonstrated whenever we come to doubt a proposition that we previously believed. Just consider what it is like to forget the multiplication table—12 x 7 = ? All of us have had moments when 84 just didn't sound quite right. At such times, we may be forced to perform some additional calculations before we can again be said to believe that 12 x 7 = 84. Or consider what it is like to fall into doubt over a familiar person's name ("Is his name really *Jeff*? Is that what I call him?"). It is clear that even very well-worn beliefs can occasionally fail to achieve credibility in the present. Such failures of truth testing have important implications, to which we now turn.

A Matter of True and False

Imagine that you are having dinner in a restaurant with several old friends. You leave the table briefly to use the restroom, and upon your return you hear one of your friends whisper, "Just be quiet. He can't know about any of this."

What are you to make of this statement? Everything turns on whether you believe that you are the "he" in question. If you are a woman, and therefore excluded by this choice of pronoun, you would probably feel nothing but curiosity. Upon retaking your seat, you might even whisper, "Who are you guys talking about?" If you are a man, on the other hand, things have just gotten interesting. What secret could your friends be keeping from you? If your birthday is just a few weeks away, you might assume that a surprise party has been planned in your honor. If not, more Shakespearean possibilities await your consideration.

Given your prior cognitive commitments, and the contextual cues in which the utterance was spoken, some credence-granting circuit inside your brain will begin to test a variety of possibilities. You will study your friends' faces. Are their expressions compatible with the more nefarious interpretations of this statement that are now occurring to you? Has one of your friends just confessed to sleeping with your wife? When could this have happened? There has always been a certain chemistry between them. . . . Suffice it to say that whichever interpretation of these events becomes a matter of belief for you will have important personal and social consequences.

At present, we have no understanding of what it means, at the level of the brain, to say that a person believes or disbelieves a given proposition—and yet it is upon this difference that all subsequent cognitive and behavioral commitments turn. To believe a proposition we must endorse, and thereby become behaviorally susceptible to, its representational content. There are good reasons to think that this process happens quite automatically—and, indeed, that the mere comprehension of an idea may be tantamount to believing it, if only for a moment. The Dutch philosopher Spinoza thought that belief and comprehension were identical, while disbelief required a subsequent act of rejection. Some very interesting work in psychology bears this out.[24] It seems rather likely that understanding a proposition is analogous to perceiving an object in physical space. Our default setting may be to accept appearances as reality until they prove to be otherwise. This would explain why merely entertaining the possibility of a friend's betrayal may have set your heart racing a moment ago.

Whether belief formation is a passive or an active process, it is clear that we continuously monitor spoken utterances (both our own and those of others) for logical and factual errors. The failure to find such errors allows us to live by the logic of what would otherwise be empty phrases. Of course, even the change of a single word can mean the difference between complaisance and death-defying feats: if your child comes to you in the middle of the night saying, "Daddy, there's an elephant in the hall," you might escort him back to bed toting an imaginary gun; if he had said, "Daddy, there's a *man* in the hall," you would probably be inclined to carry a real one.

Faith and Evidence

It does not require any special knowledge of psychology or neuroscience to observe that human beings are generally reluctant to change their minds. As many authors have noted, we are conservative in our beliefs in the sense that we do not add or subtract from our store of them without reason. Belief, in the *epistemic* sense—that is, belief that aims at representing our knowledge about the world—requires that we believe a given proposition to be *true*, not merely that we wish it were so. Such a constraint upon our thinking is undoubtedly a good thing, since unrestrained wishful thinking would uncouple our beliefs from the regularities in the world that they purport to represent. Why is it *wrong* to believe a proposition to be true just because it might feel good to believe it? One need only linger over the meaning of the word "because" (Middle English "by" + "cause") to see the problem here. "Because" suggests a *causal* connection between a proposition's *being* true and a person's believing that it is. This explains the value we generally place on evidence: because evidence is simply an account of the causal linkage between states of the world and our beliefs about them. ("I believe Oswald shot Kennedy because I found his fingerprints on the gun, and because my cousin saw him do it, and my cousin doesn't lie.") We can believe a proposition to be true only *because* something in our experience, or in our reasoning about the world, actually speaks to the truth of the proposition in question.[25]

Let's say that I believe that God exists, and some impertinent person asks me *why*. This question invites—indeed, demands—an answer of the form "I believe that God exists because..." I cannot say, however, "I believe that God exists because it is prudent to do so" (as Pascal would have us do). Of course, I can *say* this, but I cannot mean by the word "believe" what I mean when I say things like "I believe that water is really two parts hydrogen and one part oxygen because two centuries of physical experiments attest to this" or "I believe there is an oak in my yard because I can see it." Nor can I say things like "I believe in God because it makes me feel good." The fact that I would feel good if there were a God does not give me the slightest reason to believe that one exists. This is easily seen when we swap the existence of God for some other consoling proposition. Let's say that I want to believe that there is a diamond buried somewhere in my yard that is the size of a refrigerator. It is true that it would feel uncommonly good to believe this. But do I have any reason to believe that there is *actually* a diamond in my yard that is thousands of times larger than any yet discovered? No. Here we can see why

Pascal's wager, Kierkegaard's leap of faith, and other epistemological ponzi schemes won't do. To believe that God exists is to believe that I stand in some relation to his existence *such that his existence is itself the reason for my belief*. There must be some causal connection, or an appearance thereof, between the fact in question and my acceptance of it. In this way, we can see that religious beliefs, to be beliefs about the way the world *is*, must be as evidentiary in spirit as any other.

THE moment we admit that our beliefs are attempts to represent states of the world, we see that they must stand in the right relation *to* the world to be valid. It should be clear that if a person believes in God because he has had certain spiritual experiences, or because the Bible makes so much sense, or because he trusts the authority of the church, he is playing the same game of justification that we all play when claiming to know the most ordinary facts. This is probably a conclusion that many religious believers will want to resist; but resistance is not only futile but *incoherent*. There is simply no other logical space for our beliefs about the world to occupy. As long as religious propositions purport to be about the way the world is— *God can actually hear your prayers, If you take his name in vain bad things will happen to you*, etc.—they must stand in relation to the world, and to our other beliefs about it. And it is only by being so situated that propositions of this sort can influence our subsequent thinking or behavior. As long as a person maintains that his beliefs represent an actual state of the world (visible or invisible; spiritual or mundane), he must believe that his beliefs are a *consequence* of the way the world is. This, by definition, leaves him vulnerable to new evidence. Indeed, if there were no conceivable change in the world that could get a person to question his religious beliefs, this would prove that his beliefs were not predicated upon his taking any state of the world into account. He could not claim, therefore, to be *representing* the world at all.[26]

ALTHOUGH many things can be said in criticism of religious faith, there is no discounting its power. Millions among us, even now, are quite willing to die for our unjustified beliefs, and millions more, it seems, are willing to kill for them. Those who are destined to suffer terribly throughout their lives, or upon the threshold of death, often find consolation in one unfounded proposition or another. Faith enables many of us to endure life's difficulties with an equanimity that would be scarcely conceivable in a world lit only by reason. Faith also appears to have direct physical consequences in cases where mere expectations, good or bad, can incline the body toward health or untimely death.[27] But the fact that religious beliefs have a great influence on human life says nothing at all about their *validity*. For the paranoid, pursued by persecutory delusions, terror of the CIA may have great influence, but this does not mean that his phones are tapped.

What is faith, then? Is it something other than belief? The Hebrew term *'emûnâ* (verb *'mn*) is alternately translated as "to have faith," "to believe," or "to trust." The Septuagint, the Greek translation of the Hebrew Bible, retains the same meaning in the term *pisteuein*, and this Greek equivalent is adopted in the New Testament. Hebrews 11:1 defines faith as "the assurance of things hoped for, the conviction of things not seen." Read in the right way, this passage seems to render faith entirely self-justifying: perhaps the very fact that one believes in something which has not yet come to pass ("things hoped for") or for which one has no evidence ("things not seen") constitutes evidence for its actuality ("assurance"). Let's see how this works: I feel a certain, rather thrilling "conviction" that Nicole Kidman is in love with me. As we have never met, my feeling is my only evidence of her infatuation. I reason thus: my feelings suggest that Nicole and I must have a special, even metaphysical, connection— otherwise, how could I have this feeling in the first place? I decide to set up camp outside her house to make the necessary introductions; clearly, this sort of faith is a tricky business.

Throughout this book, I am criticizing faith in its ordinary, scrip-

tural sense—as belief in, and life orientation toward, certain historical and metaphysical propositions. The meaning of the term, both in
the Bible and upon the lips of the faithful, seems to be entirely
unambiguous. It is true that certain theologians and contemplatives
have attempted to recast faith as a spiritual principle that transcends
mere motivated credulity. Paul Tillich, in his *Dynamics of Faith*
(1957), rarefied the original import of the term out of existence,
casting away what he called "idolatrous faith" and, indeed, all equations between faith and belief. Surely other theologians have done
likewise. Of course, anyone is free to redefine the term "faith" however he sees fit and thereby bring it into conformity with some
rational or mystical ideal. But this is not the "faith" that has animated the faithful for millennia. The faith that I am calling into
question is precisely the gesture that Tillich himself decried as "an
act of knowledge that has a low degree of evidence." My argument,
after all, is aimed at the majority of the faithful in every religious
tradition, not at Tillich's blameless parish of one.

Despite the considerable exertions of men like Tillich who have
attempted to hide the serpent lurking at the foot of every altar, the
truth is that religious faith is simply *unjustified* belief in matters of
ultimate concern—specifically in propositions that promise some
mechanism by which human life can be spared the ravages of time
and death. Faith is what credulity becomes when it finally achieves
escape velocity from the constraints of terrestrial discourse—
constraints like reasonableness, internal coherence, civility, and
candor. However far you feel you have fled the parish (even if you
are just now adjusting the mirror on the Hubble Space Telescope),
you are likely to be the product of a culture that has elevated belief,
in the absence of evidence, to the highest place in the hierarchy of
human virtues. Ignorance is the true coinage of this realm—"Blessed
are those who have not seen and have believed" (John 20:29)—and
every child is instructed that it is, at the very least, an option, if not a
sacred duty, to disregard the facts of this world out of deference to the
God who lurks in his mother's and father's imaginations.

But faith is an impostor. This can be readily seen in the way that all the extraordinary phenomena of the religious life—a statue of the Virgin weeps, a child casts his crutches to the ground—are seized upon by the faithful as *confirmation* of their faith. At these moments, religious believers appear like men and women in the desert of uncertainty given a cool drink of data. There is no way around the fact that we crave justification for our core beliefs and believe them only because we think such justification is, at the very least, in the offing. Is there a practicing Christian in the West who would be indifferent to the appearance of incontestable physical evidence that attested to the literal truth of the Gospels? Imagine if carbon dating of the shroud of Turin[28] had shown it to be as old as Easter Sunday, AD 29: Is there any doubt that this revelation would have occasioned a spectacle of awe, exultation, and zealous remission of sins throughout the Christian world?

This is the very same faith that will not stoop to reason when it has no *good* reasons to believe. If a little supportive evidence emerges, however, the faithful prove as attentive to data as the damned. This demonstrates that faith is nothing more than a willingness to await the evidence—be it the Day of Judgment or some other downpour of corroboration. It is the search for knowledge on the installment plan: believe now, live an untestable hypothesis until your dying day, and you will discover that you were right.

But in any other sphere of life, a belief is a check that everyone insists upon cashing this side of the grave: the engineer says the bridge will hold; the doctor says the infection is resistant to penicillin—these people have defeasible reasons for their claims about the way the world is. The mullah, the priest, and the rabbi do not. Nothing could change about this world, or about the world of their experience, that would demonstrate the falsity of many of their core beliefs. This proves that these beliefs are not born of any examination of the world, or of the world of their experience. (They are, in Karl Popper's sense, "unfalsifiable.") It appears that even the Holocaust did not lead most Jews to doubt the existence of an omnipotent and benevolent God. If having half of your people systematically delivered to the furnace does not count as evidence against the notion that an all-powerful God is looking out for your interests, it seems reasonable to assume that nothing could. How does the mullah know that the Koran is the verbatim word of God? The only answer to be given in any language that does not make a mockery of the word "know" is—*he doesn't.*

A man's faith is just a subset of his beliefs about the world: beliefs about matters of ultimate concern that we, as a culture, have told him he need not justify in the present. It is time we recognized just how maladaptive this Balkanization of our discourse has become. All pretensions to theological knowledge should now be seen from the perspective of a man who was just beginning his day on the one hundredth floor of the World Trade Center on the morning of September 11, 2001, only to find his meandering thoughts— of family and friends, of errands run and unrun, of coffee in need of sweetener—inexplicably usurped by a choice of terrible starkness and simplicity: between being burned alive by jet fuel or leaping one thousand feet to the concrete below. In fact, we should take the perspective of thousands of such men, women, and children who were robbed of life, far sooner than they imagined possible, in absolute terror and confusion. The men who committed the atrocities of September 11 were certainly not "cowards," as they were repeatedly described in the Western media, nor were they lunatics in any ordinary sense. They were men of faith—*perfect* faith, as it turns out— and this, it must finally be acknowledged, is a terrible thing to be.

I AM CERTAIN that such a summary dismissal of religious faith will seem callous to many readers, particularly those who have known its comforts at first hand. But the fact that unjustified beliefs can have a consoling influence on the human mind is no argument in their favor. If every physician told his terminally ill patients that they were destined for a complete recovery, this might also set many of their minds at ease, but at the expense of the truth. Why should we be concerned about the truth? This question awaits its Socrates. For our purposes, we need only observe that the truth is of paramount concern to the faithful themselves; indeed, the *truth* of a given doctrine is the very object of their faith. The search for comfort at the expense of truth has never been a motive for religious belief, since all creeds are chock-full of terrible proposals, which are no comfort to anyone and which the faithful believe, despite the pain it causes them, for fear of leaving some dark corner of reality unacknowledged.

The faithful, in fact, hold truth in the highest esteem. And in this sense they are identical to most philosophers and scientists. People of faith claim nothing less than knowledge of sacred, redeeming, and metaphysical truths: *Christ died for your sins; He is the Son of God; All human beings have souls that will be subject to judgment after death.* These are specific claims about the way the world is. It is only the notion that a doctrine is in accord with reality at large that renders a person's faith useful, redemptive, or, indeed, logically possible, for faith in a doctrine *is* faith in its truth. What else but the truth of a given teaching could convince its adherents of the illegitimacy of all others? Heretical doctrines are deemed so, and accorded a healthy measure of disdain, for no other reason than that they are presumed to be *false*. Thus, if a Christian made no tacit claims of knowledge with regard to the literal truth of scripture, he would be just as much a Muslim, or a Jew—or an atheist—as a follower of Christ. If he were to discover (by some means that he acknowledged to be incontrovertible) that Christ had actually been born of sin and died like an animal, these revelations would surely deliver a deathblow to his faith. The faithful have never been indifferent to the truth; and yet, the principle of faith leaves them unequipped to distinguish truth from falsity in matters that most concern them.

The faithful can be expected to behave just like their secular neighbors—which is to say, more or less rationally—in their worldly affairs. When making important decisions, they tend to be as attentive to evidence and to its authentication as any unbeliever. While Jehovah's Witnesses refusing blood transfusions, or Christian Scientists forgoing modern medicine altogether, may appear to be exceptions to this rule, they are not. Such people are merely acting rationally within the framework of their religious beliefs. After all, no mother who refuses medicine for her child on religious grounds believes that prayer is merely a consoling cultural practice. Rather, she believes that her ultimate salvation demands certain displays of confidence in the power and attentiveness of God, and this is an end toward which she is willing to pledge even the life of her child as collateral. Such apparently unreasonable behavior is often in the service of reason, since it aims at the empirical authentication of religious doctrine. In fact, even the most extreme expressions of faith are often perfectly rational, given the requisite beliefs. Take the snake-dancing Pentecostals as the most colorful example: in an effort to demonstrate both their faith in the literal word of the Bible (in this case Mark 16:18) and its *truth*, they "take up serpents" (various species of rattlesnakes) and "drink any deadly thing" (generally strychnine) and test prophecy ("it shall not hurt them") to their heart's content. Some of them die in the process, of course, as did their founder, George Hensley (of snake bite, in 1955)—proof, we can be sure, not of the weakness of their faith but of the occasional efficacy of rattlesnake venom and strychnine as poisons.

Which beliefs one takes to be foundational will dictate what seems reasonable at any given moment. When the members of the "Heaven's Gate" cult failed to spot the spacecraft they knew must be trailing the comet Hale-Bopp, they returned the $4,000 telescope they had bought for this purpose, believing it to be defective.

WHERE faith really pays its dividends, however, is in the conviction that the future will be better than the past, or at least not worse. Consider the celebrated opinion of Julian of Norwich (ca. 1342–1413), who distilled the message of the Gospels in the memorable sentence

"All shall be well, and all shall be well, and all manner of thing shall be well." The allure of most religious doctrines is nothing more sublime or inscrutable than this: *things will turn out well in the end.* Faith is offered as a means by which the truth of this proposition can be savored in the present and secured in the future. It is, I think, indisputable that the *actual* existence of such a mechanism, the *fact* that uttering a few words and eating a cracker is an effective means of redemption, the *certainty* that God is watching, listening, and waiting to bestow his blessings upon one and all—in short, the literal correspondence of doctrine with reality itself—is of sole importance to the faithful.

The amazing pestilence reached Paris that June [of 1348], and it was to afflict the city for a year and a half. . . .

King Philip [VI] asked the medical faculty of the University of Paris for an explanation of the disaster. The professors reported that a disturbance in the skies had caused the sun to overheat the oceans near India, and the waters had begun to give off noxious vapors. The medical faculty offered a variety of remedies. Broth would help, for example, if seasoned with ground pepper, ginger, and cloves. Poultry, water fowl, young pork and fatty meat in general were to be avoided. Olive oil could be fatal. Bathing was dangerous, but enemas could be helpful. "Men must preserve chastity," the doctors warned, "if they value their lives."

The King still worried about the divine wrath. He issued an edict against blasphemy. For the first offense, the blasphemer's lip would be cut off; a second offense would cost him the other lip, and a third the tongue. . . .

The town authorities reacted with a series of stern measures to halt the spreading panic. They ordered the tolling of the bells to cease. They outlawed the wearing of black clothing. They forbade the gathering of more than two people at a funeral, or any display of grief in public. And to placate the angry God who had brought this affliction, they banned all work after noon on Saturdays, all gambling and swearing, and they demanded that everyone living in sin get married immediately. Li Muisis [an abbot of Tournai] recorded happily that the number of marriages increased considerably, profanity was no longer heard, and gambling declined so much that the makers of dice turned to making rosaries. He also recorded that in this newly virtuous place 25,000 citizens died of the plague and were buried in large pits on the outskirts of the town.[29]

Where did the religious beliefs of these people leave off and their worldly beliefs begin? Can there be any doubt that the beleaguered Christians of the fourteenth century were longing for *knowledge* (that is, beliefs that are both true and valid) about the plague, about its cause and mode of transmission, and hoping, thereby, to find an effective means by which to combat it? Was their reliance upon the tenets of faith enforced by anything but the starkest ignorance? If it had been known, for instance, that this pestilence was being delivered by merchant ships—that rats were climbing ashore from every hold and that upon each rat were legions of fleas carrying the plague bacillus—would the faithful have thought their energies best spent cutting the tongues out of blasphemers, silencing bells, dressing in bright colors, and making liberal use of enemas? A sure way to win an argument with these unhappy people would have been with penicillin, delivered not from a land where other "cultural perspectives" hold sway, but from higher up on the slopes of the real.

Faith and Madness

We have seen that our beliefs are tightly coupled to the structure of language and to the apparent structure of the world. Our "freedom of belief," if it exists at all, is minimal. Is a person really free to believe a proposition for which he has no evidence? No. Evidence (whether sensory or logical) is the only thing that suggests that a given belief is really *about* the world in the first place. We have names for people who have many beliefs for which there is no rational justification. When their beliefs are extremely common we call them "religious"; otherwise, they are likely to be called "mad," "psychotic," or "delusional." Most people of faith are perfectly sane, of course, even those who commit atrocities on account of their beliefs. But what is the difference between a man who believes that God will reward him with seventy-two virgins if he kills a score of Jewish teenagers, and one who believes that creatures from Alpha Centauri are beaming him messages of world peace through his hair dryer? There is a difference, to be sure, but it is not one that places religious faith in a flattering light.

It takes a certain kind of person to believe what no one else believes. To be ruled by ideas for which you have no evidence (and which therefore cannot be justified in conversation with other human beings) is generally a sign that something is seriously wrong with your mind. Clearly, there is sanity in numbers. And yet, it is merely an accident of history that it is considered normal in our society to believe that the Creator of the universe can hear your thoughts, while it is demonstrative of mental illness to believe that he is communicating with you by having the rain tap in Morse code on your bedroom window. And so, while religious people are not generally mad, their core beliefs absolutely are. This is not surprising, since most religions have merely canonized a few products of ancient ignorance and derangement and passed them down to us as though they were primordial truths. This leaves billions of us believing what no sane person could believe on his own. In fact, it is difficult to imagine a set of beliefs more suggestive of mental illness than those that lie at the heart of many of our religious traditions. Consider one of the cornerstones of the Catholic faith:

> I likewise profess that in the Mass a true, proper, and propitia-
> tory sacrifice is offered to God on behalf of the living and the
> dead, and that the Body and the Blood, together with the soul

and the divinity, of our Lord Jesus Christ is truly, really, and substantially present in the most holy sacrament of the Eucharist,
and there is a change of the whole substance of the bread into the
Body, and of the whole substance of the wine into Blood; and this
change the Catholic mass calls transubstantiation. I also profess
that the whole and entire Christ and a true sacrament is received
under each separate species.[30]

Jesus Christ—who, as it turns out, was born of a virgin, cheated
death, and rose bodily into the heavens—can now be eaten in the
form of a cracker. A few Latin words spoken over your favorite Burgundy, and you can drink his blood as well. Is there any doubt that
a lone subscriber to these beliefs would be considered mad? Rather,
is there any doubt that he would *be* mad? The danger of religious
faith is that it allows otherwise normal human beings to reap the
fruits of madness and consider them *holy*. Because each new generation of children is taught that religious propositions need not be
justified in the way that all others must, civilization is still besieged
by the armies of the preposterous. We are, even now, killing ourselves over ancient literature. Who would have thought something
so tragically absurd could be possible?

What Should We Believe?

We believe most of what we believe about the world because others
have told us to. Reliance upon the authority of experts, and upon the
testimony of ordinary people, is the stuff of which worldviews are
made. In fact, the more educated we become, the more our beliefs
come to us at second hand. A person who believes only those propositions for which he can provide full sensory or theoretical justification will know almost nothing about the world; that is, if he is not
swiftly killed by his own ignorance. How do you know that falling
from a great height is hazardous to your health? Unless you have

witnessed someone die in this way, you have adopted this belief on the authority of others.[31] This is not a problem. Life is too short, and the world too complex, for any of us to go it alone in epistemological terms. We are ever reliant on the intelligence and accuracy, if not the kindness, of strangers.

This does not suggest, however, that all forms of authority are valid; nor does it suggest that even the best authorities will always prove reliable. There are good arguments and bad ones, precise observations and imprecise ones; and each of us has to be the final judge of whether or not it is reasonable to adopt a given belief about the world.

Consider the following sources of information:

1. The anchorman on the evening news says that a large fire is burning in the state of Colorado. One hundred thousand acres have burned, and the fire is still completely uncontained.

2. Biologists say that DNA is the molecular basis for sexual reproduction. Each of us resembles our parents because we inherit a complement of their DNA. Each of us has arms and legs because our DNA coded for the proteins that produced them during our early development.

3. The pope says that Jesus was born of a virgin and resurrected bodily after death. He is the Son of God, who created the universe in six days. If you believe this, you will go to heaven after death; if you don't, you will go to hell, where you will suffer for eternity.

What is the difference between these forms of testimony? Why isn't every "expert opinion" equally worthy of our respect? Given our analysis thus far, it should not be difficult to grant authority to 1 and 2 while disregarding 3.

Proposition 1: Why do we find the news story about the fire in Colorado persuasive? It could be a hoax. But what about those televised images of hillsides engorged by flame and of planes dropping fire retardant? Maybe there is a fire, but it is in a different state. Perhaps it's really Texas that is burning. Is it reasonable to entertain such possibilities? No. Why not? Here is where the phrase "common sense" begins to earn its keep. Given our beliefs about the human mind, the success of our widespread collaboration with other human beings, and the degree to which we all rely on the news, it is scarcely conceivable that a respected television network and a highly paid anchorman are perpetrating a hoax, or that thousands of firefighters, newsmen, and terrified homeowners have mistaken Texas for Colorado. Implicit in such commonsense judgments lurks an understanding of the causal connections between various processes in the world, the likelihood of different outcomes, and the vested interests, or lack thereof, of those whose testimony we are considering. What would a professional news anchor stand to gain from lying about a fire in Colorado? We need not go into the details here; if the anchor on the evening news says that there is a fire in Colorado and then shows us images of burning trees, we can be reasonably sure that there really is a fire in Colorado.

Proposition 2: What about the "truths" of science? Are they *true*? Much has been written about the inherent provisionality of scientific theories. Karl Popper has told us that we never prove a theory right; we merely fail to prove it wrong.[32] Thomas Kuhn has told us that scientific theories undergo wholesale revision with each generation and therefore do not converge on the truth.[33] There's no telling which of our current theories will be proved wrong tomorrow, so how much confidence can we have in them? Many unwary consumers of these ideas have concluded that science is just another area of human discourse and, as such, is no more anchored to the facts of this world than literature or religion are. All truths are up for grabs.

But all spheres of discourse are not on the same footing, for the simple reason that not all spheres of discourse *seek* the same footing (or any footing whatsoever). Science is science because it represents our most committed effort to verify that our statements about the world are true (or at least not false).[34] We do this by observation and experiment within the context of a theory. To say that a given scientific theory may be wrong is not to say that it may be wrong in its every particular, or that any other theory stands an equal chance of being right. What are the chances that DNA is *not* the basis for genetic inheritance? Well, if it isn't, Mother Nature sure has a lot of explaining to do. She must explain the results of fifty years of experimentation, which have demonstrated reliable correlations between genotype and phenotype (including the reproducible effects of specific genetic mutations). Any account of inheritance that is going to supersede the present assumptions of molecular biology will have to account for the ocean of data that now conforms to these assumptions. What are the chances that we will one day discover that DNA has *absolutely nothing* to do with inheritance? They are effectively zero.

Proposition 3: Can we rely on the authority of the pope? Millions of Catholics do, of course. He is, in fact, *infallible* in matters of faith and morality. Can we really say that Catholics are *wrong* to believe that the pope knows whereof he speaks? We surely can.

We know that *no* evidence would be sufficient to authenticate many of the pope's core beliefs. How could anyone born in the twentieth century come to know that Jesus was actually born of a virgin? What process of ratiocination, mystical or otherwise, will deliver the necessary facts about a Galilean woman's sexual history (facts that run entirely counter to well-known facts of human biology)? There is no such process. Even a time machine could not help us, unless we were willing to keep watch over Mary twenty-four hours a day for the months surrounding the probable time of Jesus' conception.

Visionary experiences, in and of themselves, can never be sufficient to answer questions of historical fact. Let's say the pope had a dream about Jesus, and Jesus came to him looking fresh from Da Vinci's brush. The pope would not even be in a position to say that

the Jesus of his dream *looked like* the real Jesus. The pope's infallibility, no matter how many dreams and visions he may have had,
does not even extend to making a judgment about whether the historical Jesus wore a beard, let alone whether he was really the Son
of God, born of a virgin, or able to raise the dead. These are just not
the kinds of propositions that spiritual experience can authenticate.

Of course, we could imagine a scenario in which we would give
credence to the pope's visions, or to our own. If Jesus came saying
things like "The Vatican Library has exactly thirty-seven thousand,
two hundred and twenty-six books" and he turned out to be right,
we would then begin to feel that we were, at the very least, *in dialogue* with someone who had something to say about the way the
world is. Given a sufficient number of verifiable statements,
plucked from the ethers of papal vision, we could begin speaking
seriously about any further claims Jesus might make. The point is
that his authority would be derived in the only way that such
authority ever is—by making claims about the world that can be
corroborated by further observation. As far as proposition 3 is concerned, it is quite obvious that the pope has nothing to go on but
the Bible itself. This document is not a sufficient justification for his
beliefs, given the standards of evidence that prevailed at the time of
its composition.

WHAT about our much championed freedom of religious belief? It is
no different from our freedoms of journalistic and biological
belief—and anyone who believes that the media are perpetrating a
great fire conspiracy, or that molecular biology is just a theory that
may prove totally wrong, has merely exercised his freedom to be
thought a fool. Religious unreason should acquire an even greater
stigma in our discourse, given that it remains among the principal
causes of armed conflict in our world. Before you can get to the end
of this paragraph, another person will probably die because of what
someone else believes about God. Perhaps it is time we demanded

that our fellow human beings had better reasons for maintaining their religious differences, if such reasons even exist.

We must begin speaking freely about what is really in these holy books of ours, beyond the timid heterodoxies of modernity—the gay and lesbian ministers, the Muslim clerics who have lost their taste for public amputations, or the Sunday churchgoers who have never read their Bibles quite through. A close study of these books, and of history, demonstrates that there is no act of cruelty so appalling that it cannot be justified, or even mandated, by recourse to their pages. It is only by the most acrobatic avoidance of passages whose canonicity has never been in doubt that we can escape murdering one another outright for the glory of God. Bertrand Russell had it right when he made the following observation:

> The Spaniards in Mexico and Peru used to baptize Indian infants and then immediately dash their brains out: by this means they secured these infants went to Heaven. No orthodox Christian can find any logical reason for condemning their action, although all nowadays do so. In countless ways the doctrine of personal immortality in its Christian form has had disastrous effects upon morals. . . .[35]

It is true that there are millions of people whose faith moves them to perform extraordinary acts of self-sacrifice for the benefit of others. The help rendered to the poor by Christian missionaries in the developing world demonstrates that religious ideas can lead to actions that are both beautiful and necessary. But there are far better reasons for self-sacrifice than those that religion provides. The fact that faith has motivated many people to do good things does not suggest that faith is itself a necessary (or even a good) motivation for goodness. It can be quite possible, even reasonable, to risk one's life to save others without believing any incredible ideas about the nature of the universe.

By contrast, the most monstrous crimes against humanity have invariably been inspired by unjustified belief. This is nearly a truism. Genocidal projects tend not to reflect the rationality of their perpetrators simply because there are no *good* reasons to kill peaceful people indiscriminately. Even where such crimes have been secular, they have required the egregious credulity of entire societies to be brought off. Consider the millions of people who were killed by Stalin and Mao: although these tyrants paid lip service to rationality, communism was little more than a political religion.[36] At the heart of its apparatus of repression and terror lurked a rigid ideology, to which generations of men and women were sacrificed. Even though their beliefs did not reach beyond this world, they were both cultic and irrational. To cite only one example, the dogmatic embrace of Lysenko's "socialist" biology—as distinguished from the "capitalist" biology of Mendel and Darwin—helped pave the way for tens of millions of deaths from famine in the Soviet Union and China in the first part of the twentieth century.

In the next chapter we will examine two of the darkest episodes in the history of faith: the Inquisition and the Holocaust. I have chosen the former as a case study because there is no other instance in which so many ordinary men and women have been so deranged by their beliefs about God; nowhere else has the subversion of reason been so complete or its consequences so terrible. The Holocaust is relevant here because it is generally considered to have been an entirely secular phenomenon. It was not. The anti-Semitism that built the crematoria brick by brick—and that still thrives today—comes to us by way of Christian theology. Knowingly or not, the Nazis were agents of religion.

3

In the Shadow of God

●

WITHOUT warning you are seized and brought before a judge. Did you create a thunderstorm and destroy the village harvest? Did you kill your neighbor with the evil eye? Do you doubt that Christ is bodily present in the Eucharist? You will soon learn that questions of this sort admit of no exculpatory reply.

You are not told the names of your accusers. But their identities are of little account, for even if, at this late hour, they were to recant their charges against you, they would merely be punished as false witnesses, while their original accusations would retain their full weight as evidence of your guilt. The machinery of justice has been so well oiled by faith that it can no longer be influenced.

But you have a choice, of sorts: you can concede your guilt and name your accomplices. Yes, you must have had accomplices. No confession will be accepted unless other men and women can be implicated in your crimes. Perhaps you and three acquaintances of your choosing *did* change into hares and consort with the devil himself. The sight of iron boots designed to crush your feet seems to refresh your memory. Yes, Friedrich, Arthur, and Otto are sorcerers too. Their wives? Witches all.

You now face punishment proportionate to the severity of your crimes: flogging, a pilgrimage on foot to the Holy Land, forfeiture of property, or, more likely, a period of long imprisonment, probably for life. Your "accomplices" will soon be rounded up for torture.

Or you can maintain your innocence, which is almost certainly the truth (after all, it is the rare person who can create a thunderstorm).

In response, your jailers will be happy to lead you to the furthest reaches of human suffering, before burning you at the stake. You may be imprisoned in total darkness for months or years at a time, repeatedly beaten and starved, or stretched upon the rack. Thumbscrews may be applied, or toe screws, or a pear-shaped vise may be inserted into your mouth, vagina, or anus, and forced open until your misery admits of no possible increase. You may be hoisted to the ceiling on a *strappado* (with your arms bound behind your back and attached to a pulley, and weights tied to your feet), dislocating your shoulders. To this torment *squassation* might be added, which, being often sufficient to cause your death, may yet spare you the agony of the stake.[1] If you are unlucky enough to be in Spain, where judicial torture has achieved a transcendent level of cruelty, you may be placed in the "Spanish chair": a throne of iron, complete with iron stocks to secure your neck and limbs. In the interest of saving your soul, a coal brazier will be placed beneath your bare feet, slowly roasting them. Because the stain of heresy runs deep, your flesh will be continually larded with fat to keep it from burning too quickly. Or you may be bound to a bench, with a cauldron filled with mice placed upside-down upon your bare abdomen. With the requisite application of heat to the iron, the mice will begin to burrow into your belly in search of an exit.[2]

Should you, while in extremis, admit to your torturers that you are indeed a heretic, a sorcerer, or a witch, you will be made to confirm your story before a judge—and any attempt to recant, to claim that your confession has been coerced through torture, will deliver you either to your tormentors once again or directly to the stake. If, once condemned, you repent of your sins, these compassionate and learned men—whose concern for the fate of your eternal soul really knows no bounds—will do you the kindness of strangling you before lighting your pyre.[3]

THE medieval church was quick to observe that the Good Book was good enough to suggest a variety of means for eradicating heresy, ranging from a communal volley of stones to cremation while alive.[4] A literal reading of the Old Testament not only permits but *requires* heretics to be put to death. As it turns out, it was never difficult to find a mob willing to perform this holy office, and to do so purely on the authority of the Church—since it was still a capital offense to possess a Bible in any of the vernacular languages of Europe.[5] In fact, scripture was not to become generally accessible to the common man until the sixteenth century. As we noted earlier, Deuteronomy was the preeminent text in every inquisitor's canon, for it explicitly enjoins the faithful to murder anyone in their midst, even members of their own families, who profess a sympathy for foreign gods. Showing a genius for totalitarianism that few mortals have ever fully implemented, the author of this document demands that anyone too squeamish to take part in such religious killing must be killed as well (Deuteronomy 17:12–13).[6] Anyone who imagines that no justification for the Inquisition can be found in scripture need only consult the Bible to have his view of the matter clarified:

> If you hear that in one of the towns which Yahweh your God has given you for a home, there are men, scoundrels from your own stock, who have led their fellow-citizens astray, saying, "Let us go and serve other gods," hitherto unknown to you, it is your duty to look into the matter, examine it, and inquire most carefully. If it is proved and confirmed that such a hateful thing has taken place among you, you must put the inhabitants of that town to the sword; you must lay it under the curse of destruction—the town and everything in it. You must pile up all its loot in the public square and burn the town and all its loot, offering it all to Yahweh your God. It is to be a ruin for all time and never rebuilt. (Deuteronomy 13:12–16).

For obvious reasons, the church tended to ignore the final edict: the destruction of heretic property.

In addition to demanding that we fulfill every "jot" and "tittle" of Old Testament law,[7] Jesus seems to have suggested, in John 15:6, further refinements to the practice of killing heretics and unbelievers: "If a man abide not in me, he is cast forth as a branch, and is withered; and men gather them, and cast them into the fire, and they are burned." Whether we want to interpret Jesus metaphorically is, of course, our business. The problem with scripture, however, is that many of its possible interpretations (including most of the literal ones) can be used to justify atrocities in defense of the faith.

The Holy Inquisition formally began in 1184 under Pope Lucius III, to crush the popular movement of Catharism. The Cathars (from the Greek *katharoi*, "the pure ones") had fashioned their own brand of Manicheanism (Mani himself was flayed alive at the behest of Zoroastrian priests in 276 CE), which held that the material world had been created by Satan and was therefore inherently evil. The Cathars were divided by a schism of their own and within each of their sects by the distinction between the renunciate *perfecti* and the lay *credentes* ("the believers") who revered them. The *perfecti* ate no meat, eggs, cheese, or fat, fasted for days at a time, maintained strict celibacy, and abjured all personal wealth. The life of the *perfecti* was so austere that most *credentes* only joined their ranks once they were safely on their deathbeds, so that, having lived as they pleased, they might yet go to God in holiness. Saint Bernard, who had tried in vain to combat this austere doctrine with that of the church, noted the reasons for his failure: "As to [the Cathars'] conversation, nothing can be less reprehensible . . . and what they speak, they prove by deeds. As for the morals of the heretic, he cheats no one, he oppresses no one, he strikes no one; his cheeks are pale with fasting, . . . his hands labor for his livelihood."[8]

There seems, in fact, to have been nothing wrong with these people apart from their attachment to certain unorthodox beliefs about the creation of the world. But heresy is heresy. Any person who believes that the Bible contains the infallible word of God will understand why these people had to be put to death.

The Inquisition took rather genteel steps at first (the use of torture to extract confessions was not "officially" sanctioned until 1215, at the Fourth Lateran Council), but two developments conspired to lengthen its strides. The first came in 1199 when Pope Innocent III decreed that all property belonging to a convicted heretic would be forfeited to the church; the church then shared it both with local officials and with the victim's accusers, as a reward for their candor. The second was the rise of the Dominican order.[9] Saint Dominic himself, displaying the conviction of every good Catholic of the day, announced to the Cathars, "For many years I have exhorted you in vain, with gentleness, preaching, praying, weeping. But according to the proverb of my country, 'where blessing can accomplish nothing, blows may avail.' We shall rouse against you princes and prelates, who, alas, will arm nations and kingdoms against this land. . . ."[10] It would appear that sainthood comes in a variety of flavors. With the founding of Dominic's holy order of mendicant friars, the Inquisition was ready to begin its work in earnest. It is important to remember, lest the general barbarity of time inure us to the horror of these historical accounts, that the perpetrators of the Inquisition—the torturers, informers, and those who commanded their actions—were ecclesiastics of one rank or another. They were men of God—popes, bishops, friars, and priests. They were men who had devoted their lives, in word if not in deed, to Christ as we find him in the New Testament, healing the sick and challenging those without sin to cast the first stone:

In 1234, the canonization of Saint Dominic was finally proclaimed in Toulouse, and Bishop Raymond du Fauga was washing his hands in preparation for dinner when he heard the rumor that a fever-ridden old woman in a nearby house was about to undergo the Cathar ritual. The bishop hurried to her bedside and managed to convince her that he was a friend, then interrogated her on her beliefs, then denounced her as a heretic. He called on her to recant. She refused. The bishop thereupon had her bed carried out into a field, and there she was burned. "And after the bishop and the friars and their companions had seen the business completed," Brother Guillaume wrote, "they returned to the refectory and, giving thanks to God and the Blessed Dominic, ate with rejoicing what had been prepared for them."[11]

The question of how the church managed to transform Jesus' principal message of loving one's neighbor and turning the other cheek into a doctrine of murder and rapine seems to promise a harrowing mystery; but it is no mystery at all. Apart from the Bible's heterogeneity and outright self-contradiction, allowing it to justify diverse and irreconcilable aims,[12] the culprit is clearly the doctrine of faith itself. Whenever a man imagines that he need only believe the truth of a proposition, without evidence—that unbelievers will go to hell, that Jews drink the blood of infants—he becomes capable of anything.

The practice for which the Inquisition is duly infamous, and the innovation that secured it a steady stream of both suspects and guilty verdicts, was its use of torture to extract confessions from the accused, to force witnesses to testify, and to persuade a confessing heretic to name those with whom he had collaborated in sin. The justification for this behavior came straight from Saint Augustine, who reasoned that if torture was appropriate for those who broke the laws of men, it was even more fitting for those who broke the laws of God.[13] As practiced by medieval Christians, judicial torture was merely a final, mad inflection of their faith. That anyone imagined that *facts* were being elicited by such a lunatic procedure seems a miracle in itself. As Voltaire wrote in 1764, "There is something divine here, for it is incomprehensible that men should have patiently borne this yoke."[14]

A contemporaneous account of the Spanish auto-da-fé (the public spectacle at which heretics were sentenced and often burned) will serve to complete our picture. The Spanish Inquisition did not cease its persecution of heretics until 1834 (the last auto-da-fé took place in Mexico in 1850), about the time Charles Darwin set sail on the

Beagle and Michael Faraday discovered the relationship between electricity and magnetism.

> The condemned are then immediately carried to the Riberia, the place of execution, where there are as many stakes set up as there are prisoners to be burnt. The negative and relapsed being first strangled and then burnt; the professed mount their stakes by a ladder, and the Jesuits, after several repeated exhortations to be reconciled to the church, consign them to eternal destruction, and then leave them to the fiend, who they tell them stands at their elbow to carry them into torments. On this a great shout is raised, and the cry is, "Let the dogs' beards be made"; which is done by thrusting flaming bunches of furze, fastened to long poles, against their beards, till their faces are burnt black, the surrounding populace rending the air with the loudest acclamations of joy. At last fire is set to the furze at the bottom of the stake, over which the victims are chained, so high that the flame seldom reaches higher than the seat they sit on, and thus they are rather roasted than burnt. Although there cannot be a more lamentable spectacle and the sufferers continually cry out as long as they are able, "Pity for the love of God!" yet it is beheld by persons of all ages and both sexes with transports of joy and satisfaction.[15]

And while Protestant reformers broke with Rome on a variety of counts, their treatment of their fellow human beings was no less disgraceful. Public executions were more popular than ever: heretics were still reduced to ash, scholars were tortured and killed for impertinent displays of reason, and fornicators were murdered without a qualm.[16] The basic lesson to be drawn from all this was summed up nicely by Will Durant: "Intolerance is the natural concomitant of strong faith; tolerance grows only when faith loses certainty; certainty is murderous."[17]

There really seems to be very little to perplex us here. Burning people who are destined to burn for all time seems a small price to pay to protect the people you love from the same fate. Clearly, the common law marriage between reason and faith—wherein otherwise reasonable men and women can be motivated by the content of unreasonable beliefs—places society upon a slippery slope, with confusion and hypocrisy at its heights, and the torments of the inquisitor waiting below.

Witch and Jew

Historically, there have been two groups targeted by the church that deserve special mention. Witches are of particular interest in this context because their persecution required an extraordinary degree of credulity to get underway, for the simple reason that a confederacy of witches in medieval Europe seems never to have existed. There were no covens of pagan dissidents, meeting in secret, betrothed to Satan, abandoning themselves to the pleasures of group sex, cannibalism, and the casting of spells upon neighbors, crops, and cattle. It seems that such notions were the product of folklore, vivid dreams, and sheer confabulation—and confirmed by confessions elicited under the most gruesome torture. Anti-Semitism is of interest here, both for the scale of the injustice that it has wrought and for its explicitly theological roots. From the perspective of Christian teaching, Jews are even worse than run-of-the-mill heretics; they are heretics who explicitly repudiate the divinity of Jesus Christ.

While the stigmas applied to witches and Jews throughout Christendom shared curious similarities—both were often accused of the lively and improbable offense of murdering Christian infants and drinking their blood[18]—their cases remain quite distinct. Witches, in all likelihood, did not even exist, and those murdered in their stead numbered perhaps 40,000 to 50,000 over three hundred years of persecution;[19] Jews have lived side by side with Christians for nearly two millennia, fathered their religion, and for reasons that are no more substantial than those underlying the belief in the Resurrection have been the objects of murderous intolerance since the first centuries after Christ.

THE accounts of witch hunts resemble, in most respects, the more widespread persecution of heretics throughout the Inquisition: imprisonment on the basis of accusations alone, torture to extract confession, confessions deemed unacceptable until accomplices were named, death by slow fire, and the rounding up of the freshly accused. The following anecdote is typical:

> In 1595, an old woman residing in a village near Constance, angry at not being invited to share the sports of the country people on a day of public rejoicing, was heard to mutter something to herself, and was afterwards seen to proceed through the fields towards a hill, where she was lost sight of. A violent thunderstorm arose about two hours afterwards, which wet the dancers to the skin, and did considerable damage to the plantations. This woman, suspected before of witchcraft, was seized and imprisoned, and accused of having raised the storm, by filling a hole with wine, and stirring it about with a stick. She was tortured till she confessed, and burned alive the next evening.[20]

Though it is difficult to generalize about the many factors that conspired to make villagers rise up against their neighbors, it is obvious that belief in the existence of witches was the sine qua non of the phenomenon. But what was it, precisely, that people believed? They appear to have believed that their neighbors were having sex with the devil, enjoying nocturnal flights upon broomsticks, changing into cats and hares, and eating the flesh of other human beings. More important, they believed utterly in *maleficium*—that is, in the efficacy of harming others by occult means. Among the many disasters that could befall a person over the course of a short and difficult life, medieval Christians seemed especially concerned that a neighbor might cast a spell and thereby undermine their health or good fortune. Only the advent of science could successfully undercut such an idea, along with the fantastical displays of cruelty to which it gave rise. We must remember that it was not until the mid-nineteenth century that the germ theory of disease emerged, laying to rest much superstition about the causes of illness.

Occult beliefs of this sort are clearly an inheritance from our primitive, magic-minded ancestors. The Fore people of New Guinea, for instance, besides being enthusiastic cannibals, exacted a gruesome revenge upon suspected sorcerers:

> Besides attending public meetings, Fore men also hunted down men they believed to be sorcerers and killed them in reprisal. The hunters used a specialized attack called *tukabu* against sorcerers: they ruptured their kidneys, crushed their genitals and broke their thigh bones with stone axes, bit into their necks and tore out their tracheas, jammed bamboo splinters into their veins to bleed them.[21]

No doubt each of these gestures held metaphysical significance. This behavior seems to have been commonplace among the Fore at least until the 1960s. The horrible comedy of human ignorance achieves a rare moment of transparency here: the Fore were merely responding to an epidemic of kuru—a fatal spongiform infection of the brain—brought on not by sorcerers in their midst but by their own religious observance of eating the bodies and brains of their dead.[22]

Throughout the Middle Ages and the Renaissance, it was perfectly apparent that disease could be inflicted by demons and black magic. There are accounts of frail, old women charged with killing able-bodied men and breaking the necks of their horses—actions which they were made to confess under torture—and few people, it seems, found such accusations implausible. Even the relentless torture of the accused was given a perverse rationale: the devil, it was believed, made his charges insensible to pain, despite their cries for mercy. And so it was that, for centuries, men and women who were guilty of little more than being ugly, old, widowed, or mentally ill were convicted of impossible crimes and then murdered for God's sake.

After nearly four hundred years some ecclesiastics began to appreciate how insane all this was. Consider the epiphany of Frederick Spee: "Torture fills our Germany with witches and unheard-of wickedness, and not only Germany but any nation that attempts it. . . . If all of us have not confessed ourselves witches, that is only because we have not all been tortured."[23] But Spee was led to this reasonable surmise only after a skeptical friend, the duke of Brunswick, had a woman suspected of witchcraft artfully tortured and interrogated in his presence. This poor woman testified that she has seen Spee himself on the Brocken, shape-shifting into a wolf, a goat, and other beasts and fathering numerous children by the assembled witches born with the heads of toads and the legs of spiders. Spee, lucky indeed to be in the company of a friend, and certain of his own innocence, immediately set to work on his *Cautio Criminalis* (1631), which detailed the injustice of witch trials.[24]

Bertrand Russell observed, however, that not all reasonable men were as fortunate as Spee:

Some few bold rationalists ventured, even while the persecution was at its height, to doubt whether tempests, hail-storms, thunder and lightning were really caused by the machinations of women. Such men were shown no mercy. Thus towards the end of the sixteenth century Flade, Rector of the University of Trèves, and Chief Judge of the Electoral Court, after condemning countless witches, began to think that perhaps their confessions were due to the desire to escape from the tortures of the rack, with the result that he showed unwillingness to convict. He was accused of having sold himself to Satan, and was subjected to the same tortures as he had inflicted upon others. Like them, he confessed his guilt, and in 1589 he was strangled and then burnt.[25]

As late as 1718 (just as the inoculation against smallpox was being introduced to England and the English mathematician Brook Taylor was making refinements to the calculus), we find the madness of the witch hunt still a potent social force. Charles Mackay relates an incident in Caithness (northeast Scotland):

A silly fellow, named William Montgomery, a carpenter, had a mortal antipathy to cats; and somehow or other these animals generally chose his back-yard as the scene of their catterwaulings. He puzzled his brains for a long time to know why he, above all his neighbors, should be so pestered. At last he came to the sage conclusion that his tormentors were no cats, but witches. In this opinion he was supported by his maid-servant, who swore a round oath that she had often heard the aforesaid cats talking together in human voices. The next time the unlucky tabbies assembled in his back-yard, the valiant carpenter was on the alert. Arming himself with an axe, a dirk, and a broadsword, he rushed out among them. One of them he wounded in the back, a second in the hip, and the leg of a third he maimed with his axe; but he could not capture any of them. A few days afterwards, two old women of the parish died; and it was said, that when their bodies were laid out, there appeared upon the back of one the mark as of a recent wound, and a similar scar upon the hip of the other. The carpenter and his maid were convinced that they were the very cats, and the whole county repeated the same story. Every one was upon the look-out for proofs corroborative; a very remarkable one was soon discovered. Nancy Gilbert, a wretched old creature upwards of seventy years of age, was found in bed with her leg broken. As she was ugly enough for a witch, it was asserted that she also was one of the cats that had fared so ill at the hands of the carpenter. The latter, when informed of the popular suspicion, asserted that he distinctly remembered to have struck one of the cats a blow with the back of his broadsword, which ought to have broken her leg. Nancy was immediately dragged from her bed and thrown into prison. Before she was put to the torture, she explained in a very natural and intelligible manner how she had broken her limb; but this account did not give satisfaction. The professional persuasions of the torturer made her tell a different tale, and she confessed that she was indeed a witch, and had been wounded by Montgomery on the night stated; that the two old women recently deceased were witches also, besides about a score of others whom she named. The poor creature suffered so much by the removal from her own home, and the tortures inflicted upon her, that she died the next day in prison.[26]

Apart from observing, yet again, the astonishing consequences of certain beliefs, we should take note of the reasonable way these witch-hunters attempted to confirm their suspicions. They looked for correlations that held apparent significance: not *any* old woman would do; they needed one who had suffered a wound similar to the one inflicted upon the cat. Once you accept the premise that old women can shape-shift into cats and back again, the rest is practically *science*.

The church did not officially condemn the use of torture until the bull of Pope Pius VII in 1816.

ANTI-SEMITISM[27] is as integral to church doctrine as the flying buttress is to a Gothic cathedral, and this terrible truth has been published in Jewish blood since the first centuries of the common era. Like that of the Inquisition, the history of anti-Semitism can scarcely be given sufficient treatment in the context of this book. I raise the subject, however briefly, because the irrational hatred of Jews has produced a spectrum of effects that have been most acutely felt in our own time. Anti-Semitism is intrinsic to both Christianity and Islam; both traditions consider the Jews to be bunglers of God's initial revelation. Christians generally also believe that the Jews murdered Christ, and their continued existence as Jews constitutes a perverse denial of his status as the Messiah. Whatever the context, the hatred of Jews remains a product of faith: Christian, Muslim, as well as Jewish.

Contemporary Muslim anti-Semitism is heavily indebted to its Christian counterpart. *The Protocols of the Elders of Zion*, a Russian anti-Semitic forgery that is the source of most conspiracy theories relating to the Jews, is now considered an authoritative text in the Arab-speaking world.[28] A recent contribution to *Al-Akhbar*, one of Cairo's mainstream newspapers, suggests that the problem of Muslim anti-Semitism is now deeper than any handshake in the White House Rose Garden can remedy: "Thanks to Hitler, of blessed memory, who on behalf of the Palestinians took revenge in advance, against the most vile criminals on the face of the Earth. . . . Although we do have a complaint against him, for his revenge was not enough."[29] This is from *moderate* Cairo, where Muslims drink alcohol, go to the movies, and watch belly dancing—and where the government actively represses fundamentalism. Clearly, hatred of the Jews is white-hot in the Muslim world.

The gravity of Jewish suffering over the ages, culminating in the Holocaust, makes it almost impossible to entertain any suggestion that Jews might have brought their troubles upon themselves. This is, however, in a rather narrow sense, the truth. Prior to the rise of the church, Jews became the objects of suspicion and occasional persecution for their refusal to assimilate, for the insularity and professed superiority of their religious culture—that is, for the content of their own unreasonable, sectarian beliefs. The dogma of a "chosen people," while at least implicit in most faiths, achieved a stridence in Judaism that was unknown in the ancient world. Among cultures that worshiped a plurality of Gods, the later monotheism of the Jews proved indigestible. And while their explicit demonization as a people required the mad work of the Christian church, the ideology of Judaism remains a lightning rod for intolerance to this day. As a system of beliefs, it appears among the least suited to survive in a theological state of nature. Christianity and Islam both acknowledge the sanctity of the Old Testament and offer easy conversion to their faiths. Islam honors Abraham, Moses, and Jesus as forerunners of Muhammad. Hinduism embraces almost anything in sight with its manifold arms (many Hindus, for instance, consider Jesus an avatar of Vishnu). Judaism alone finds itself surrounded by unmitigated errors. It seems little wonder, therefore, that it has drawn so much sectarian fire. Jews, insofar as they are religious, believe that they are bearers of a unique covenant with God. As a consequence, they have spent the last two thousand years collaborating with those who see them as different by seeing themselves as irretrievably so. Judaism is as intrinsically divisive, as ridiculous in its literalism, and as at odds with the civilizing insights of modernity as any other religion. Jewish settlers, by exercising their "freedom of belief" on contested land, are now one of the principal obstacles to peace in the Middle East. They will be a direct cause of war between Islam and the West should one ever erupt over the Israeli-Palestinian conflict.[30]

THE problem for first-century Christians was simple: they belonged to a sect of Jews that had recognized Jesus as the messiah (Greek *christos*), while the majority of their coreligionists had not. Jesus was a Jew, of course, and his mother a Jewess. His apostles, to the last man, were also Jews. There is no evidence whatsoever, apart from the tendentious writings of the later church, that Jesus ever conceived of himself as anything other than a Jew among Jews, seeking the fulfillment of Judaism—and, likely, the return of Jewish sovereignty in a Roman world. As many authors have observed, the numerous strands of Hebrew prophecy that were made to coincide with Jesus' ministry betray the apologetics, and often poor scholarship, of the gospel writers.

The writers of Luke and Matthew, for instance, in seeking to make the life of Jesus conform to Old Testament prophecy, insist that Mary conceived as a virgin (Greek *parthenos*), harking to the

Greek rendering of Isaiah 7:14. Unfortunately for fanciers of Mary's virginity, the Hebrew word *alma* (for which *parthenos* is an erroneous translation) simply means "young woman," without any implication of virginity. It seems all but certain that the Christian dogma of the virgin birth, and much of the church's resulting anxiety about sex, was the result of a mistranslation from the Hebrew.[31]

Another strike against the doctrine of the virgin birth is that the other evangelists, Mark and John, seem to know nothing about it—though both appear troubled by accusations of Jesus' illegitimacy.[32] Paul apparently thinks that Jesus is the son of Joseph and Mary. He refers to Jesus as being "born of the seed of David according to the flesh" (Romans 1:3—meaning Joseph was his father), and "born of woman" (Galatians 4:4—meaning that Jesus was really human), with no reference to Mary's virginity.[33]

Mary's virginity has always been suggestive of God's attitude toward sex: it is intrinsically sinful, being the mechanism through which original sin was bequeathed to the generations after Adam. It would appear that Western civilization has endured two millennia of consecrated sexual neurosis simply because the authors of Matthew and Luke could not read Hebrew. For the Jews, the true descendants of Jesus and the apostles, the dogma of the virgin birth has served as a perennial justification for their persecution, because it has been one of the principal pieces of "evidence" demonstrating the divinity of Jesus.

We should note that the emphasis on miracles in the New Testament, along with the attempts to make the life of Jesus conform to Old Testament prophecy, reveal the first Christians' commitment, however faltering, to making their faith seem *rational*. Given the obvious significance of any miracle, and the widespread acceptance of prophecy, it would have been only reasonable to have considered these purported events to be evidence for Christ's divinity. Augustine, for his part, came right out and said it: "I should not be a Christian but for the miracles." A millennium later, Blaise Pascal—

mathematical prodigy, philosopher, and physicist—was so impressed by Christ's confirmation of prophecy that he devoted the last years of his short life to defending Christian doctrine in writing:

> Through Jesus we know God. All those who have claimed to know God and prove his existence without Jesus Christ have only had futile proofs to offer. But to prove Christ we have the prophecies which are solid and palpable proofs. By being fulfilled and proved true by the event, these prophecies show that these truths are certain and thus prove that Jesus is divine.[34]

"Solid and palpable"? That so nimble a mind could be led to labor under such dogma was surely one of the great wonders of the age.[35] Even today, the apparent confirmation of prophecy detailed in the New Testament is offered as the chief reason to accept Jesus as the messiah. The "leap of faith" is really a fiction. No Christians, not even those of the first century, have ever been content to rely upon it.

WHILE God had made his covenant with Israel, and delivered his Son in the guise of a Jew, the earliest Christians were increasingly gentile, and as the doctrine spread, the newly baptized began to see the Jews' denial of Jesus' divinity as the consummate evil. This sectarian ethos is already well established by the time of Paul:

> For ye, brethren, became followers of the churches of God which in Judæa are in Christ Jesus: for ye also like things of your own countrymen, even as they have of the Jews: Who both killed the Lord Jesus, and their own prophets, and have persecuted us; and they please not God, and are contrary to all men: Forbidding us to speak to the Gentiles that they might be saved, to fill up their sins alway: for the wrath is come upon them to the uttermost. (Thessalonians 2:14–16)

The explicit demonization of the Jews appears in the Gospel of John:

> Jesus said unto them [the Jews], If God were your Father, ye
> would love me: for I proceeded forth and came from God; neither
> came I of myself, but he sent me. Why do ye not understand my
> speech? Even because ye cannot hear my word. Ye are of your
> father the devil, and the lusts of your father ye will do. He was a
> murderer from the beginning, and abode not in the truth, because
> there is no truth in him. When he speaketh a lie, he speaketh of
> his own: for he is a liar, and the father of it. And because I tell you
> the truth, ye believe me not. (John 8:41–45)

With the destruction of the Temple in 70 CE, Christians—gentile
and Jew alike—felt that they were witnessing the fulfillment of
prophecy, imagining that the Roman legions were meting out God's
punishment to the betrayers of Christ. Anti-Semitism soon
acquired a triumphal smugness, and with the ascension of Christianity as the state religion in 312 CE, with the conversion of
Constantine, Christians began openly to relish and engineer the
degradation of world Jewry.[36] Laws were passed that revoked many
of the civic privileges previously granted to Jews. Jews were
excluded from the military and from holding high office and were
forbidden to proselytize or to have sexual relations with Christian
women (both under penalty of death). The Justinian Code, in the
sixth century, essentially declared the legal status of the Jews null
and void—outlawing the Mishnah (the codification of Jewish
oral law) and making disbelief in the Resurrection and the Last
Judgment a capital offense.[37] Augustine, ever the ready sectarian,
rejoiced at the subjugation of the Jews and took special pleasure in
the knowledge that they were doomed to wander the earth bearing
witness to the truth of scripture and the salvation of the gentiles.
The suffering and servitude of the Jews was proof that Christ had
been the messiah after all.[38]

Like witches, the Jews of Europe were often accused of incredible crimes, the most prevalent of which has come to be known as the "blood libel"—born of the belief that Jews require the blood of Christians (generally newborn) for use in a variety of rituals. Throughout the Middle Ages, Jews were regularly accused of murdering Christian infants, a crime for which they were duly despised. It was well known that all Jews menstruated, male and female alike, and required the blood of a Christian to replenish their lost stores. They also suffered from terrible hemorrhoids and oozing sores as a punishment for the murder of Christ—and as a retort to their improbable boast before the "innocent" Pontius Pilate (Matthew 27:25), "His blood be on us and on our children." It should come as no surprise that Jews were in the habit of applying Christian blood as a salve upon these indignities. Christian blood was also said to ease the labor pains of any Jewess fortunate enough to have it spread upon pieces of parchment and placed into her clenched fists. It was common knowledge, too, that all Jews were born blind and that, when smeared upon their eyes, Christian blood granted them the faculty of sight. Jewish boys were frequently born with their fingers attached to their foreheads, and only the blood of a Christian could allow this pensive gesture to be broken without risk to the child.

Once born, a Jew's desire for Christian blood could scarcely be slaked. During the rite of circumcision it took the place of consecrated oil (*crissam*, an exclusively Christian commodity); and later in life, Jewish children of both sexes had their genitalia smeared with the blood of some poor, pious man—waylaid upon the road and strangled in a ditch—to make them fertile. Medieval Christians believed that Jews used their blood for everything from a rouge to a love philter and as a prophylactic against leprosy. Given this state of affairs, who could doubt that Jews of all ages would be fond of sucking blood out of Christian children "with quills and small reeds," for later use by their elders during wedding feasts? Finally, with a mind to covering all their bases, Jews smeared their dying brethren with the blood of an innocent Christian babe (recently baptized and then suffocated), saying, "If the Messiah promised by the prophets has really come, and he be Jesus, may this innocent blood ensure for you eternal life!"[39]

The blood libel totters on shoulders of other giant misconceptions, of course, especially the notion, widely accepted at the time, that the various constituents of the human body possess magical and medicinal power. This explains the acceptance of similar accusations leveled at witches, such as the belief that candles made from human fat could render a man invisible while lighting up his surroundings.[40] One wonders just how many a thief was caught striding through his neighbor's foyer in search of plunder, bearing a malodorous candle confidently aloft, before these miraculous tools of subterfuge fell out of fashion.

But for sheer gothic absurdity nothing surpasses the medieval concern over *host desecration*, the punishment of which preoccupied pious Christians for centuries. The doctrine of transubstantiation was formally established in 1215 at the Fourth Lateran Council (the same one that sanctioned the use of torture by inquisitors and prohibited Jews from owning land or embarking upon civil or military careers), and thereafter became the centerpiece of the Christian (now Catholic) faith. (The relevant passage from *The Profession of Faith of the Roman Catholic* was cited in chapter 2.) Henceforth, it was an indisputable fact of this world that the communion host is actually transformed at the Mass into the living body of Jesus Christ. After this incredible dogma had been established, by mere reiteration, to the satisfaction of everyone, Christians began to worry that these living wafers might be subjected to all manner of mistreatment, and even physical torture, at the hands of heretics and Jews. (One might wonder why *eating* the body of Jesus would be any less of a torment to him.) Could there be any doubt that the Jews would seek to harm the Son of God again, knowing that his body was now readily accessible in the form of defenseless crackers? Historical accounts suggest that as many as three thousand Jews were murdered in response to a *single* allegation of this imaginary crime. The crime of host desecration was punished throughout Europe for centuries.[41]

It is out of this history of theologically mandated persecution that secular anti-Semitism emerged. Even explicitly anti-Christian movements, as in the cases of German Nazism and Russian socialism, managed to inherit and enact the doctrinal intolerance of the church. Astonishingly, ideas as spurious as the blood libel are still very much with us, having found a large cult of believers in the Muslim world.[42]

The Holocaust

The National Socialism of all of us is anchored in uncritical loyalty, in the surrender to the Führer that does not ask for the why in individual cases, in the silent execution of his orders. We believe that the Führer is obeying a higher call to fashion German history. There can be no criticism of this belief.

Rudolf Hess, in a speech, June 1934.[43]

The rise of Nazism in Germany required much in the way of "uncritical loyalty." Beyond the abject (and *religious*) loyalty to Hitler, the Holocaust emerged out of people's acceptance of some very implausible ideas.

Heinrich Himmler thought the SS should have leeks and mineral water for breakfast. He thought people could be made to confess by telepathy. Following King Arthur and the round table, he would have only twelve people to dinner. He believed that Aryans had not evolved from monkeys and apes like other races, but had come down to earth from the heavens, where they had been preserved in ice from the beginning of time. He established a meteorology division which was given the task of proving this cosmic ice theory. He also thought he was a reincarnation of Heinrich the

First. Himmler was an extreme case: the picture is perhaps one of someone quite mad. But one of his characteristics was much more widely shared—his mind had not been encouraged to grow. Filled with information and opinion, he had no critical powers.[44]

At the heart of every totalitarian enterprise, one sees outlandish dogmas, poorly arranged, but working ineluctably like gears in some ludicrous instrument of death. Nazism evolved out of a variety of economic and political factors, of course, but it was held together by a belief in the racial purity and superiority of the German people. The obverse of this fascination with race was the certainty that all impure elements—homosexuals, invalids, Gypsies, and, above all, Jews—posed a threat to the fatherland. And while the hatred of Jews in Germany expressed itself in a predominately secular way, it was a direct inheritance from medieval Christianity. For centuries, religious Germans had viewed the Jews as the worst species of heretics and attributed every societal ill to their continued presence among the faithful. Daniel Goldhagen has traced the rise of the German conception of the Jews as a "race" and a "nation," which culminated in an explicitly nationalistic formulation of this ancient Christian animus.[45] Of course, the *religious* demonization of the Jews was also a contemporary phenomenon. (Indeed, the Vatican itself perpetuated the blood libel in its newspapers as late as 1914.)[46] Ironically, the very fact that Jews had been mistreated in Germany (and elsewhere) since time immemorial—by being confined to ghettos and deprived of civic status—gave rise to the modern, secular strand of anti-Semitism, for it was not until the emancipation efforts of the early nineteenth century that the hatred of the Jews acquired an explicitly racial inflection. Even the self-proclaimed "friends of the Jews" who sought the admission of Jews into German society with the full privileges of citizenship did so only on the assumption that the Jews could be reformed thereby and rendered pure by sustained association with the German race.[47] Thus, the voices of liberal tolerance within Germany were often as anti-Semitic as their conservative opponents, for they differed only in the belief that the Jew was capable of moral regeneration. By the end of the nineteenth century, after the liberal experiment had failed to dissolve the Jews in the pristine solvent of German tolerance, the erstwhile "friends of the Jews" came to regard these strangers in their midst with the same loathing that their less idealistic contemporaries had nurtured all along. An analysis of prominent anti-Semitic writers and publications from 1861 to 1895 reveals just how murderous the German anti-Semites were inclined to be: fully two-thirds of those that purported to offer "solutions" to the "Jewish problem" openly advocated the physical extermination of the Jews—and this, as Goldhagen points out, was several decades before the rise of Hitler. Indeed, the possibility of exterminating a whole people was considered before "genocide" was even a proper concept, and long before killing on such a massive scale had been shown to be practically feasible in the First and Second World Wars.

While Goldhagen's controversial charge that the Germans were Hitler's "willing executioners" seems generally fair, it is true that the people of other nations were equally willing. Genocidal anti-Semitism had been in the air for some time, particularly in Eastern Europe. In the year 1919, for instance, sixty-thousand Jews were murdered in Ukraine alone.[48] Once the Third Reich began its overt persecution of Jews, anti-Semitic pogroms erupted in Poland, Rumania, Hungary, Austria, Czechoslovakia, Croatia, and elsewhere.[49]

With passage of the Nuremberg laws in 1935 the transformation of German anti-Semitism was complete. The Jews were to be considered a race, one that was inimical to a healthy Germany in principle. As such, they were fundamentally irredeemable, for while one can cast away one's religious ideology, and even accept baptism into the church, one cannot cease to be what one is. And it is here that we encounter the overt complicity of the church in the attempted murder of an entire people. German Catholics showed themselves remarkably acquiescent to a racist creed that was at cross-purposes with at least one of their core beliefs: for if baptism truly had the power to redeem, then Jewish converts should have been considered saved without residue in the eyes of the church. But, as we have seen, coherence in any system of beliefs is never perfect—and the German churches, in order to maintain order during their services, were finally obliged to print leaflets admonishing their flock not to attack Jewish converts *during times of worship*. That a person's race could not be rescinded was underscored as early as 1880, in a Vatican-approved paper: "Oh how wrong and deluded are those who think Judaism is just a religion, like Catholicism, Paganism, Protestantism, and not in fact a race, a people, and a nation! . . . For the Jews are not only Jews because of their religion . . . they are Jews also and especially because of their race."[50] The German Catholic episcopate issued its own guidelines in 1936: "Race, soil, blood and people are precious natural values, which God the Lord has created and the care of which he has entrusted to us Germans."[51]

But the truly sinister complicity of the church came in its willingness to open its genealogical records to the Nazis and thereby enable them to trace the extent of a person's Jewish ancestry. A historian of the Catholic Church, Guenther Lewy, has written:

> The very question of whether the [Catholic] Church should lend its help to the Nazi state in sorting out people of Jewish descent was never debated. On the contrary. "We have always unselfishly worked for the people without regard to gratitude or ingratitude," a priest wrote in *Klerusblatt* in September 1934. "We shall also do our best to help in this service to the people." And the co-operation of the Church in this matter continued right through the war years, when the price of being Jewish was no longer dismissal from a government job and loss of livelihood, but deportation and outright physical destruction.[52]

All of this, despite the fact that the Catholic Church was in very real opposition to much of the Nazi platform, which was bent upon curtailing its power. Goldhagen also reminds us that not a single

German Catholic was excommunicated before, during, or after the war, "after committing crimes as great as any in human history." This is really an extraordinary fact. Throughout this period, the church continued to excommunicate theologians and scholars in droves for holding unorthodox views and to proscribe books by the hundreds, and yet not a single perpetrator of genocide—of whom there were countless examples—succeeded in furrowing Pope Pius XII's censorious brow.

This astonishing situation merits a slight digression. At the end of the nineteenth century, the Vatican attempted to combat the unorthodox conclusions of modern Bible commentators with its own rigorous scholarship. Catholic scholars were urged to adopt the techniques of modern criticism, to demonstrate that the results of a meticulous and dispassionate study of the Bible could be compatible with church doctrine. The movement was known as "modernism," and soon occasioned considerable embarrassment, as many of the finest Catholic scholars found that they, too, were becoming skeptical about the literal truth of scripture. In 1893 Pope Leo XIII announced,

> All those books . . . which the church regards as sacred and canon-
> ical were written with all their parts under the inspiration of the
> Holy Spirit. Now, far from admitting the coexistence of error,
> Divine inspiration by itself excludes all error, and that also of
> necessity, since God, the Supreme Truth, must be incapable of
> teaching error.[53]

In 1907, Pope Pius X declared modernism a heresy, had its exponents within the church excommunicated, and put all critical studies of the Bible on the Index of proscribed books. Authors similarly distinguished include Descartes (selected works), Montaigne (*Essais*), Locke (*Essay on Human Understanding*), Swift (*Tale of a Tub*), Swedenborg (*Principia*), Voltaire (*Lettres philosophiques*), Diderot (*Encyclopédie*), Rousseau (*Du contrat social*), Gibbon (*The Decline and Fall of the Roman Empire*), Paine (*The Rights of Man*), Sterne

(*A Sentimental Journey*), Kant (*Critique of Pure Reason*), Flaubert (*Madame Bovary*), and Darwin (*On the Origin of Species*). As a censorious afterthought, Descartes' *Meditations* was added to the Index in 1948. With all that had occurred earlier in the decade, one might have thought that the Holy See could have found greater offenses with which to concern itself. Although not a single leader of the Third Reich—not even Hitler himself—was ever excommunicated, Galileo was not absolved of heresy until 1992.

In the words of the present pope, John Paul II, we can see how the matter now stands: "This Revelation is definitive; one can only accept it or reject it. One can accept it, professing belief in God, the Father Almighty, Creator of heaven and earth, and in Jesus Christ, the Son, of the same substance as the Father and the Holy Spirit, who is Lord and the Giver of life. Or one can reject all of this."[54] While the rise and fall of modernism in the church can hardly be considered a victory for the forces of rationality, it illustrates an important point: wanting to know how the world is leaves one vulnerable to new evidence. It is no accident that religious doctrine and honest inquiry are so rarely juxtaposed in our world.

When we consider that so few generations had passed since the church left off disemboweling innocent men before the eyes of their families, burning old women alive in public squares, and torturing scholars to the point of madness for merely speculating about the nature of the stars, it is perhaps little wonder that it failed to think anything had gone terribly amiss in Germany during the war years. Indeed, it is also well known that certain Vatican officials (the most notorious of whom was Bishop Alois Hudal) helped members of the SS like Adolf Eichmann, Martin Bormann, Heinrich Mueller, Franz Stangl, and hundreds of others escape to South America and the Middle East in the aftermath of the war.[55] In this context, one is often reminded that others in the Vatican helped Jews escape as well. This is true. It is also true, however, that Vatican aid was often contingent upon whether or not the Jews in question had been previously baptized.[56]

There were, no doubt, innumerable instances in which European Christians risked their lives to protect the Jews in their
midst, and did so because of their Christianity.[57] But they were
not innumerable enough. The fact that people are sometimes
inspired to heroic acts of kindness by the teaching of Christ says
nothing about the wisdom or necessity of believing that he, exclusively, was the Son of God. Indeed, we will find that we need not
believe anything on insufficient evidence to feel compassion for
the suffering of others. Our common humanity is reason enough
to protect our fellow human beings from coming to harm. Genocidal intolerance, on the other hand, must inevitably find its inspiration elsewhere. Whenever you hear that people have begun
killing noncombatants intentionally and indiscriminately, ask
yourself what dogma stands at their backs. What do these freshly
minted killers *believe*? You will find that it is always—*always*—
preposterous.

MY PURPOSE in this chapter has been to intimate, in as concise a
manner as possible, some of the terrible consequences that have
arisen, logically and inevitably, out of Christian faith. Unfortunately, this catalog of horrors could be elaborated upon indefinitely. Auschwitz, the Cathar heresy, the witch hunts—these
phrases signify depths of human depravity and human suffering
that would surely elude description were a writer to set himself
no other task. As I have cast a very wide net in the present chapter, I can only urge readers who may feel they have just been
driven past a roadside accident at full throttle to consult the literature on these subjects. Such extracurricular studies will reveal
that the history of Christianity is principally a story of
mankind's misery and ignorance rather than of its requited love
of God.

While Christianity has few living inquisitors today, Islam has many. In the next chapter we will see that in our opposition to the worldview of Islam, we confront a civilization with an arrested history. It is as though a portal in time has opened, and fourteenth-century hordes are pouring into our world. Unfortunately, they are now armed with twenty-first-century weapons.

4

The Problem with Islam

·

WHILE my argument in this book is aimed at faith itself, the differences between faiths are as relevant as they are unmistakable. There is a reason, after all, why we must now confront Muslim, rather than Jain terrorists, in every corner of the world. Jains do not believe anything that is remotely likely to inspire them to commit acts of suicidal violence against unbelievers. By any measure of normativity we might wish to adopt (ethical, practical, epistemological, economic, etc.), there are good beliefs and there are bad ones—and it should now be obvious to everyone that Muslims have more than their fair share of the latter.[1]

Of course, like every religion, Islam has had its moments. Muslim scholars invented algebra, translated the writings of Plato and Aristotle, and made important contributions to a variety of nascent sciences at a time when European Christians were luxuriating in the most abysmal ignorance. It was only through the Muslim conquest of Spain that classical Greek texts found their way into Latin translation and seeded the Renaissance in western Europe. Thousands of pages could be written cataloging facts of this sort for every religion, but to what end? Would it suggest that religious faith is good, or even benign? It is a truism to say that people of faith have created almost everything of value in our world, because nearly every person who has ever swung a hammer or trimmed a sail has been a devout member of one or another religious culture. There has been simply no one else to do the job. We can also say that every human achievement prior to the twentieth century was accomplished by men and women who were perfectly ignorant of the molecular basis of life. Does this suggest that a nineteenth-century view of biology would have been worth maintaining? There is no telling what our world would now be like had some great kingdom of Reason emerged at the time of the Crusades and pacified the credulous multitudes of Europe and the Middle East. We might have had modern democracy and the Internet by the year 1600. The fact that religious faith has left its mark on every aspect of our civilization is not an argument in its favor, nor can any particular faith be exonerated simply because certain of its adherents made foundational contributions to human culture.

Given the vicissitudes of Muslim history, however, I suspect that the starting point I have chosen for this book—that of a single suicide bomber following the consequences of his religious beliefs—is bound to exasperate many readers, since it ignores most of what commentators on the Middle East have said about the roots of Muslim violence. It ignores the painful history of the Israeli occupation of the West Bank and Gaza. It ignores the collusion of Western powers with corrupt dictatorships. It ignores the endemic poverty and lack of economic opportunity that now plague the Arab world. But I will argue that we can ignore all of these things—or treat them only to place them safely on the shelf—because the world is filled with poor, uneducated, and exploited peoples who do not commit acts of terrorism, indeed who would never commit terrorism of the sort that has become so commonplace among Muslims; and the Muslim world has no shortage of educated and prosperous men and women, suffering little more than their infatuation with Koranic eschatology, who are eager to murder infidels for God's sake.[2]

We are at war with Islam. It may not serve our immediate foreign policy objectives for our political leaders to openly acknowledge this fact, but it is unambiguously so. It is not merely that we are at war with an otherwise peaceful religion that has been "hijacked" by extremists. We are at war with precisely the vision of life that is prescribed to all Muslims in the Koran, and further elaborated in the literature of the hadith, which recounts the sayings and actions of the Prophet. A future in which Islam and the West do not stand on the brink of mutual annihilation is a future in which most Muslims have learned to ignore most of their canon, just as most Christians have learned to do. Such a transformation is by no means guaranteed to occur, however, given the tenets of Islam.

A Fringe without a Center

Many authors have pointed out that it is problematic to speak of Muslim "fundamentalism" because it suggests that there are large doctrinal differences between fundamentalist Muslims and the mainstream. The truth, however, is that most Muslims appear to be "fundamentalist" in the Western sense of the word—in that even "moderate" approaches to Islam generally consider the Koran to be the literal and inerrant word of the one true God. The difference between fundamentalists and moderates—and certainly the difference between all "extremists" and moderates—is the degree to which they see political and military action to be intrinsic to the practice of their faith. In any case, people who believe that Islam must inform every dimension of human existence, including politics and law, are now generally called not "fundamentalists" or "extremists" but, rather, "Islamists."

The world, from the point of view of Islam, is divided into the "House of Islam" and the "House of War," and this latter designation should indicate how many Muslims believe their differences with those who do not share their faith will be ultimately resolved. While there are undoubtedly some "moderate" Muslims who have decided to overlook the irrescindable militancy of their religion, Islam is undeniably a religion of conquest. The only future devout Muslims can envisage—*as Muslims*—is one in which all infidels have been converted to Islam, subjugated, or killed. The tenets of Islam simply do not admit of anything but a temporary sharing of power with the "enemies of God."

Like most other religions, Islam has suffered a variety of schisms. Since the seventh century, the Sunni (the majority) have considered the Shia to be heterodox, and the Shia have returned the compliment. Divisions have emerged within each of these sects as well, and even within the ranks of those who are unmistakably Islamist. We need not go into the sectarian algebra in any detail, apart from noting that these schisms have had the salutary effect of dividing the House of Islam against itself. While this mitigates the threat that Islam currently poses to the West, Islam and Western liberalism remain irreconcilable. Moderate Islam—*really* moderate, *really* critical of Muslim irrationality—scarcely seems to exist. If it does, it is doing as good a job at hiding as moderate Christianity did in the fourteenth century (and for similar reasons).

The feature of Islam that is most troubling to non-Muslims, and which apologists for Islam do much to obfuscate, is the principle of jihad. Literally, the term can be translated as "struggle" or "striving," but it is generally rendered in English as "holy war," and this is no accident. While Muslims are quick to observe that there is an inner (or "greater") jihad, which involves waging war against one's own sinfulness, no amount of casuistry can disguise the fact that the outer (or "lesser") jihad—war against infidels and apostates—is a central feature of the faith. Armed conflict in "defense of Islam" is a religious obligation for every Muslim man. We are misled if we believe that the phrase "in defense of Islam" suggests that all Muslim fighting must be done in "self-defense." On the contrary, the duty of jihad is an unambiguous call to world conquest. As Bernard Lewis writes, "the presumption is that the duty of jihad will continue, interrupted only by truces, until all the world either adopts the Muslim faith or submits to Muslim rule."[3] There is just no denying that Muslims expect victory in *this* world, as well as in the next. As Malise Ruthven points out, "The Prophet had been his own Caesar. . . . If *imitatio Christi* meant renouncing worldly ambition and seeking salvation by deeds of private virtue, *imitatio Muhammadi* meant sooner or later taking up arms against those forces which seemed to threaten Islam from within or without."[4] While the Koran is more than sufficient to establish these themes, the literature of the hadith elaborates:

> Jihad is your duty under any ruler, be he godly or wicked.

> A single endeavor (of fighting) in Allah's Cause in the forenoon or in the afternoon is better than the world and whatever is in it.

> A day and a night fighting on the frontier is better than a month of fasting and prayer.

> Nobody who dies and finds good from Allah (in the Hereafter) would wish to come back to this world even if he were given the whole world and whatever is in it, except the martyr who, on seeing the superiority of martyrdom, would like to come back to the world and get killed again (in Allah's Cause).

> He who dies without having taken part in a campaign dies in a kind of unbelief.

> Paradise is in the shadow of swords.[5]

Many hadiths of this sort can be found, and Islamists regularly invoke them as a justification for attacks upon infidels and apostates.

Those looking for ways to leaven the intrinsic militancy of Islam have observed that there are a few lines in the Koran that seem to speak directly against indiscriminate violence. Those who wage jihad are enjoined not to attack first (Koran 2:190), since "God does not love aggressors." But this injunction restrains no one. Given the long history of conflict between Islam and the West, almost any act of violence against infidels can now be plausibly construed as an action in defense of the faith. Our recent adventures in Iraq provide all the rationale an aspiring martyr needs to wage jihad against "the friends of Satan" for decades to come. Lewis notes that one who would fight for God is also enjoined not to kill women, children, or the aged, unless in self-defense, but a little casuistry on the notion of self-defense allows Muslim militants to elude this stricture as well. The bottom line is that devout Muslims can have no doubt about the reality of paradise or about the efficacy of martyrdom as a means of getting there. Nor can they question the wisdom and reasonableness of killing people for what amount to theological grievances. In Islam, it is the "moderate" who is left to split hairs, because the basic thrust of the doctrine is undeniable: convert, subjugate, or kill unbelievers; kill apostates; and conquer the world.

The imperative of world conquest is an interesting one, given that "imperialism" is one of the chief sins that Muslims attribute to the West:

> Imperialism is a particularly important theme in the Middle Eastern and more especially the Islamic case against the West. For them, the word imperialism has a special meaning. This word is, for example, never used by Muslims of the great Muslim empires—the first one founded by the Arabs, the later ones by the Turks, who conquered vast territories and populations and incorporated them in the House of Islam. It was perfectly legitimate for Muslims to conquer and rule Europe and Europeans and thus enable them—but not compel them—to embrace the true faith. It was a crime and a sin for Europeans to conquer and rule Muslims and, still worse, to try to lead them astray. In the Muslim perception, conversion to Islam is a benefit to the convert and a merit in those who convert him. In Islamic law, conversion from Islam is apostasy—a capital offense for both the one who is misled and the one who misleads him. On this question, the law is clear and unequivocal. If a Muslim renounces Islam, even if a new convert reverts to his previous faith, the penalty is death.[6]

We will return to the subject of apostasy in a moment. We should first note, however, that Lewis' comment about not compelling the conquered to embrace the true faith is misleading in this context. It is true that the Koran provides a handbrake, of sorts, for Muslim "moderates"—"There shall be no compulsion in religion" (Koran 2:256)—but a glance at the rest of the Koran, and at Muslim history, reveals that we should not expect too much from its use. As it stands, this line offers a very slender basis for Muslim tolerance. First, the Muslim conception of tolerance applies only to Jews and Christians—"People of the Book"—while the practices of Buddhists, Hindus, and other idolators are considered so spiritually depraved as to be quite beyond the pale.[7] Even People of the Book must keep to themselves and "humbly" tithe (pay the *jizya*) to their Muslim rulers. Fareed Zakaria observes,[8] as many have, that Jews lived for centuries under Muslim rule and had a relatively easy time of it— but this is only compared with the horrors of life under theocratic Christendom. The truth is that life for Jews within the House of Islam has been characterized by ceaseless humiliation and regular pogroms. A state of apartheid has been the norm, in which Jews have been forbidden to bear arms, to give evidence in court, and to ride horses. They have been forced to wear distinctive clothing (the yellow badge originated in Baghdad, not in Nazi Germany) and to avoid certain streets and buildings. They have been obliged, under penalty of violence and even death, to pass Muslims only on their left (impure) side while keeping their eyes lowered. In parts of the Arab world it has been a local custom for Muslim children to throw stones at Jews and spit upon them.[9] These and other indignities have been regularly punctuated by organized massacres and pogroms: in Morocco (1728, 1790, 1875, 1884, 1890, 1903, 1912, 1948, 1952, and 1955), in Algeria (1805 and 1934), in Tunisia (1864, 1869, 1932, and 1967), in Persia (1839, 1867, and 1910), in Iraq (1828, 1936, 1937, 1941, 1946, 1948, 1967, and 1969), in Libya (1785, 1860, 1897, 1945, 1948, and 1967), in Egypt (1882, 1919, 1921, 1924, 1938–39, 1945, 1948, 1956, and 1967), in Palestine (1929 and 1936), in Syria (1840, 1945, 1947, 1948, 1949, and 1967), in Yemen (1947), etc.[10] Life for Christians under Islam has been scarcely more cheerful.

As a matter of doctrine, the Muslim conception of tolerance is one in which non-Muslims have been politically and economically subdued, converted, or put to sword. The fact that the Muslim world has not been united under a single government for most of its history, and may never be again, is immaterial where this aspiration for hegemony is concerned. For each political community within Islam, "it is the task of the Islamic state to bring about obedience to the revealed law."[11]

Zakaria observes that Muslims living in the West generally appear tolerant of the beliefs of others. Let us accept this characterization for the moment—though it ignores the inconvenient reality that many Western countries now appear to be "hotbeds of Islamic militancy."[12] Before we chalk this up to Muslim tolerance, however, we should ask ourselves how Muslim intolerance would reveal itself in the West. What minority, even a radicalized one, isn't generally "tolerant" of the majority for most of its career? Even avowed terrorists and revolutionaries spend most of their days just biding their time. We should not mistake the "tolerance" of political, economic, and numerical weakness for genuine liberalism.

Lewis observes that "for Muslims, no piece of land once added to the realm of Islam can ever be finally renounced."[13] We might also add that no *mind*, once added to the realm, can ever be finally renounced—because, as Lewis also notes, the penalty for apostasy is death. We would do well to linger over this fact for a moment, because it is the black pearl of intolerance that no liberal exegesis will ever fully digest. Within the House of Islam, the penalty for learning too much about the world—so as to call the tenets of the faith into question—is death. If a twenty-first-century Muslim loses his faith, though he may have been a Muslim only for a single hour, the normative response, everywhere under Islam, is to kill him.

While the Koran merely describes the punishments that await the apostate in the next world (Koran 3:86–91), the hadith is emphatic about the justice that must be meted out in this one: "Whoever changes his religion, kill him." No metaphor hides this directive, and it would seem that no process of liberal hermeneutics can brush it aside. We might be tempted to accord great significance to the fact that the injunction does not appear in the Koran itself, but in practical terms the hadith literature seems to be every bit as constitutive of the Muslim worldview. Given the fact that the hadith is often used as the lens through which to interpret the Koran, many Muslim jurists consider it to be an even greater authority on the practice of Islam.[14] It is true that some liberal jurists require that the apostate subsequently speak against Islam before sanctioning his murder, but the penalty itself is generally not considered "extreme." The justice of killing apostates is a matter of mainstream acceptance, if not practice. This explains why there did not appear to be a single reasonable Muslim living on earth when the Ayatollah Khomeini put a bounty on the head of Salman Rushdie. Many Westerners wondered why millions of "moderate" Muslims did not publicly disavow this fatwa. The answer follows directly from the tenets of Islam, according to which not even Cat Stevens, a Western-born folk singer (now Yosuf Islam), could doubt the justice of it.[15]

As we have seen, Christianity and Judaism can be made to sound the same, intolerant note—but it has been a few centuries since either has done so. It is, however, a current reality under Islam that if you open the wrong door in your free inquiry of the world, the brethren deem that you should die for it. We might well wonder, then, in what sense Muslims believe that there should be "no compulsion in religion."

In reviewing Lewis's recent book on Islam, Kenneth Pollack raised a criticism that could be applied with even greater felicity to my account thus far:

Lewis still has not grappled with the deeper questions for his readers. He still has not offered his explanation for why the Islamic Middle East stagnated, why its efforts at reform failed, why it is notably failing to become integrated into the global economy in a meaningful way and why these failures have produced not a renewed determination to succeed (as in East Asia over the past 50 years, and arguably in India, Latin America and even parts of sub-Saharan Africa today) but an anger and frustration with the West so pervasive and vitriolic that it has bred murderous, suicidal terrorism despite all of the Islamic prohibitions against such action.[16]

These are all good questions—and Zakaria offers plausible answers to them—but they are not the "deeper questions." If you believe anything like what the Koran says you must believe in order to escape the fires of hell, you will, at the very least, be sympathetic with the actions of Osama bin Laden. The prohibitions against "suicidal terrorism" are not nearly as numerous as Pollack suggests. The Koran contains a single ambiguous line, "Do not destroy yourselves" (4:29). Like most commentators on these matters, Pollack seems unable to place himself in the position of one who *actually believes* the propositions set forth in the Koran—that paradise awaits, that our senses deliver nothing but evidence of a fallen world in desperate need of conquest for the glory of God. Open the Koran, which is perfect in its every syllable, and simply read it with the eyes of faith. You will see how little compassion need be wasted on those whom God himself is in the process of "mocking," "cursing," "shaming," "punishing," "scourging," "judging," "burning," "annihilating," "not forgiving," and "not reprieving." God, who is infinitely wise, has cursed the infidels with their doubts. He prolongs their life and prosperity so that they may continue heaping sin upon sin and all the more richly deserve the torments that await them beyond the grave. In this light, the people who died on September 11 were nothing more than fuel for the eternal fires of God's justice. To convey the relentlessness with which unbelievers are vilified in the text of the Koran, I provide a long compilation of quotations below, in order of their appearance in the text. This is what the Creator of the universe apparently has on his mind (when he is not fussing with gravitational constants and atomic weights):

"It is the same whether or not you forwarn them [the unbelievers], they will have no faith" (2:6). "God will mock them and keep them long in sin, blundering blindly along" (2:15). A fire "whose fuel is men and stones" awaits them (2:24). They will be "rewarded with disgrace in this world and with grievous punishment on the Day of Resurrection" (2:85). "God's curse be upon the infidels!" (2:89). "They have incurred God's most inexorable wrath. An ignominious punishment awaits [them]" (2:90). "God is the enemy of the unbelievers" (2:98). "The unbelievers among the People of the Book [Christians and Jews], and the pagans, resent that any blessing should have been sent down to you from your Lord" (2:105). "They shall be held up to shame in this world and sternly punished in the hereafter" (2:114). "Those to whom We [God] have given the Book, and who read it as it ought to be read, truly believe in it; those that deny it shall assuredly be lost" (2:122). "[We] shall let them live awhile, and then shall drag them to the scourge of the Fire. Evil shall be their fate" (2:126). "The East and the West are God's. He guides whom He will to a straight path" (2:142). "Do not say that those slain in the cause of God are dead. They are alive, but you are not aware of them" (2:154). "But the infidels who die unbelievers shall incur the curse of God, the angels, and all men. Under it they shall remain for ever; their punishment shall not be lightened, nor shall they be reprieved" (2:162). "They shall sigh with remorse, but shall never come out of the Fire" (2:168). "The unbelievers are like beasts which, call out to them as one may, can hear nothing but a shout and a cry. Deaf, dumb, and blind, they understand nothing" (2:172). "Theirs shall be a woeful punishment" (2:175). "How steadfastly they seek the Fire! That is because God has revealed the Book with truth; those that disagree about it are in extreme schism" (2:176). "Slay them wherever you find them. Drive them out of the places from which they drove you. Idolatry is worse than carnage. . . . [I]f they attack you put them to the sword. Thus shall the unbelievers be rewarded: but if they desist, God is forgiving and merciful. Fight against them until idolatry is no more and God's religion reigns supreme. But if they desist, fight none except the evil-doers"(2:190–93). "Fighting is obligatory for you, much as you dislike it. But you may hate a thing although it is good for you, and love a thing although it is bad for you. God knows, but you know not" (2:216). "They will not cease to fight against you until they force you to renounce your faith—if they are able. But whoever of you recants and dies an unbeliever, his works shall come to nothing in this world and in the world to come. Such men shall be the tenants of Hell, wherein they shall abide forever. Those that have embraced the Faith, and those that have fled their land and fought for the cause of God, may hope for God's mercy" (2:217–18). "God does not guide the evil-doers" (2:258). "God does not guide the unbelievers" (2:264). "The evil-doers shall have none to help them" (2:270). "God gives guidance to whom He will" (2:272).

"Those that deny God's revelations shall be sternly punished; God is mighty and capable of revenge" (3:5). "As for the unbelievers, neither their riches nor their children will in the least save them from God's judgment. They shall become fuel for the Fire" (3:10). "Say to the unbelievers: 'You shall be overthrown and driven into Hell—an evil resting place!'" (3:12). "The only true faith in God's sight is Islam. . . . He that denies God's revelations should know that swift is God's reckoning" (3:19). "Let the believers not make friends with infidels in preference to the faithful—he that does this has nothing to hope for from God—except in self-defense" (3:28). "Believers, do not make friends with any but your own people. They will spare no pains to corrupt you. They desire nothing but your ruin. Their hatred is evident from what they utter with their mouths, but greater is the hatred which their breasts conceal" (3:118). "If you have suffered a defeat, so did the enemy. We alternate these vicissitudes among mankind so that God may know the true believers and choose martyrs from among you (God does not love the evil-doers); and that God may test the faithful and annihilate the infidels" (3:140). "Believers, if you yield to the infidels they will drag you back to unbelief and you will return headlong to perdition. . . . We will put terror into the hearts of the unbelievers. . . . The

Fire shall be their home" (3:149–51). "Believers, do not follow the example of the infidels, who say of their brothers when they meet death abroad or in battle: 'Had they stayed with us they would not have died, nor would they have been killed.' God will cause them to regret their words. . . . If you should die or be slain in the cause of God, God's forgiveness and His mercy would surely be better than all the riches they amass" (3:156). "Never think that those who were slain in the cause of God are dead. They are alive, and well provided for by their Lord; pleased with His gifts and rejoicing that those they left behind, who have not yet joined them, have nothing to fear or to regret; rejoicing in God's grace and bounty. God will not deny the faithful their reward" (3:169). "Let not the unbelievers think that We prolong their days for their own good. We give them respite only so that they may commit more grievous sins. Shameful punishment awaits them" (3:178). "Those that suffered persecution for My sake and fought and were slain: I shall forgive them their sins and admit them to gardens watered by running streams, as a reward from God; God holds the richest recompense. Do not be deceived by the fortunes of the unbelievers in the land. Their prosperity is brief. Hell shall be their home, a dismal resting place" (3:195–96).

"God has cursed them in their unbelief" (4:46). "God will not forgive those who serve other gods besides Him; but He will forgive whom He will for other sins. He that serves other gods besides God is guilty of a heinous sin. . . . Consider those to whom a portion of the Scriptures was given. They believe in idols and false gods and say of the infidels: 'These are better guided than the believers'" (4:50–51). "Those that deny Our revelation We will burn in fire. No sooner will their skins be consumed than We shall give them other skins, so that they may truly taste the scourge. God is mighty and wise" (4:55–56).

"Believers, do not seek the friendship of the infidels and those who were given the Book before you, who have made of your religion a jest and a pastime" (5:57). "That which is revealed to you from your Lord will surely increase the wickedness and unbelief of many among them. We have stirred among them enmity and hatred, which will endure till the Day of Resurrection" (5:65). "God does not guide the unbelievers" (5:67). "That which is revealed to you from your Lord will surely increase the wickedness and unbelief of many among them. But do not grieve for the unbelievers" (5:69). "You see many among them making friends with unbelievers. Evil is that to which their souls prompt them. They have incurred the wrath of God and shall endure eternal torment. . . . You will find that the most implacable of men in their enmity to the faithful are the Jews and the pagans, and that the nearest in affection to them are those who say: 'We are Christians'" (5:80–82). "[T]hose that disbelieve and deny Our revelations shall become the inmates of Hell" (5:86).

"[T]hey deny the truth when it is declared to them: but they shall learn the consequences of their scorn" (6:5). "We had made them more powerful in the land than yourselves [the Meccans], sent down for them abundant water from the sky and gave them rivers that rolled at their feet. Yet because they sinned We destroyed them all and raised up other generations after them. If We sent down to you a Book inscribed on real parchment and they touched it with their own hands, the unbelievers would still assert: 'This is but plain sorcery.' They ask: 'Why has no angel been sent down to him [Muhammad]?' If We had sent down an angel, their fate would have been sealed and they would have never been reprieved" (6:5–8). "Who is more wicked than the man who invents falsehoods about God or denies His revelations?" (6:21). "Some of them listen to you. But We have cast veils over their hearts and made them hard of hearing lest they understand your words. They will believe in none of Our signs, even if they see them one and all. When they come to argue with you the unbelievers say: 'This is nothing but old fictitious tales.' They forbid it and depart from it. They ruin none but themselves, though they do not perceive it. If you could see them when they are set before the Fire! They will say: 'Would that we could return! Then we would not deny the revelations of our Lord and would be true believers' (6:23–27). "But if they were sent back, they would return to that which they have been forbidden. They are liars all" (6:29). "Had God pleased He would have given them guidance, one and all" (6:35). "Deaf and dumb are those that deny Our revelations: they blunder about in darkness. God confounds whom He will, and guides to a straight path whom He pleases." (6:39) "[T]heir hearts were hardened, and Satan made their deeds seem fair to them. And when they had clean forgotten Our admonition We granted them all that they desired; but just as they were rejoicing in what they were given, We suddenly smote them and they were plunged into utter despair. Thus were the evil-doers annihilated. Praise be to God, Lord of the Universe!" (6:43–45). "[T]hose that deny Our revelations shall be punished for their misdeeds" (6:49). "Such are those that are damned by their own sins. They shall drink scalding water and be sternly punished for their unbelief" (6:70). "Could you but see the wrongdoers when death overwhelms them! With hands outstretched, the angels will say: 'Yield up your souls. You shall be rewarded with the scourge of shame this day, for you have said of God what is untrue and scorned His revelations" (6:93). "Avoid the pagans. Had God pleased, they would not have worshipped idols. . . . We will turn away their hearts and eyes from the Truth since they refused to believe in it at first. We will let them blunder about in their wrongdoing. If We sent the angels down to them, and caused the dead to speak to them, . . . and ranged all things in front of them, they would still not believe, unless God willed otherwise. . . . Thus have We assigned for every prophet an enemy: the devils among men and jinn, who inspire each other with vain and varnished falsehoods. But had your Lord pleased, they would not have done so. Therefore leave them to their own inventions, so that the hearts of those who have no faith in the life to come may be inclined to what they say and, being pleased, persist in their sinful ways" (6:107–12). "The devils will teach their votaries to argue with you. If you obey them you shall yourselves become idolaters. . . . God will humiliate the transgressors and mete out to them a grievous punishment for their scheming" (6:121–25). "If God wills to guide a man, He opens his bosom to Islam. But if he pleases to confound him, He makes his bosom small and narrow as though he were climbing up to heaven. Thus shall God lay the scourge on the unbelievers" (6:125).

THIS is all desperately tedious, of course.[17] But there is no substitute for confronting the text itself. I cannot judge the quality of the Arabic; perhaps it is sublime. But the book's contents are not. On almost every page, the Koran instructs observant Muslims to despise non-believers. On almost every page, it prepares the ground for religious conflict. Anyone who can read passages like those quoted above and still not see a link between Muslim faith and Muslim violence should probably consult a neurologist.

Islam, more than any other religion human beings have devised, has all the makings of a thoroughgoing cult of death. Sayyid Qutb, one of the most influential thinkers in the Islamic world, and the father of modern Islamism among the Sunni, wrote, "The Koran points to another contemptible characteristic of the Jews: their craven desire to live, no matter at what price and regardless of quality, honor, and dignity."[18] This statement is really a miracle of concision. While it may seem nothing more than a casual fillip against the Jews, it is actually a powerful distillation of the Muslim worldview. Stare at it for a moment or two, and the whole machinery of intolerance and suicidal grandiosity will begin to construct itself before your eyes. The Koran's ambiguous prohibition against suicide appears to be an utter non-issue. Surely there are Muslim jurists who might say that suicide bombing is contrary to the tenets of Islam (where are these jurists, by the way?) and that suicide bombers are therefore not martyrs but fresh denizens of hell. Such a minority opinion, if it exists, cannot change the fact that suicide bombings have been rationalized by much of the Muslim world (where they are called "sacred explosions"). Indeed, such rationalization is remarkably easy, given the tenets of Islam. In light of what devout Muslims believe—about jihad, about martyrdom, about paradise, and about infidels—suicide bombing hardly appears to be an aberration of their faith. And it is no surprise at all that those who die in this way are considered martyrs by many of their coreligionists. A military action that entails sufficient risk of death could be considered "suicidal" in any case, rendering moot the distinction between suicide and death in the line of duty for one who would "fight for the cause of God." The bottom line for the aspiring martyr seems to be this: as long as you are killing infidels or apostates "in defense of Islam," Allah doesn't care whether you kill yourself in the process or not.

Over 38,000 people recently participated in a global survey conducted by the Pew Research Center for the People and the Press. The results constitute the first publication of its Global Attitudes Project entitled "What the World Thinks in 2002."[19] The survey included the following question, posed only to Muslims:

Some people think that suicide bombing and other forms of violence against civilian targets are justified in order to defend Islam from its enemies. Other people believe that, no matter what the reason, this kind of violence is never justified. Do you personally feel that this kind of violence is often justified to defend Islam, sometimes justified, rarely justified, or never justified?

Before we look at the results of this study, we should appreciate the significance of the juxtaposed phrases "suicide bombing" and "civilian targets." We now live in a world in which Muslims have been scientifically polled (with margins of error ranging from 2 to 4 percent) as to whether they support ("often," "sometimes," "rarely," or "never") the deliberate murder and maiming of noncombatant men, women, and children in defense of Islam. Here are some of the results of the Pew study (not all percentages sum to 100):

SUICIDE BOMBING IN DEFENSE OF ISLAM
Justifiable?

	Yes	No	DK/Refused
Lebanon	73	21	6
Ivory Coast	56	44	0
Nigeria	47	45	8
Bangladesh	44	37	19
Jordan	43	48	8
Pakistan	33	43	23
Mali	32	57	11
Ghana	30	57	12
Uganda	29	63	8
Senegal	28	69	3
Indonesia	27	70	3
Turkey	13	73	14

If you do not find these numbers sufficiently disturbing, consider that places like Saudia Arabia, Yemen, Egypt, Iran, Sudan, Iraq, and the Palestinian territories were not included in the survey. Had they been, it is safe to say, the Lebanese would have lost their place at the top of the list several times over. Suicide bombing also entails *suicide*, of course, which most Muslims believe is expressly forbidden by God. Consequently, had the question been "Is it ever justified to target civilians in defense of Islam," we could expect even greater Muslim support for terrorism.

But the Pew results are actually bleaker than the above table indicates. A closer look at the data reveals that the pollsters skewed their results by binning the responses "rarely justified" and "never justified" together, thus giving a false sense of Muslim pacifism. Take another look at the data from Jordan: 43 percent of Jordanians apparently favor terrorism, while 48 percent do not. The problem, however, is that 22 percent of Jordanians actually responded "rarely justified," and this accounts for nearly half of their "No" responses. "Rarely justified" still means that under certain circumstances, these respondents would sanction the indiscriminate murder of noncombatants (*plus* suicide), not as an accidental by-product of a military operation but as its intended outcome. A more accurate picture of Muslim tolerance for terrorism emerges when we focus on the percentage of respondents who could not find it in their hearts to say "never justified" (leaving aside the many people who still lurk in the shadows of "Don't Know/Refused"). If we divide the data in this way, the sun of modernity sets even further over the Muslim world:

SUICIDE BOMBING IN DEFENSE OF ISLAM
Is It Ever *Justifiable?*

	YES	No	DK/REFUSED
Lebanon	82	12	6
Ivory Coast	73	27	0
Nigeria	66	26	8
Jordan	65	26	8
Bangladesh	58	23	19
Mali	54	35	11
Senegal	47	50	3
Ghana	44	43	12
Indonesia	43	54	3
Uganda	40	52	8
Pakistan	38	38	23
Turkey	20	64	14

These are hideous numbers. If all Muslims had responded as Turkey did (where a mere 4 percent think suicide bombings are "often" justified, 9 percent "sometimes," and 7 percent "rarely"), we would still have a problem worth worrying about; we would, after all, be talking about more than 200 million avowed supporters of terrorism. But Turkey is an island of ambassadorial goodwill compared with the rest of the Muslim world.

Let us imagine that peace one day comes to the Middle East. What will Muslims say of the suicide bombings that they so widely endorsed? Will they say, "We were driven mad by the Israeli occupation"? Will they say, "We were a generation of sociopaths"? How will they account for the celebrations that followed these "sacred explosions"? A young man, born into relative privilege, packs his clothing with explosives and ball bearings and unmakes himself along with a score of children in a discotheque, and his mother is promptly congratulated by hundreds of her neighbors. What will the Palestinians think about such behavior once peace has been established? If they are still devout Muslims here is what they *must* think: "Our boys are in paradise, and they have prepared the way for us to follow. Hell has been prepared for the infidels." It seems to me to be an almost axiomatic truth of human nature that no peace, should it ever be established, will survive beliefs of this sort for very long.

We must not overlook the fact that a significant percentage of the world's Muslims believe that the men who brought down the World Trade Center are now seated at the right hand of God, amid "rivers of purest water, and rivers of milk forever fresh; rivers of wine delectable to those that drink it, and rivers of clearest honey" (47:15). These men—who slit the throats of stewardesses and delivered young couples with their children to their deaths at five hundred miles per hour—are at present being "attended by boys graced with eternal youth" in a "kingdom blissful and glorious." They are "arrayed in garments of fine green silk and rich brocade, and adorned with bracelets of silver" (76:15). The list of their perquisites is long. But what is it that gets a martyr out of bed early on his last day among the living? Did any of the nineteen hijackers make haste to Allah's garden simply to get his hands on his allotment of silk? It seems doubtful. The irony here is almost a miracle in its own right: the most sexually repressive people found in the world today—people who are stirred to a killing rage by reruns of *Baywatch*—are lured to martyrdom by a conception of paradise that resembles nothing so much as an al fresco bordello.[20]

Apart from the terrible ethical consequences that follow from this style of otherworldliness, we should observe just how deeply implausible the Koranic paradise is. For a seventh-century prophet to say that paradise is a garden, complete with rivers of milk and honey, is rather like a twenty-first-century prophet's saying that it is a gleaming city where every soul drives a new Lexus. A moment's reflection should reveal that such pronouncements suggest nothing at all about the afterlife and much indeed about the limits of the human imagination.

Jihad and the Power of the Atom

For devout Muslims, religious identity seems to trump all others. Despite the occasional influence of Pan-Arabism, the concept of an ethnic or national identity has never taken root in the Muslim world as it has in the West. The widespread support for Saddam Hussein among Muslims, in response to the American attack upon Iraq, is as good a way as any of calibrating the reflexivity of Muslim solidarity. Saddam Hussein was, as both a secularist and a tyrant, widely despised in the Muslim world prior to the American invasion; and yet the reaction of most Muslims revealed that no matter what his crimes against the Iraqi people, against the Kuwaitis, and against the Iranians, the idea of an army of infidels occupying Baghdad simply could not be countenanced, no matter what humanitarian purpose it might serve. Saddam may have tortured and killed more Muslims than any person in living memory, but the Americans are the "enemies of God."

It is important to keep the big picture in view, because the details, being absurd to an almost crystalline degree, are truly meaningless. In our dialogue with the Muslim world, we are confronted by people who hold beliefs for which there is no rational justification and which therefore cannot even be discussed, and yet these are the very beliefs that underlie many of the demands they are likely to make upon us.

It should be of particular concern to us that the beliefs of Muslims pose a special problem for nuclear deterrence. There is little possibility of our having a *cold* war with an Islamist regime armed with long-range nuclear weapons. A cold war requires that the parties be mutually deterred by the threat of death. Notions of martyrdom and jihad run roughshod over the logic that allowed the United

States and the Soviet Union to pass half a century perched, more or less stably, on the brink of Armageddon. What will we do if an Islamist regime, which grows dewy-eyed at the mere mention of paradise, ever acquires long-range nuclear weaponry? If history is any guide, we will not be sure about where the offending warheads are or what their state of readiness is, and so we will be unable to rely on targeted, conventional weapons to destroy them. In such a situation, the only thing likely to ensure our survival may be a nuclear first strike of our own. Needless to say, this would be an unthinkable crime—as it would kill tens of millions of innocent civilians in a single day—but it may be the only course of action available to us, given what Islamists believe. How would such an unconscionable act of self-defense be perceived by the rest of the Muslim world? It would likely be seen as the first incursion of a genocidal crusade. The horrible irony here is that *seeing could make it so*: this very perception could plunge us into a state of hot war with any Muslim state that had the capacity to pose a nuclear threat of its own. All of this is perfectly insane, of course: I have just described a plausible scenario in which much of the world's population could be annihilated on account of religious ideas that belong on the same shelf with Batman, the philosopher's stone, and unicorns. That it would be a horrible absurdity for so many of us to die for the sake of myth does not mean, however, that it could not happen. Indeed, given the immunity to all reasonable intrusions that faith enjoys in our discourse, a catastrophe of this sort seems increasingly likely. We must come to terms with the possibility that men who are every bit as zealous to die as the nineteen hijackers may one day get their hands on long-range nuclear weaponry. The Muslim world in particular must anticipate this possibility and find some way to prevent it. Given the steady proliferation of technology, it is safe to say that time is not on our side.

The Clash

Samuel Huntington has famously described the conflict between Islam and the West as a "clash of civilizations." Huntington observed that wherever Muslims and non-Muslims share a border, armed conflict tends to arise. Finding a felicitous phrase for an infelicitous fact, he declared that "Islam has bloody borders."[21] Many scholars have attacked Huntington's thesis, however. Edward Said wrote that "a great deal of demagogy and downright ignorance is involved in presuming to speak for a whole religion or civilization."[22] Said, for his part, maintained that the members of Al Qaeda are little more than "crazed fanatics" who, far from lending credence to Huntington's thesis, should be grouped with the Branch Davidians, the disciples of the Reverend Jim Jones in Guyana, and the cult of Aum Shinrikyo: "Huntington writes that the world's billion or so Muslims are 'convinced of the superiority of their culture, and obsessed with the inferiority of their power.' Did he canvas 100 Indonesians, 200 Moroccans, 500 Egyptians and fifty Bosnians? Even if he did, what sort of sample is that?" It is hard not to see this kind of criticism as disingenuous. Undoubtedly we should recognize the limits of generalizing about a culture, but the idea that Osama bin Laden is the Muslim equivalent of the Reverend Jim Jones is risible. Bin Laden has not, contrary to Said's opinion on the matter, "become a vast, over-determined symbol of everything America hates and fears."[23] One need only read the Koran to know, with something approaching mathematical certainty, that all truly devout Muslims will be "convinced of the superiority of their culture, and obsessed with the inferiority of their power," just as Huntington alleges. And this is all that his thesis requires.

Whether or not one likes Huntington's formulation, one thing is clear: the evil that has finally reached our shores is not merely the evil of terrorism. It is the evil of religious faith at the moment of its political ascendancy. Of course, Islam is not uniquely susceptible to undergoing such horrible transformations, though it is, at this moment in history, uniquely ascendant.[24] Western leaders who insist that our conflict is not with Islam are mistaken; but, as I argue throughout this book, we have a problem with Christianity and Judaism as well. It is time we recognized that all reasonable men and women have a common enemy. It is an enemy so near to us, and so deceptive, that we keep its counsel even as it threatens to destroy the very possibility of human happiness. Our enemy is nothing other than faith itself.

While it would be comforting to believe that our dialogue with the Muslim world has, as one of its possible outcomes, a future of mutual tolerance, nothing guarantees this result—least of all the tenets of Islam. Given the constraints of Muslim orthodoxy, given the penalties within Islam for a radical (and reasonable) adaptation to modernity, I think it is clear that Islam must find some way to revise itself, peacefully or otherwise. What this will mean is not at all obvious. What is obvious, however, is that the West must either win the argument or win the war. All else will be bondage.

The Riddle of Muslim "Humiliation"

Thomas Friedman, a tireless surveyor of the world's discontents for the *New York Times*, has declared that Muslim "humiliation" is at the root of Muslim terrorism. Others have offered the same diagnosis, and Muslims themselves regularly assert that Western imperialism has offended their dignity, their pride, and their honor. What should we make of this? Can anyone point to a greater offender of Muslim dignity than Islamic law itself? For a modern example of the kind of society that can be fashioned out of an exclusive reliance upon the tenets of Islam, simply recall what Afghanistan was like under the Taliban. Who are those improbable creatures scurrying about in shrouds and being regularly beaten for showing an exposed ankle? Those were the dignified (and illiterate) women of the House of Islam.

Zakaria and many others have noted that as repressive as Arab dictators generally are, they tend to be more liberal than the people they oppress. The Saudi Prince Abdullah, for instance—a man who has by no means distinguished himself as a liberal—recently proposed that women should be permitted to drive automobiles in his country. As it turns out, his greatly oppressed people would not stand for this degree of spiritual oppression, and the prince was forced to back down. At this point in their history, give most Muslims the freedom to vote, and they will freely vote to tear out their political freedoms by the root. We should not for a moment lose sight of the possibility that they would curtail our freedoms as well, if they only had the power to do so.

There is no doubt that our collusion with Muslim tyrants—in Iraq, Syria, Algeria, Iran, Egypt, and elsewhere—has been despicable. We have done nothing to discourage the mistreatment and outright slaughter of tens of thousands of Muslims by their own regimes—regimes that, in many cases, we helped bring to power. Our failure to support the Shiite uprising in southern Iraq in 1991, which we encouraged, surely ranks among the most unethical and consequential foreign policy blunders of recent decades. But our culpability on this front must be bracketed by the understanding that were democracy to suddenly come to these countries, it would be little more than a gangplank to theocracy. There does not seem to be anything within the principles of Islam by which to resist the slide into sharia (Islamic law), while there is everything to encourage it. This is a terrible truth that we have to face: the only thing that currently stands between us and the roiling ocean of Muslim unreason is a wall of tyranny and human rights abuses that we have helped to erect. This situation must be remedied, but we cannot merely force Muslim dictators from power and open the polls. It would be like opening the polls to the Christians of the fourteenth century.

It is also true that poverty and lack of education play a role in all of this, but it is not a role that suggests easy remedies. The Arab world is now economically and intellectually stagnant to a degree that few could have thought possible, given its historical role in advancing and preserving human knowledge. In the year 2002 the GDP in all Arab countries combined did not equal that of Spain. Even more troubling, Spain translates as many books into Spanish each year as the entire Arab world has translated into Arabic since the ninth century.[25] This degree of insularity and backwardness is shocking, but it should not lead us to believe that poverty and lack of education are the roots of the problem. That a generation of poor and illiterate children are being fed into the fundamentalist machinery of the *madrassas* (Saudi-financed religious schools) should surely terrify us.[26] But Muslim terrorists have not tended to come from the ranks of the uneducated poor; many have been middle class, educated, and without any obvious dysfunction in their personal lives. As Zakaria points out, compared with the nineteen hijackers, John Walker Lindh (the young man from California who joined the Taliban) was "distinctly undereducated." Ahmed Omar Sheikh, who organized the kidnapping and murder of the *Wall Street Journal* reporter Daniel Pearl studied at the London School of Economics. Hezbollah militants who die in violent operations are actually *less* likely to come from poor homes than their nonmilitant contemporaries and *more* likely to have a secondary school education.[27] The leaders of Hamas are all college graduates, and some have master's degrees.[28] These facts suggest that even if every Muslim enjoyed a standard of living comparable to that of the average middle-class American, the West might still be in profound danger of colliding with Islam. I suspect that Muslim prosperity might even make matters worse, because the only thing that seems likely to persuade most Muslims that their worldview is problematic is the demonstrable failure of their societies.[29] If Muslim orthodoxy were as economically and technologically viable as Western liberalism, we would probably be doomed to witness the Islamification of the earth.

As we see in the person of Osama bin Laden, a murderous religious fervor is compatible with wealth and education. Indeed, the technical proficiency of many Muslim terrorists demonstrates that it is compatible with a *scientific* education. That is why there is no cognitive or cultural substitute for desacralizing faith itself. As long as it is acceptable for a person to believe that he knows how God wants everyone on earth to live, we will continue to murder one another on account of our myths. In our dealings with the Muslim world, we must acknowledge that Muslims have not found anything of substance to say against the actions of the September 11 hijackers, apart from the ubiquitous canard that they were really Jews.[30] Muslim discourse is currently a tissue of myths, conspiracy theories,[31] and exhortations to recapture the glories of the seventh century. There is no reason to believe that economic and political improvements in the Muslim world, in and of themselves, would remedy this.

The Danger of Wishful Thinking

Paul Berman has written a beautiful primer on totalitarianism—of the left and the right, East and West—and observed that it invariably contains a genocidal, and even suicidal, dimension. He notes that the twentieth century was a great incubator of "pathological mass movements"—political movements that "get drunk on the idea of slaughter."[32] He also points out that liberal thinkers are often unable to recognize these terrors for what they are. There is indeed a great tradition, in Berman's phrase, of "liberalism as denial." The French Socialists in the 1930s seem to have had a peculiar genius for this style of self-deception, for despite the billowing clouds of unreason wafting over from the East, they could not bring themselves to believe that the Nazis posed a problem worth taking seriously. In the face of the German menace, they simply blamed their own government and defense industry for warmongering. As Berman suggests, the same forces of wishful thinking and self-doubt have been gathering strength in the West in the aftermath of September 11. Because they assume that people everywhere are animated by the same desires and fears, many Western liberals now blame their own governments for the excesses of Muslim terrorists. Many suspect that we have somehow heaped this evil upon our own heads. Berman observes, for instance, that much of the world now blames Israel for the suicidal derangement of the Palestinians. Rather than being an expression of mere anti-Semitism (though it is surely this as well), this view is the product of a quaint moral logic: people are just people, so the thinking goes, and they do not behave *that* badly unless they have some very good reasons. The excesses of Palestinian suicide bombers, therefore, must attest to the excesses of the Israeli occupation. Berman points out that this sort of thinking has led the Israelis to be frequently likened to the Nazis in the European press.[33] Needless to say, the comparison is grotesque. The truth is, as Dershowitz points out, that "no other nation in history faced with comparable challenges has ever adhered to a higher standard of human rights, been more sensitive to the safety of innocent civilians, tried harder to operate under the rule of law, or been willing to take more risks for peace."[34] The Israelis have shown a degree of restraint in their use of violence that the Nazis never contemplated and that, more to the point, no Muslim society would contemplate today. Ask yourself, what are the chances that the Palestinians would show the same restraint in killing Jews if the Jews were a powerless minority living under their occupation and disposed to acts of suicidal terrorism? It would be no more likely than Muhammad's flying to heaven on a winged horse.[35]

Berman also takes issue with Huntington's thesis, however, in that the concept of a "civilization," to his mind, fails to pick out the real variable at issue. Rather than a clash of civilizations, we have a "clash of ideologies," between "liberalism and the apocalyptic and phantasmagorical movements that have risen up against liberal civilization ever since the calamities of the First World War."[36] The distinction appears valid, but unimportant. The problem is that certain of our beliefs cannot survive the proximity of certain others. War and conversation are our options, and nothing guarantees that we will always have a choice between them.

Berman sums up our situation beautifully:

What have we needed for these terrorists to prosper? We have
needed immense failures of political courage and imagination
within the Muslim world. We have needed an almost willful lack
of curiosity about those failures by people in other parts of the
world—the lack of curiosity that allowed us to suppose that totalitarianism had been defeated, even as totalitarianism was reaching a new zenith. We have needed handsome doses of wishful
thinking—the kind of simpleminded faith in a rational world
that, in its inability to comprehend reality, sparked the totalitarian movements in the first place. . . . We have needed a provincial
ignorance about intellectual currents in other parts of the world.
We have needed foolish resentments in Europe, and a foolish
arrogance in America. We have needed so many things! But
there has been no lack—every needed thing has been here in
abundance.[37]

But we have needed one more thing to bring us precisely to this
moment. We have needed a religious doctrine, spread over much of
the developing world, that makes sacraments of illiberalism, ignorance, and suicidal violence. Contrary to Berman's analysis,
Islamism is not merely the latest flavor of totalitarian nihilism.
There is a difference between nihilism and a desire for supernatural
reward. Islamists could smash the world to atoms and still not be
guilty of nihilism, because everything in their worldview has been
transfigured by the light of paradise. Given what Islamists believe, it
is perfectly rational for them to strangle modernity wherever they
can lay hold of it. It is rational, even, for Muslim women to encourage the suicides of their children, as long as they are fighting for the
cause of God. Devout Muslims simply *know* that they are going to
a better place. God is both infinitely powerful and infinitely just.
Why not, then, delight in the death throes of a sinful world? There
are other ideologies with which to expunge the last vapors of reasonableness from a society's discourse, but Islam is undoubtedly one
of the best we've got.

SECULARISTS tend to argue that the role of Islam, or religion in general, is secondary to that of politics in determining the character of a society. On this account, people are motivated by their political interests first and find a religious rationale to suit the occasion. No doubt there are numerous examples of political leaders' invoking religion for purely pragmatic, and even cynical, reasons (the tenure of Pakistan's Zia ul-Haq seems a good example). But we should not draw the wrong lesson here. A lever works only if it is attached to *something*. Someone, after all, must believe in God, for talk of God to be politically efficacious. And I take it to be more or less self-evident that whenever large numbers of people begin turning themselves into bombs, or volunteer their children for use in the clearing of minefields (as was widespread in the Iran-Iraq war),[38] the rationale behind their actions has ceased to be merely political. This is not to say that the aspiring martyr does not relish what he imagines will be the thunderous political significance of his final act, but unless a person believes some rather incredible things about this universe—in particular, about what happens after death—he is very unlikely to engage in behavior of this sort. Nothing explains the actions of Muslim extremists, and the widespread tolerance of their behavior in the Muslim world, better than the tenets of Islam.

Given what many Muslims believe, is genuine peace in this world possible? Is the relative weakness of Muslim states the only thing that prevents outright war between Islam and the West? I'm afraid that encouraging answers to such questions are hard to come by. The basis for liberalism in the doctrine of Islam seems meager to the point of being entirely illusory. Although we have seen that the Bible is itself a great reservoir of intolerance, for Christians and Jews alike—as everything from the writings of Augustine to the present actions of Israeli settlers demonstrates—it is not difficult to find great swaths of the Good Book, as well as Christian and Jewish exegesis, that offer counterarguments. The Christian who wants to live in the full presence of rationality and modernity can keep the Jesus of Matthew sermonizing upon the mount and simply ignore the world-consuming rigmarole of Revelation. Islam appears to offer no such refuge for one who would live peacefully in a pluralistic world. Of course, glimmers of hope can be found in even the shadiest of places: as Berman points out, the diatribes of Muslim orthodoxy are predicated upon the fear that Western liberalism is in the process of invading the Muslim mind and "stealing his loyalty"—indicating that Muslims, like other people, are susceptible to the siren's song of liberalism.[39] We must surely hope so. The character of their religious beliefs, however, suggests that they will be less susceptible than the rest of us.

For reasons we have already begun to explore, there is a deep bias in our discourse against conclusions of this sort. With respect to Islam, the liberal tendency is to blame the West for raising the ire of the Muslim world, through centuries of self-serving conquest and meddling, while conservatives tend to blame other contingent features of Middle East, Arab, or Muslim history. The problem seems to have been located everywhere except at the core of the Muslim faith—but faith is precisely what differentiates every Muslim from every infidel. Without faith, most Muslim grievances against the West would be impossible even to formulate, much less avenge.

Leftist Unreason and the Strange Case of Noam Chomsky

Nevertheless, many people are now convinced that the attacks of September 11 say little about Islam and much about the sordid career of the West—in particular, about the failures of U.S. foreign policy. The French philosopher Jean Baudrillard gives these themes an especially luxuriant expression, declaring that terrorism is a necessary consequence of American "hegemony." He goes so far as to suggest that we were secretly hoping that such devastation would be visited upon us:

> At a pinch we can say that they *did it*, but we *wished for* it. . . . When global power monopolizes the situation to this extent, when there is such a formidable condensation of all functions in

the technocratic machinery, and when no alternative form of thinking is allowed, what other way is there but a *terroristic situational transfer.* It was the system itself which created the objective conditions for this brutal retaliation. . . . This is terror against terror—there is no longer any ideology behind it. We are far beyond ideology and politics now. . . . As if the power bearing these towers suddenly lost all energy, all resilience; as though that arrogant power suddenly gave way under the pressure of too intense an effort: the effort always to be the unique world model.[40]

If one were feeling charitable, one might assume that something essential to these profundities got lost in translation. I think it far more likely, however, that it did not survive translation into *French.* If Baudrillard had been obliged to live in Afghanistan under the Taliban, would he have thought that the horrible abridgments of his freedom were a matter of the United States's "effort always to be the unique world model"? Would the peculiar halftime entertainment at every soccer match—where suspected fornicators, adulterers, and thieves were regularly butchered in the dirt at centerfield—have struck him as the first rumblings of a "terroristic situational transfer"? We may be beyond politics, but we are not in the least "beyond ideology" now. Ideology is all that our enemies have.[41]

And yet, thinkers far more sober than Baudrillard view the events of September 11 as a consequence of American foreign policy. Perhaps the foremost among them is Noam Chomsky. In addition to making foundational contributions to linguistics and the psychology of language, Chomsky has been a persistent critic of U.S. foreign policy for over three decades. He has also managed to demonstrate a principal failing of the liberal critique of power. He appears to be an exquisitely moral man whose political views prevent him from making the most basic moral distinctions—between types of violence, and the variety of human purposes that give rise to them.

In his book *9-11*, with rubble of the World Trade Center still piled high and smoldering, Chomsky urged us not to forget that "the U.S. itself is a leading terrorist state." In support of this claim he catalogs a number of American misdeeds, including the sanctions that the United States imposed upon Iraq, which led to the death of "maybe half a million children," and the 1998 bombing of the Al-Shifa pharmaceuticals plant in Sudan, which may have set the stage for tens of thousands of innocent Sudanese to die of tuberculosis, malaria, and other treatable diseases. Chomsky does not hesitate to draw moral equivalences here: "For the first time in modern history, Europe and its offshoots were subjected, on home soil, to the kind of atrocity that they routinely have carried out elsewhere."[42]

Before pointing out just how wayward Chomsky's thinking is on this subject, I would like to concede many of his points, since they have the virtue of being both generally important and irrelevant to the matter at hand. There is no doubt that the United States has much to atone for, both domestically and abroad. In this respect, we can more or less swallow Chomsky's thesis whole. To produce this horrible confection at home, start with our genocidal treatment of the Native Americans, add a couple hundred years of slavery, along with our denial of entry to Jewish refugees fleeing the death camps of the Third Reich, stir in our collusion with a long list of modern despots and our subsequent disregard for their appalling human rights records, add our bombing of Cambodia and the Pentagon Papers to taste, and then top with our recent refusals to sign the Kyoto protocol for greenhouse emissions, to support any ban on land mines, and to submit ourselves to the rulings of the International Criminal Court. The result should smell of death, hypocrisy, and fresh brimstone.

We have surely done some terrible things in the past. Undoubtedly, we are poised to do terrible things in the future. Nothing I have written in this book should be construed as a denial of these facts, or as defense of state practices that are manifestly abhorrent. There may be much that Western powers, and the United States in particular, should pay reparations for. And our failure to acknowledge our misdeeds over the years has undermined our credibility in the international community. We can concede all of this, and even share

Chomsky's acute sense of outrage, while recognizing that his analysis of our current situation in the world is a masterpiece of moral blindness.

Take the bombing of the Al-Shifa pharmaceuticals plant: according to Chomsky, the atrocity of September 11 pales in comparison with that perpetrated by the Clinton administration in August 1998. But let us now ask some very basic questions that Chomsky seems to have neglected to ask himself: What did the U.S. government think it was doing when it sent cruise missiles into Sudan? Destroying a chemical weapons site used by Al Qaeda. Did the Clinton administration *intend* to bring about the deaths of thousands of Sudanese children? No. Was our goal to kill as many Sudanese as we could? No. Were we trying to kill anyone at all? Not unless we thought members of Al Qaeda would be at the Al-Shifa facility in the middle of the night. Asking these questions about Osama bin Laden and the nineteen hijackers puts us in a different moral universe entirely.

If we are inclined to follow Chomsky down the path of moral equivalence and ignore the role of human intentions, we can forget about the bombing of the Al-Shifa plant, because many of the things we did *not* do in Sudan had even greater consequences. What about all the money and food we simply never thought to give the Sudanese prior to 1998? How many children did we kill (that is, *not save*) just by living in blissful ignorance of the conditions in Sudan? Surely if we had all made it a priority to keep death out of Sudan for as long as possible, untold millions could have been saved from whatever it was that wound up killing them. We could have sent teams of well-intentioned men and women into Khartoum to ensure that the Sudanese wore their seatbelts. Are we culpable for all the preventable injury and death that we did nothing to prevent? We may be, up to a point. The philosopher Peter Unger has made a persuasive case that a single dollar spent on anything but the absolute essentials of our survival is a dollar that has some starving child's blood on it.[43] Perhaps we do have far more moral responsibility for the state of the world than most of us seem ready to contemplate. This is not Chomsky's argument, however.

Arundhati Roy, a great admirer of Chomsky, has summed up his position very well:

> [T]he U.S. government refuses to judge itself by the same moral standards by which it judges others. . . . Its technique is to position itself as the well-intentioned giant whose good deeds are confounded in strange countries by their scheming natives, whose markets it's trying to free, whose societies it's trying to modernize, whose women it's trying to liberate, whose souls it's trying to save. . . . [T]he U.S. government has conferred upon itself the right and freedom to murder and exterminate people "for their own good."[44]

But we are, in many respects, just such a "well-intentioned giant." And it is rather astonishing that intelligent people, like Chomsky and Roy, fail to see this. What we need to counter their arguments is a device that enables us to distinguish the morality of men like Osama bin Laden and Saddam Hussein from that of George Bush and Tony Blair. It is not hard to imagine the properties of such a tool. We can call it "the perfect weapon."

Perfect Weapons and the Ethics of "Collateral Damage"

What we euphemistically describe as "collateral damage" in times of war is the direct result of limitations in the power and precision of our technology. To see that this is so, we need only imagine how any of our recent conflicts would have looked if we had possessed *perfect weapons*—weapons that allowed us either to temporarily impair or to kill a particular person, or group, at any distance, without harming others or their property. What would we do with such technology? Pacifists would refuse to use it, despite the variety of monsters currently loose in the world: the killers and torturers of children, the genocidal sadists, the men who, for want of the right genes, the right upbringing, or the right ideas, cannot possibly be expected to live peacefully with the rest of us. I will say a few things about pacifism in a later chapter—for it seems to me to be a deeply immoral position that comes to us swaddled in the dogma of highest moralism—but most of us are not pacifists. Most of us would elect to use weapons of this sort. A moment's thought reveals that a person's use of such a weapon would offer a perfect window onto the soul of his ethics.

Consider the all too facile comparisons that have recently been made between George Bush and Saddam Hussein (or Osama bin Laden, or Hitler, etc.)—in the pages of writers like Roy and Chomsky, in the Arab press, and in classrooms throughout the free world. How would George Bush have prosecuted the recent war in Iraq with perfect weapons? Would he have targeted the thousands of Iraqi civilians who were maimed or killed by our bombs? Would he have put out the eyes of little girls or torn the arms from their mothers? Whether or not you admire the man's politics—or the man—there is no reason to think that he would have sanctioned the injury or death of even a single innocent person. What would Saddam Hussein or Osama bin Laden do with perfect weapons? What would Hitler have done? They would have used them rather differently.

It is time for us to admit that not all cultures are at the same stage of moral development. This is a radically impolitic thing to say, of course, but it seems as objectively true as saying that not all societies have equal material resources. We might even conceive of our moral differences in just these terms: not all societies have the same degree of *moral wealth*. Many things contribute to such an endowment. Political and economic stability, literacy, a modicum of social equality—where such things are lacking, people tend to find many compelling reasons to treat one another rather badly. Our recent history offers much evidence of our own development on these fronts, and a corresponding change in our morality. A visit to New York in the summer of 1863 would have found the streets ruled by roving gangs of thugs; blacks, where not owned outright by white slaveholders, were regularly lynched and burned. Is there any doubt that many

New Yorkers of the nineteenth century were barbarians by our present standards? To say of another culture that it lags a hundred and fifty years behind our own in social development is a terrible criticism indeed, given how far we've come in that time. Now imagine the benighted Americans of 1863 coming to possess chemical, biological, and nuclear weapons. This is more or less the situation we confront in much of the developing world.

Consider the horrors that Americans perpetrated as recently as 1968, at My Lai:

> Early in the morning the soldiers were landed in the village by helicopter. Many were firing as they spread out, killing both people and animals. There was no sign of the Vietcong battalion and no shot was fired at Charlie Company all day, but they carried on. They burnt down every house. They raped women and girls and then killed them. They stabbed some women in the vagina and disemboweled others, or cut off their hands or scalps. Pregnant women had their stomachs slashed open and were left to die. There were gang rapes and killings by shooting or with bayonets. There were mass executions. Dozens of people at a time, including old men, women and children, were machine-gunned in a ditch. In four hours nearly 500 villagers were killed.[45]

This is about as bad as human beings are capable of behaving. But what distinguishes us from many of our enemies is that this indiscriminate violence appalls us. The massacre at My Lai is remembered as a signature moment of shame for the American military. Even at the time, U.S. soldiers were dumbstruck with horror by the behavior of their comrades. One helicopter pilot who arrived on the scene ordered his subordinates to use their machine guns against their own troops if they would not stop killing villagers.[46] As a culture, we have clearly outgrown our tolerance for the deliberate torture and murder of innocents. We would do well to realize that much of the world has not.

Wherever there are facts of any kind to be known, one thing is certain: not all people will discover them at the same time or understand them equally well. Conceding this leaves but a short step to hierarchical thinking of a sort that is at present inadmissible in most liberal discourse. Wherever there are right and wrong answers to important questions, there will be better or worse ways to get those answers, and better or worse ways to put them to use. Take child rearing as an example: How can we keep children free from disease? How can we raise them to be happy and responsible members of society? There are undoubtedly both good and bad answers to questions of this sort, and not all belief systems and cultural practices will be equally suited to bringing the good ones to light. This is not to say that there will always be only *one* right answer to every question, or a single, best way to reach every specific goal. But given the inescapable specificity of our world, the range of optimal solutions to any problem will generally be quite limited. While there might not be one best food to eat, we cannot eat stones—and any culture that would make stone eating a virtue, or a religious precept, will suffer mightily for want of nourishment (and teeth). It is inevitable, therefore, that some approaches to politics, economics, science, and even spirituality and ethics will be objectively better than their competitors (by any measure of "better" we might wish to adopt), and gradations here will translate into very real differences in human happiness.

Any systematic approach to ethics, or to understanding the necessary underpinnings of a civil society, will find many Muslims standing eye deep in the red barbarity of the fourteenth century. There are undoubtedly historical and cultural reasons for this, and enough blame to go around, but we should not ignore the fact that we must now confront whole societies whose moral and political development—in their treatment of women and children, in their prosecution of war, in their approach to criminal justice, and in their very intuitions about what constitutes cruelty—lags behind our own. This may seem like an unscientific and potentially racist thing to say, but it is neither. It is not in the least racist, since it is not at all likely that there are *biological* reasons for the disparities here, and it is unscientific only because science has not yet addressed the moral sphere in a systematic way. Come back in a hundred years, and if we haven't returned to living in caves and killing one another with clubs, we will have some scientifically astute things to say about ethics. Any honest witness to current events will realize that there is no moral equivalence between the kind of force civilized democracies project in the world, warts and all, and the internecine violence that is perpetrated by Muslim militants, or indeed by Muslim governments. Chomsky seems to think that the disparity either does not exist or runs the other way.

Consider the recent conflict in Iraq: If the situation had been reversed, what are the chances that the Iraqi Republican Guard, attempting to execute a regime change on the Potomac, would have taken the same degree of care to minimize civilian casualties? What are the chances that Iraqi forces would have been deterred by our use of human shields? (What are the chances we would have *used* human shields?) What are the chances that a routed American government would have called for its citizens to volunteer to be suicide bombers? What are the chances that Iraqi soldiers would have wept upon killing a carload of American civilians at a checkpoint unnecessarily? You should have, in the ledger of your imagination, a mounting column of zeros.

Nothing in Chomsky's account acknowledges the difference between intending to kill a child, because of the effect you hope to produce on its parents (we call this "terrorism"), and inadvertently killing a child in an attempt to capture or kill an avowed child murderer (we call this "collateral damage"). In both cases a child has died, and in both cases it is a tragedy. But the ethical status of the perpetrators, be they individuals or states, could hardly be more distinct.

Chomsky might object that to knowingly place the life of a child in jeopardy is unacceptable in any case, but clearly this is not a principle we can follow. The makers of roller coasters know, for instance, that despite rigorous safety precautions, sometime, somewhere, a child will be killed by one of their contraptions. Makers of automobiles know this as well. So do makers of hockey sticks, baseball bats, plastic bags, swimming pools, chain-link fences, or nearly anything else that could conceivably contribute to the death of a child. There is a reason we do not refer to the inevitable deaths of children on our ski slopes as "skiing atrocities." But you would not know this from reading Chomsky. For him, intentions do not seem to matter. Body count is all.

We are now living in a world that can no longer tolerate well-armed, malevolent regimes. Without perfect weapons, collateral damage—the maiming and killing of innocent people—is unavoidable. Similar suffering will be imposed on still more innocent people because of our lack of perfect automobiles, airplanes, antibiotics, surgical procedures, and window glass. If we want to draw conclusions about ethics—as well as make predictions about what a given person or society will do in the future—we cannot ignore human intentions. Where ethics are concerned, intentions are everything.[47]

A Waste of Precious Resources

Many commentators on the Middle East have suggested that the problem of Muslim terrorism cannot be reduced to what religious Muslims believe. Zakaria has written that the roots of Muslim violence lie not in Islam but in the recent history of the Arab Middle East. He points out that a mere fifty years ago, the Arab world stood on the cusp of modernity and then, tragically, fell backward. The true cause of terrorism, therefore, is simply the tyranny under which most Arabs have lived ever since. The problem, as Zakaria puts it, "is wealth, not poverty."[48] The ability to pull money straight out of the ground has led Arab governments to be entirely unresponsive to the concerns of their people. As it turns out, not needing to collect taxes is highly corrupting of state power. The result is just what we see—rich, repressive regimes built upon political and economic swampland. Little good is achieved for the forces of modernity when its mere products—fast food, television, and advanced weaponry—are hurled into the swamp as well.

According to Zakaria, "if there is one great cause of the rise of Islamic fundamentalism, it is the total failure of political institutions in the Arab world."[49] Perhaps. But "the rise of Islamic fundamentalism" is only a problem because the *fundamentals of Islam* are a problem. A rise of Jain fundamentalism would endanger no one. In fact, the uncontrollable spread of Jainism throughout the world would improve our situation immensely. We would lose more of our crops to pests, perhaps (observant Jains generally will not kill anything, including insects), but we would not find ourselves surrounded by suicidal terrorists or by a civilization that widely condones their actions.

Zakaria points out that Islam is actually notably antiauthoritarian, since obedience to a ruler is necessary only if he rules in accordance with God's law. But, as we have seen, few formulas for tyranny are more potent than obedience to "God's law." Still, Zakaria thinks that any emphasis on religious reform is misplaced:

> The truth is that little is to be gained by searching the Quran for clues to Islam's true nature. . . . The trouble with thundering declarations about "Islam's nature" is that Islam, like any religion, is not what books make it but what people make it. Forget the rantings of fundamentalists, who are a minority. Most Muslims' daily lives do not confirm the idea of a faith that is intrinsically anti-Western or anti-modern.[50]

According to Zakaria, the key to Arab redemption is to modernize politically, economically, and socially—and this will force Islam to follow along the path to liberalism, as Christianity has in the West. As evidence for this, he observes that millions of Muslims live in the United States, Canada, and Europe and "have found ways of being devout without being obscurantist, and pious without embracing fury."[51] There may be some truth to this, though, as we have seen, Zakaria ignores some troubling details. If, as I contend throughout this book, all that is good in religion can be had elsewhere—if, for instance, ethical and spiritual experience can be cultivated and talked about without our claiming to know things we manifestly do not know—then all the rest of our religious activity represents, at best, a massive waste of time and energy. Think of all the good things human beings will not do in this world tomorrow because they believe that their most pressing task is to build another church or mosque, or to enforce some ancient dietary practice, or to print volumes upon volumes of exegesis on the disordered thinking of ignorant men. How many hours of human labor will be devoured, today, by an imaginary God? Think of it: if a computer virus shuts down a nation's phone system for five minutes, the loss in human productivity is measured in billions of dollars. Religious faith has crashed our lines daily, for millennia. I'm not suggesting that the value of every human action should be measured in terms of productivity. Indeed, much of what we do would wither under such an analysis. But we should still recognize what a fathomless sink for human resources (both financial and attentional) organized religion is. Witness the rebuilding of Iraq: What was the first thing hundreds of thousands of Iraqi Shiites thought to do upon their liberation? Flagellate themselves. Blood poured from their scalps and backs as they walked miles of cratered streets and filth-strewn alleys to converge on the holy city Karbala, home to the tomb of Hussein, the grandson of the Prophet. Ask yourself whether this was really the best use of their time. Their society was in tatters. Fresh water and electricity were scarce. Their schools and hospitals were being looted. And an occupying army was trying to find reasonable people with whom to collaborate to form a civil society. Self-mortification and chanting should have been rather low on their list of priorities.

But the problem of religion is not merely that it competes for time and resources. While Zakaria is right to observe that faith has grown rather tame in the West—and this is undoubtedly a good thing—he neglects to notice that it still has very long claws. As we will see in the next chapter, even the most docile forms of Christianity currently present insuperable obstacles to AIDS prevention and family planning in the developing world, to medical research, and to the development of a rational drug policy—and these contributions to human misery alone constitute some of the most appalling failures of reasonableness in any age.

What Can We Do?

In thinking about Islam, and about the risk it now poses to the West, we should imagine what it would take to live peacefully with the Christians of the fourteenth century—Christians who were still eager to prosecute people for crimes like host desecration and witchcraft. We are in the presence of the past. It is by no means a straightforward task to engage such people in constructive dialogue, to convince them of our common interests, to encourage them on the path to democracy, and to mutually celebrate the diversity of our cultures.

It is clear that we have arrived at a period in our history where civil society, on a global scale, is not merely a nice idea; it is essential for the maintenance of civilization. Given that even failed states now possess potentially disruptive technology, we can no longer afford to live side by side with malign dictatorships or with the armies of ignorance massing across the oceans.

What constitutes a civil society? At minimum, it is a place where ideas, of all kinds, can be criticized without the risk of physical violence. If you live in a land where certain things cannot be said about the king, or about an imaginary being, or about certain books, because such utterances carry the penalty of death, torture, or imprisonment, you do not live in a civil society. It appears that one of the most urgent tasks we now face in the developed world is to find some way of facilitating the emergence of civil societies everywhere else. Whether such societies have to be democratic is not at all clear. Zakaria has persuasively argued that the transition from tyranny to liberalism is unlikely to be accomplished by plebiscite. It seems all but certain that some form of benign dictatorship will generally be necessary to bridge the gap. But benignity is the key— and if it cannot emerge from within a state, it must be imposed from without. The means of such imposition are necessarily crude: they amount to economic isolation, military intervention (whether open or covert), or some combination of both.[52] While this may seem an exceedingly arrogant doctrine to espouse, it appears we have no alternatives. We cannot wait for weapons of mass destruction to dribble out of the former Soviet Union—to pick only one horrible possibility—and into the hands of fanatics.

We should, I think, look upon modern despotisms as hostage crises. Kim Jong Il has thirty million hostages. Saddam Hussein had twenty-five million. The clerics in Iran have seventy million more. It does not matter that many hostages have been so brainwashed that they will fight their would-be liberators to the death. They are held prisoner twice over—by tyranny and by their own ignorance. The developed world must, somehow, come to their rescue. Jonathan Glover seems right to suggest that we need "something along the lines of a strong and properly funded permanent UN force, together with clear criteria for intervention and an international court to authorize it."[53] We can say it even more simply: we need a world government. How else will a war between the United States and China ever become as unlikely as a war between Texas and Vermont? We are a very long way from even thinking about the possibility of a world government, to say nothing of creating one. It would require a degree of economic, cultural, and moral integration that we may never achieve. The diversity of our religious beliefs constitutes a primary obstacle here. Given what most of us believe about God, it is at present unthinkable that human beings will ever identify themselves merely as *human beings*, disavowing all lesser affiliations. World government does seem a long way off—so long that we may not survive the trip.

Is Islam compatible with a civil society? Is it possible to believe what you must believe to be a good Muslim, to have military and economic power, and to not pose an unconscionable threat to the civil societies of others? I believe that the answer to this question is no. If a stable peace is ever to be achieved between Islam and the West, Islam must undergo a radical transformation. This transformation, to be palatable to Muslims, must also appear to come from Muslims themselves. It does not seem much of an exaggeration to say that the fate of civilization lies largely in the hands of "moderate" Muslims. Unless Muslims can reshape their religion into an ideology that is basically benign—or outgrow it altogether—it is difficult to see how Islam and the West can avoid falling into a continual state of war, and on innumerable fronts. Nuclear, biological, and chemical weapons cannot be uninvented. As Martin Rees points out, there is no reason to expect that we will be any more successful at stopping their proliferation, in small quantities, than we have been with respect to illegal drugs.[54] If this is true, weapons of mass destruction will soon be available to anyone who wants them.

Perhaps the West will be able to facilitate a transformation of the Muslim world by applying outside pressure. It will not be enough, however, for the United States and a few European countries to take a hard line while the rest of Europe and Asia sell advanced weaponry and "dual-use" nuclear reactors to all comers. To achieve the necessary economic leverage, so that we stand a chance of waging this war of ideas by peaceful means, the development of alternative energy technologies should become the object of a new Manhattan Project. There are, needless to say, sufficient economic and environmental justifications for doing this, but there are political ones as well. If oil were to become worthless, the dysfunction of the most prominent Muslim societies would suddenly grow as conspicuous as the sun. Muslims might then come to see the wisdom of moderating their thinking on a wide variety of subjects. Otherwise, we will be obliged to protect our interests in the world with force—continually. In this case, it seems all but certain that our newspapers will begin to read more and more like the book of Revelation.

5

West of Eden

•

COMPARED with the theocratic terrors of medieval Europe, or those that persist in much of the Muslim world, the influence of religion in the West now seems rather benign. We should not be misled by such comparisons, however. The degree to which religious ideas still determine government policies—especially those of the United States—presents a grave danger to everyone. It has been widely reported, for instance, that Ronald Reagan perceived the paroxysms in the Middle East through the lens of biblical prophecy. He went so far as to include men like Jerry Falwell and Hal Lindsey in his national security briefings.[1] It should go without saying that theirs are not the sober minds one wants consulted about the deployment of nuclear weaponry. For many years U.S. policy in the Middle East has been shaped, at least in part, by the interests that fundamentalist Christians have in the future of a Jewish state. Christian "support for Israel" is, in fact, an example of religious cynicism so transcendental as to go almost unnoticed in our political discourse. Fundamentalist Christians support Israel because they believe that the final consolidation of Jewish power in the Holy Land—specifically, the rebuilding of Solomon's temple—will usher in both the Second Coming of Christ and the final destruction of the Jews.[2] Such smiling anticipations of genocide seem to have presided over the Jewish state from its first moments: the first international support for the Jewish return to Palestine, Britain's Balfour Declaration of 1917, was inspired, at least in part, by a conscious conformity to biblical prophecy.[3] These intrusions of eschatology into modern politics suggest that the dangers of religious faith can scarcely be overstated. Millions of Christians and Muslims now organize their lives around prophetic traditions that will only find fulfillment once rivers of blood begin flowing from Jerusalem. It is not at all difficult to imagine how prophecies of internecine war, once taken seriously, could become self-fulfilling.

The Eternal Legislator

Many members of the U.S. government currently view their professional responsibilities in religious terms. Consider the case of Roy Moore, chief justice of the Alabama Supreme Court. Finding himself confronted by the sixth-highest murder rate in the nation, Justice Moore thought it expedient to install a two-and-a-half-ton monument of the Ten Commandments in the rotunda of the state courthouse in Montgomery. Almost no one disputes that this was a violation of the spirit (if not the letter) of the "establishment" clause of the First Amendment to the U.S. Constitution. When a federal court ordered Justice Moore to remove the monument, he refused. Not wanting to have an obvious hand in actually *separating* church and state, the U.S. Congress amended an appropriations bill to ensure that federal funds could not be used for the monument's removal.[4] Attorney General John Ashcroft, whose sole business is to enforce the nation's laws, maintained a pious silence all the while. This was not surprising, given that when he does speak, he is in the habit of saying things like "We are a nation called to defend freedom—freedom that is not the grant of any government or document, but is our endowment from God."[5] According to a Gallup poll, Ashcroft and the Congress were on firm ground as far as the American people were concerned, because 78 percent of those polled objected to the removal of the monument.[6] One wonders whether Moore, Ashcroft, the U.S. Congress, and three-quarters of the American people would like to see the *punishments* for breaking these hallowed commandments also specified in marble and placed in our nation's courts. What, after all, is the punishment for taking the Lord's name in vain? It happens to be death (Leviticus 24:16). What is the punishment for working on the Sabbath? Also death (Exodus 31:15). What is the punishment for cursing one's father or mother? Death again (Exodus 21:17). What is the punishment for adultery? You're catching on (Leviticus 20:10). While the commandments themselves are difficult to remember (especially since chapters 20 and 34 of Exodus provide us with incompatible lists), the penalty for breaking them is simplicity itself.

Contemporary examples of governmental piety are everywhere to be seen. Many prominent Republicans belong to the Council for National Policy, a secretive Christian pressure group founded by the fundamentalist Tim LaHaye (coauthor of the apocalyptic "Left Behind" series of novels). This organization meets quarterly to discuss who knows what. George W. Bush gave a closed-door speech to the council in 1999, after which the Christian Right endorsed his candidacy.[7] Indeed, 40 percent of those who eventually voted for Bush were white evangelicals.[8] Beginning with his appointment of John Ashcroft as his attorney general, President Bush found no lack of occasions on which to return the favor. The departments of Justice, Housing and Urban Development, Health and Human Services, and Education now regularly issue directives that blur the separation between church and state.[9] In his "faith-based initiative" Bush has managed to funnel tens of millions of taxpayer dollars directly to church groups, to be used more or less however they see fit.[10] One of his appointments to the Food and Drug Administration was Dr. W. David Hager, a pro-life obstetrician who has declared publicly that premarital sex is a sin and that any attempt to separate "Christian truth" and "secular truth" is "dangerous."[11] Lieutenant General William G. Boykin was recently appointed deputy undersecretary of defense for intelligence at the Pentagon. A highly decorated Special Forces officer, he now sets policy with respect to the search for Osama bin Laden, Mullah Omar, and the rest of

America's enemies in hiding. He is also, as it turns out, an ardent opponent of Satan. Analyzing a photograph of Mogadishu after the fateful routing of his forces there in 1993, Boykin remarked that certain shadows in the image revealed "the principalities of darkness . . . a demonic presence in that city that God revealed to me as the enemy."[12] On the subject of the war on terror, he has asserted that our "enemy is a guy named Satan."[13] While these remarks sparked some controversy in the media, most Americans probably took them in stride. After all, 65 percent of us are quite certain that Satan exists.[14]

Men eager to do the Lord's work have been elected to other branches of the federal government as well. The House majority leader, Tom DeLay, is given to profundities like "Only Christianity offers a way to live in response to the realities that we find in this world. Only Christianity." He claims to have gone into politics "to promote a Biblical worldview." Apparently feeling that it is impossible to say anything stupid while in the service of this worldview, he attributed the shootings at the Columbine High School in Colorado to the fact that our schools teach the theory of evolution.[15] We might wonder how it is that pronouncements this floridly irrational do not lead to immediate censure and removal from office.

Facts of this sort can be cataloged without apparent end—to the vexation of reader and writer alike. I will cite just one more, now from the judicial branch: In January of 2002, Supreme Court Justice Antonin Scalia, a devout Catholic, delivered a speech at the University of Chicago Divinity School on the subject of the death penalty. I quote Scalia at some length, because his remarks reveal just how close we are to living in a theocracy:

> This is not the Old Testament, I emphasize, but St. Paul. . . . [T]he *core* of his message is that government—however you want to limit that concept—derives its moral authority from God. . . . Indeed, it seems to me that the more Christian a country is the *less* likely it is to regard the death penalty as immoral. . . . I

attribute that to the fact that, for the believing Christian, death is no big deal. Intentionally killing an innocent person is a big deal: it is a grave sin, which causes one to lose his soul. But losing this life, in exchange for the next? . . . For the nonbeliever, on the other hand, to deprive a man of his life is to end his existence. What a horrible act! . . .

The reaction of people of faith to this tendency of democracy to obscure the divine authority behind government should not be resignation to it, but the resolution to combat it as effectively as possible. We have done that in this country (and continental Europe has not) by preserving in our public life many visible reminders that—in the words of a Supreme Court opinion from the 1940s—"we are a religious people, whose institutions presuppose a Supreme Being." . . . All this, as I say, is most un-European, and helps explain why our people are more inclined to understand, as St. Paul did, that government carries the sword as "the minister of God," to "execute wrath" upon the evildoer.[16]

All of this should be terrifying to anyone who expects that reason will prevail in the inner sanctums of power in the West. Scalia is right to observe that what a person believes happens after death determines his view of it—and, therefore, his ethics. Although he is a Catholic, Scalia differs from the pope on the subject of capital punishment, but then so do a majority of Americans (74 percent).[17] It is remarkable that we are the last civilized nation to put "evildoers" to death, and Justice Scalia rightly attributes this to our style of religiosity. Perhaps we can take a moment, in this context, to wonder whether our unique position in the world is really the moral accomplishment that Scalia imagines it to be. We know, for instance, that no human being creates his own genes or his early life experiences, and yet most of us believe that these factors determine his character throughout life. It seems true enough to say that the men and women on death row either have bad genes, bad parents, bad ideas, or bad luck. Which of these quantities are they responsible for? Resorting to biblical justifications for capital punishment does nothing to reconcile our growing understanding of human behavior with our desire for retribution in the face of the most appalling crimes. There is undoubtedly an important secular debate to be had about the ethics of the death penalty, but it is just as obvious that we should be drawing upon sources that show a greater understanding of the human mind and modern society than is evident in Saint Paul.

But men like Scalia—men who believe that we already have God's eternal decrees on paper—have been inoculated against doubts on this subject or, indeed, against the nuances of a scientific worldview. It is not surprising that Scalia is the kind of judge that President Bush has sought to appoint to the federal courts.[18] Scalia supports the use of capital punishment even in cases where the defendant is acknowledged to be mentally retarded.[19] He also upholds state sodomy laws (in this case, even when they are applied in an exclusive and discriminating way to homosexuals).[20] Needless to say, Scalia has found *legal* reasons to insist that the Supreme Court not leaven the religious dogmatism of the states, but he leaves little doubt that he looks to Saint Paul, and perhaps to the barbarous author of Leviticus, for guidance on these matters.

The War on Sin

In the United States, and in much of the rest of the world, it is currently illegal to seek certain experiences of pleasure. Seek pleasure by a forbidden means, even in the privacy of your own home, and men with guns may kick in the door and carry you away to prison for it. One of the most surprising things about this situation is how unsurprising most of us find it. As in most dreams, the very faculty of reason that would otherwise notice the strangeness of these events seems to have succumbed to sleep.

Behaviors like drug use, prostitution, sodomy, and the viewing of obscene materials have been categorized as "victimless crimes." Of course, society is the tangible victim of almost everything human beings do—from making noise to manufacturing chemical waste—but we have not made it a crime to do such things within certain limits. Setting these limits is invariably a matter of assessing risk. One could argue that it is, at the very least, conceivable that certain activities engaged in private, like the viewing of sexually violent pornography, might incline some people to commit genuine crimes against others.[21] There is a tension, therefore, between private freedom and public risk. If there were a drug, or a book, or a film, or a sexual position that led 90 percent of its users to rush into the street and begin killing people at random, concerns over private pleasure would surely yield to those of public safety. We can also stipulate that no one is eager to see generations of children raised on a steady diet of methamphetamine and Marquis de Sade. Society as a whole has an interest in how its children develop, and the private behavior of parents, along with the contents of our media, clearly play a role in this. But we must ask ourselves, why would anyone want to punish people for engaging in behavior that brings no significant risk of harm to anyone? Indeed, what is startling about the notion of a victimless crime is that even when the behavior in question is genuinely victimless, its criminality is still affirmed by those who are eager to punish it. It is in such cases that the true genius lurking behind many of our laws stands revealed. The idea of a victimless crime is nothing more than a judicial reprise of the Christian notion of *sin*.

IT is no accident that people of faith often want to curtail the private freedoms of others. This impulse has less to do with the history of religion and more to do with its logic, because the very idea of privacy is incompatible with the existence of God. If God sees and knows all things, and remains so provincial a creature as to be scandalized by certain sexual behaviors or states of the brain, then what people do in the privacy of their own homes, though it may not have the slightest implication for their behavior in public, will still be a matter of public concern for people of faith.[22]

A variety of religious notions of wrongdoing can be seen converging here—concerns over nonprocreative sexuality and idolatry especially—and these seem to have given many of us the sense that it is ethical to punish people, often severely, for engaging in private behavior that harms no one. Like most costly examples of irrationality, in which human happiness has been blindly subverted for generations, the role of religion here is both explicit and foundational. To see that our laws against "vice" have actually nothing to do with keeping people from coming to physical or psychological harm, and everything to do with not angering God, we need only consider that oral or anal sex between consenting adults remains a criminal offense in thirteen states. Four of the states (Texas, Kansas, Oklahoma, and Missouri) prohibit these acts between same-sex couples and, therefore, effectively prohibit homosexuality. The other nine ban consensual sodomy for everyone (these places of equity are Alabama, Florida, Idaho, Louisiana, Mississippi, North Carolina, South Carolina, Utah, and Virginia).[23] One does not have to be a demographer to grasp that the impulse to prosecute consenting adults for nonprocreative sexual behavior will correlate rather strongly with religious faith.

The influence of faith on our criminal laws comes at a remarkable price. Consider the case of drugs. As it happens, there are many substances—many of them naturally occurring—the consumption of which leads to transient states of inordinate pleasure. Occasionally, it is true, they lead to transient states of misery as well, but there is no doubt that pleasure is the norm, otherwise human beings would not have felt the continual desire to take such substances for millennia. Of course, pleasure is precisely the problem with these substances, since pleasure and piety have always had an uneasy relationship.

When one looks at our drug laws—indeed, at our vice laws altogether—the only organizing principle that appears to make sense of them is that anything which might radically eclipse prayer or procreative sexuality as a source of pleasure has been outlawed. In particular, any drug (LSD, mescaline, psilocybin, DMT, MDMA, marijuana, etc.) to which spiritual or religious significance has been ascribed by its users has been prohibited. Concerns about the health of our citizens, or about their productivity, are red herrings in this debate, as the legality of alcohol and cigarettes attests.

The fact that people are being prosecuted and imprisoned for using marijuana, while alcohol remains a staple commodity, is surely the reductio ad absurdum of any notion that our drug laws are designed to keep people from harming themselves or others.[24] Alcohol is by any measure the more dangerous substance. It has no approved medical use, and its lethal dose is rather easily achieved. Its role in causing automobile accidents is beyond dispute. The manner in which alcohol relieves people of their inhibitions contributes to human violence, personal injury, unplanned pregnancy, and the spread of sexual disease. Alcohol is also well known to be addictive. When consumed in large quantities over many years, it can lead to devastating neurological impairments, to cirrhosis of the liver, and to death. In the United States alone, more than 100,000 people annually die from its use. It is also more toxic to a developing fetus than any other drug of abuse. (Indeed, "crack babies" appear to have been really suffering from fetal-alcohol syndrome.)[25] None of these charges can be leveled at marijuana. As a drug, marijuana is nearly unique in having several medical applications and no known lethal dosage. While adverse reactions to drugs like aspirin and ibuprofen account for an estimated 7,600 deaths (and 76,000 hospitalizations) each year in the United States alone, marijuana kills no one.[26] Its role as a "gateway drug" now seems less plausible than ever (and it was never plausible).[27] In fact, nearly everything human beings do—driving cars, flying planes, hitting golf balls—is more dangerous than smoking marijuana in the privacy of one's own home. Anyone who would seriously attempt to argue that marijuana is worthy of prohibition because of the risk it poses to human beings will find that the powers of the human brain are simply insufficient for the job.

And yet, we are so far from the shady groves of reason now that people are still receiving life sentences without the possibility of parole for growing, selling, possessing, or buying what is, in fact, a naturally occurring plant.[28] Cancer patients and paraplegics have been sentenced to decades in prison for marijuana possession. Owners of garden-supply stores have received similar sentences because some of their *customers* were caught growing marijuana. What explains this astonishing wastage of human life and material resources? The only explanation is that our discourse on this subject has never been obliged to function within the bounds of rationality. Under our current laws, it is safe to say, if a drug were invented that posed no risk of physical harm or addiction to its users but produced a brief feeling of spiritual bliss and epiphany in 100 percent of those who tried it, this drug would be illegal, and people would be punished mercilessly for its use. Only anxiety about the biblical crime of idolatry would appear to make sense of this retributive impulse. Because we are a people of faith, taught to concern ourselves with the sinfulness of our neighbors, we have grown tolerant of irrational uses of state power.

Our prohibition of certain substances has led thousands of otherwise productive and law-abiding men and women to be locked away for decades at a stretch, sometimes for life. Their children have become wards of the state. As if such cascading horror were not disturbing enough, *violent* criminals—murders, rapists, and child molesters—are regularly paroled to make room for them.[29] Here we appear to have overstepped the banality of evil and plunged to the absurdity at its depths.[30]

The consequences of our irrationality on this front are so egregious that they bear closer examination. Each year, over 1.5 million men and women are arrested in the United States because of our drug laws. At this moment, somewhere on the order of 400,000 men and women languish in U.S. prisons for *nonviolent* drug offenses. One million others are currently on probation.[31] More people are imprisoned for nonviolent drug offenses in the United States than are incarcerated, for any reason, in all of Western Europe (which has a larger population). The cost of these efforts, at the federal level alone, is nearly \$20 billion dollars annually.[32] The total cost of our drug laws—when one factors in the expense to state and local governments and the tax revenue lost by our failure to regulate the sale of drugs—could easily be in excess of \$100 billion dollars each year.[33] Our war on drugs consumes an estimated 50 percent of the trial time of our courts and the full-time energies of over 400,000 police officers.[34] These are resources that might otherwise be used to fight violent crime and terrorism.

In historical terms, there was every reason to expect that such a policy of prohibition would fail. It is well known, for instance, that the experiment with the prohibition of alcohol in the United States did little more than precipitate a terrible comedy of increased drinking, organized crime, and police corruption. What is not generally remembered is that Prohibition was an explicitly religious exercise, being the joint product of the Woman's Christian Temperance Union and the pious lobbying of certain Protestant missionary societies.

The problem with the prohibition of any desirable commodity is money. The United Nations values the drug trade at \$400 billion a year. This exceeds the annual budget for the U.S. Department of Defense. If this figure is correct, the trade in illegal drugs constitutes 8 percent of all international commerce (while the sale of textiles makes up 7.5 percent and motor vehicles just 5.3 percent).[35] And yet, prohibition itself is what makes the manufacture and sale of drugs so extraordinarily profitable. Those who earn their living in this way enjoy a 5,000 to 20,000 percent return on their investment, tax-free. Every relevant indicator of the drug trade—rates of drug use and interdiction, estimates of production, the purity of drugs on the street, etc.—shows that the government can do nothing to stop it as long as such profits exist (indeed, these profits are highly corrupting of law enforcement in any case). The crimes of the addict, to finance the stratospheric cost of his lifestyle, and the crimes of the dealer, to protect both his territory and his goods, are likewise the results of prohibition.[36] A final irony, which seems good enough to be the work of Satan himself, is that the market we have created by our drug laws has become a steady source of revenue for terrorist organizations like Al Qaeda, Islamic Jihad, Hezbollah, Shining Path, and others.[37]

Even if we acknowledge that stopping drug use is a justifiable social goal, how does the financial cost of our war on drugs appear in light of the other challenges we face? Consider that it would require only a onetime expenditure of $2 billion to secure our commercial seaports against smuggled nuclear weapons. At present we have allocated a mere $93 million for this purpose.[38] How will our prohibition of marijuana use look (this comes at a cost of $4 billion *annually*) if a new sun ever dawns over the port of Los Angeles? Or consider that the U.S. government can afford to spend only $2.3 billion each year on the reconstruction of Afghanistan. The Taliban and Al Qaeda are now regrouping. Warlords rule the countryside beyond the city limits of Kabul. Which is more important to us, reclaiming this part of the world for the forces of civilization or keeping cancer patients in Berkeley from relieving their nausea with marijuana? Our present use of government funds suggests an uncanny skewing—we might even say derangement—of our national priorities. Such a bizarre allocation of resources is sure to keep Afghanistan in ruins for many years to come. It will also leave Afghan farmers with no alternative but to grow opium. Happily for them, our drug laws still render this a highly profitable enterprise.[39]

Anyone who believes that God is watching us from beyond the stars will feel that punishing peaceful men and women for their private pleasure is perfectly reasonable. We are now in the twenty-first century. Perhaps we should have better reasons for depriving our neighbors of their liberty at gunpoint. Given the magnitude of the real problems that confront us—terrorism, nuclear proliferation, the spread of infectious disease, failing infrastructure, lack of adequate funds for education and health care, etc.—our war on sin is so outrageously unwise as to almost defy rational comment. How have we grown so blind to our deeper interests? And how have we managed to enact such policies with so little substantive debate?

The God of Medicine

While there is surely an opposition between reason and faith, we will see that there is none between reason and love or reason and spirituality. The basis for this claim is simple. Every experience that a human being can have admits of rational discussion about its causes and consequences (or about our ignorance thereof). Although this leaves considerable room for the exotic, it leaves none at all for faith. There may yet be good reasons to believe in psychic phenomena, alien life, the doctrine of rebirth, the healing power of prayer, or anything else—*but our credulity must scale with the evidence.* The doctrine of faith denies this. From the perspective of faith, it is better to ape the behavior of one's ancestors than to find creative ways to uncover new truths in the present.

There are sources of irrationality other than religious faith, of course, but none of them are celebrated for their role in shaping public policy. Supreme Court justices are not in the habit of praising our nation for its reliance upon astrology, or for its wealth of UFO sightings, or for exemplifying the various reasoning biases that psychologists have found to be more or less endemic to our species.[40] Only mainstream religious dogmatism receives the unqualified support of government. And yet, religious faith obscures uncertainty where uncertainty manifestly exists, allowing the unknown, the implausible, and the patently false to achieve primacy over the facts.

Consider the present debate over research on human embryonic stem cells. The problem with this research, from the religious point of view, is simple: it entails the destruction of human embryos. The embryos in question will have been cultured in vitro (not removed from a woman's body) and permitted to grow for three to five days. At this stage of development, an embryo is called a blastocyst and consists of about 150 cells arranged in a microscopic sphere. Interior to the blastocyst is a small group of about 30 embryonic stem cells. These cells have two properties that make them of such abiding interest to scientists: as stem cells, they can remain in an unspecialized state, reproducing themselves through cell division for long periods of time (a population of such cells living in culture is known as a cell line); stem cells are also pluripotent, which means they have the potential to become any specialized cell in the human body— neurons of the brain and spinal cord, insulin-producing cells of the pancreas, muscle cells of the heart, and so forth.

Here is what we know. We know that much can be learned from research on embryonic stem cells. In particular, such research may give us further insight into the processes of cell division and cell differentiation. This would almost certainly shed new light on those medical conditions, like cancer and birth defects, that seem to be merely a matter of these processes gone awry. We also know that research on embryonic stem cells requires the destruction of human embryos at the 150-cell stage. There is not the slightest reason to believe, however, that such embryos have the capacity to sense pain, to suffer, or to experience the loss of life in any way at all. What is indisputable is that there are millions of human beings who do have these capacities, and who currently suffer from traumatic injuries to the brain and spinal cord. Millions more suffer from Parkinson's and Alzheimer's diseases. Millions more suffer from stroke and heart disease, from burns, from diabetes, from rheumatoid arthritis, from Purkinje cell degeneration, from Duchenne muscular dystrophy, and from vision and hearing loss. We know that embryonic stem cells promise to be a renewable source of tissues and organs that might alleviate such suffering in the not too distant future.

Enter faith: we now find ourselves living in a world in which college-educated politicians will hurl impediments in the way of such research because they are concerned about the fate of *single cells*. Their concern is not merely that a collection of 150 cells may suffer its destruction. Rather, they believe that even a human zygote (a fertilized egg) should be accorded all the protections of a fully developed human being. Such a cell, after all, has the potential to *become* a fully developed human being. But given our recent advances in the biology of cloning, as much can be said of almost every cell in the human body. By the measure of a cell's *potential*, whenever the president scratches his nose he is now engaged in a diabolical culling of souls.

Out of deference to some rather poorly specified tenets of Christian doctrine (after all, nothing in the Bible suggests that killing human embryos, or even human fetuses, is the equivalent of killing a human being), the U.S. House of Representatives voted effectively to ban embryonic stem-cell research on February 27, 2003.

No rational approach to ethics would have led us to such an impasse. Our present policy on human stem cells has been shaped by beliefs that are divorced from every reasonable intuition we might form about the possible experience of living systems. In neurological terms, we surely visit more suffering upon this earth by killing a fly than by killing a human blastocyst, to say nothing of a human zygote (flies, after all, have 100,000 cells in their brains alone). Of course, the point at which we fully acquire our humanity, and our capacity to suffer, remains an open question. But anyone who would dogmatically insist that these traits must arise coincident with the moment of conception has nothing to contribute, apart from his ignorance, to this debate. Those opposed to therapeutic stem-cell research on religious grounds constitute the biological and ethical equivalent of a flat-earth society. Our discourse on the subject should reflect this. In this area of public policy alone, the accommodations that we have made to faith will do nothing but enshrine a perfect immensity of human suffering for decades to come.

BUT the tendrils of unreason creep further. President Bush recently decided to cut off funding to any overseas family-planning group that provides information on abortion. According to the *New York Times*, this "has effectively stopped condom provision to 16 countries and reduced it in 13 others, including some with the world's highest rates of AIDS infection."[41] Under the influence of Christian notions of the sinfulness of sex outside of marriage, the U.S. government has required that one-third of its AIDS prevention funds allocated to Africa be squandered on teaching abstinence rather than condom use. It is no exaggeration to say that millions could die as a direct result of this single efflorescence of religious dogmatism. As Nicholas Kristof points out, "sex kills, and so does this kind of blushing prudishness."[42]

And yet, even those who see the problem in all its horror find it impossible to criticize faith itself. Take Kristof as an example: in the very act of exposing the medievalism that prevails in the U.S. government, and its likely consequences abroad, he goes on to chastise anyone who would demand that the faithful be held fully accountable for their beliefs:

> I tend to disagree with evangelicals on almost everything, and I see no problem with aggressively pointing out the dismal consequences of this increasing religious influence. For example, evangelicals' discomfort with condoms and sex education has led the administration to policies that are likely to lead to more people dying of AIDS at home and abroad, not to mention more pregnancies and abortions.
>
> But liberal critiques sometimes seem not just filled with outrage at evangelical-backed policies, which is fair, but also to have a sneering tone about conservative Christianity itself. Such mockery of religious faith is inexcusable. And liberals sometimes show more intellectual curiosity about the religion of Afghanistan than that of Alabama, and more interest in reading the Upanishads than in reading the Book of Revelation.[43]

This is reason in ruins. Kristof condemns the "dismal consequences" of faith while honoring their cause.[44] It is true that the rules of civil discourse currently demand that Reason wear a veil whenever she ventures out in public. But the rules of civil discourse must change.

Faith drives a wedge between ethics and suffering. Where certain actions cause no suffering at all, religious dogmatists still maintain that they are evil and worthy of punishment (sodomy, marijuana use, homosexuality, the killing of blastocysts, etc.). And yet, where suffering and death are found in abundance their causes are often deemed to be good (withholding funds for family planning in the third world, prosecuting nonviolent drug offenders, preventing stem-cell research, etc). This inversion of priorities not only victimizes innocent people and squanders scarce resources; it completely falsifies our ethics. It is time we found a more reasonable approach to answering questions of right and wrong.

6

A Science of Good and Evil

•

Is THE difference between good and evil just a matter of what any particular group of human beings says it is? Consider that one of the greatest sources of amusement in sixteenth-century Paris was *cat burning*. At the midsummer's fair an impresario would gather dozens of cats in a net, hoist them high into the air from a special stage, and then, to everyone's delight, lower the whole writhing bundle onto a bonfire. The assembled spectators "shrieked with laughter as the animals, howling with pain, were singed, roasted, and finally carbonized."[1] Most of us would recoil from such a spectacle today. But would we be *right* to do so? Can we say that there are ethical truths of which all avid torturers of cats are ignorant?

Many people appear to believe that ethical truths are culturally contingent in a way that scientific truths are not. Indeed, this loss of purchase upon ethical *truth* seems to be one of the principal shortcomings of secularism. The problem is that once we abandon our belief in a rule-making God, the question of *why* a given action is good or bad becomes a matter of debate. And a statement like "Murder is wrong," while being uncontroversial in most circles, has never seemed anchored to the facts of this world in the way that statements about planets or molecules appear to be. The problem, in philosophical terms, has been one of characterizing just what sort of "facts" our moral intuitions can be said to track—if, indeed, they track anything of the kind.

A rational approach to ethics becomes possible once we realize that questions of right and wrong are really questions about the happiness and suffering of sentient creatures. If we are in a position to affect the happiness or suffering of others, we have ethical responsibilities toward them[2]—and many of these responsibilities are so grave as to become matters of civil and criminal law. Taking happiness and suffering as our starting point, we can see that much of what people worry about under the guise of morality has nothing to do with the subject. It is time we realized that crimes without victims are like debts without creditors. They do not even exist.[3] Any person who lies awake at night worrying about the private pleasures of other consenting adults has more than just too much time on his hands; he has some unjustifiable beliefs about the nature of right and wrong.

The fact that people of different times and cultures disagree about ethical questions should not trouble us. It suggests nothing at all about the status of moral truth. Imagine what it would be like to consult the finest thinkers of antiquity on questions of basic science: "What," we might ask, "is fire? And how do living systems reproduce themselves? And what are the various lights we see in the night sky?" We would surely encounter a bewildering lack of consensus on these matters. Even though there was no shortage of brilliant minds in the ancient world, they simply lacked the physical and conceptual tools to answer questions of this sort. Their lack of consensus signified their ignorance of certain physical truths, not that no such truths exist.

If there are right and wrong answers to ethical questions, these answers will be best sought in the living present. Whether our search takes us to a secluded cave or to a modern laboratory makes no difference to the existence of the facts in question. If ethics represents a genuine sphere of knowledge, it represents a sphere of potential progress (and regress). The relevance of tradition to this area of discourse, as to all others, will be as a support for present inquiry. Where our traditions are not supportive, they become mere vehicles of ignorance. The pervasive idea that religion is somehow the *source* of our deepest ethical intuitions is absurd. We no more get our sense that cruelty is wrong from the pages of the Bible than we get our sense that two plus two equals four from the pages of a textbook on mathematics. Anyone who does not harbor some rudimentary sense that cruelty is wrong is unlikely to learn that it is by reading—and, indeed, most scripture offers rather equivocal testimony to this fact in any case. Our ethical intuitions must have their precursors in the natural world, for while nature is indeed red in tooth and claw, it is not merely so. Even monkeys will undergo extraordinary privations to avoid causing harm to another member of their species.[4] Concern for others was not the invention of any prophet.

The fact that our ethical intuitions have their roots in biology reveals that our efforts to ground ethics in religious conceptions of "moral duty" are misguided. Saving a drowning child is no more a moral duty than understanding a syllogism is a logical one. We simply do not need religious ideas to motivate us to live ethical lives. Once we begin thinking seriously about happiness and suffering, we find that our religious traditions are no more reliable on questions of ethics than they have been on scientific questions generally.

The anthropocentrism that is intrinsic to every faith cannot help appearing impossibly quaint—and therefore *impossible*—given what we now know about the natural world. Biological truths are simply not commensurate with a designer God, or even a good one. The perverse wonder of evolution is this: the very mechanisms that create the incredible beauty and diversity of the living world guarantee monstrosity and death. The child born without limbs, the sightless fly, the vanished species—these are nothing less than Mother Nature caught in the act of throwing her clay. No perfect God could maintain such incongruities. It is worth remembering that if God created the world and all things in it, he created smallpox, plague, and filariasis. Any person who intentionally loosed such horrors upon the earth would be ground to dust for his crimes.

The deity who stalked the deserts of the Middle East millennia ago—and who seems to have abandoned them to bloodshed in his name ever since—is no one to consult on questions of ethics. Indeed, to judge him on the basis of his works is a highly invidious undertaking. Bertrand Russell got here first: "Apart from logical cogency, there is to me something a little odd about the ethical valuations of those who think that an omnipotent, omniscient, and benevolent Deity, after preparing the ground by many millions of years of lifeless nebulae, would consider Himself adequately rewarded by the final emergence of Hitler and Stalin and the H bomb."[5] This is a devastating observation, and there is no retort to it. In the face of God's obvious inadequacies, the pious have generally held that one cannot apply earthly norms to the Creator of the universe. This argument loses its force the moment we notice that the Creator who purports to be beyond human judgment is consistently ruled by human passions—jealousy, wrath, suspicion, and the lust to dominate. A close study of our holy books reveals that the God of Abraham is a ridiculous fellow—capricious, petulant, and cruel—and one with whom a covenant is little guarantee of health or happiness.[6] If these are the characteristics of God, then the worst among us have been created far more in his image than we ever could have hoped.

The problem of vindicating an omnipotent and omniscient God in the face of evil (this is traditionally called the problem of theodicy) is insurmountable. Those who claim to have surmounted it, by recourse to notions of free will and other incoherencies, have merely heaped bad philosophy onto bad ethics.[7] Surely there must come a time when we will acknowledge the obvious: theology is now little more than a branch of human ignorance. Indeed, it is ignorance with wings.

Ethics and the Sciences of Mind

The connection between ethics and the scientific understanding of consciousness, while rarely made, is ineluctable, for other creatures become the objects of our ethical concern only insofar as we attribute consciousness (or perhaps *potential* consciousness) to them. That most of us feel no ethical obligations toward rocks—to treat them with kindness, to make sure they do not suffer unduly—can be derived from the fact that most of us do not believe that there is anything that it is like to *be* a rock.[8] While a science of consciousness is still struggling to be born, it is sufficient for our purposes to note that the problem of ascertaining our ethical obligations to non-human animals (as well as to humans who have suffered neurological injury, to human fetuses, to blastocysts, etc.) requires that we better understand the relationship between mind and matter. Do crickets suffer? I take it as a given that this question is both coherently posed and has an answer, whether or not we will ever be in a position to answer it ourselves.

This is the point at which our notions about mind and matter directly influence our notions of right and wrong. We should recall that the practice of vivisection was given new life by certain missteps in the philosophy of mind—when Descartes, in thrall to both Christian dogma and mechanistic physics, declared that all nonhuman animals were mere automata, devoid of souls and therefore insensible to pain.[9] One of his contemporaries observed the immediate consequences of this view:

> The scientists administered beatings to dogs with perfect indifference and made fun of those who pitied the creatures as if they felt pain. They said the animals were clocks; that the cries they emitted when struck were only the noise of a little spring that had been touched, but that the whole body was without feeling. They nailed the poor animals up on boards by their four paws to vivisect them to see the circulation of blood, which was a great subject of controversy.[10]

Cognitive chauvinism of this sort has not merely been a problem for animals. The doubt, on the part of Spanish explorers, about whether or not South American Indians had "souls" surely contributed to the callousness with which they treated them during their conquest of the New World. Admittedly, it is difficult to say just how far down the phylogenic tree our ethical responsibilities run. Our intuitions about the consciousness of other animals are driven by a variety of factors, many of which probably have no bearing upon whether or not they are conscious. For instance, creatures that lack facial expressiveness—or faces at all—are more difficult to include within the circle of our moral concern. It seems that until we more fully understand the relationship between brains and minds, our judgments about the possible scope of animal suffering will remain relatively blind and relatively dogmatic.[11]

THERE will probably come a time when we achieve a detailed understanding of human happiness, and of ethical judgments themselves, at the level of the brain.[12] Just as defects in color vision can result from genetic and developmental disorders, problems can undoubtedly arise in our ethical and emotional circuitry as well. To say that a person is "color-blind" or "achromatopsic" is now a straightforward statement about the state of the visual pathways in his brain, while to say that he is "an evil sociopath" or "lacking in moral fiber" seems hopelessly unscientific. This will almost certainly change. If there are truths to be known about how human beings conspire to make one another happy or miserable, there are truths to be known about ethics.[13] A scientific understanding of the link between intentions, human relationships, and states of happiness would have much to say about the nature of good and evil and about the proper response to the moral transgressions of others. There is every reason to believe that sustained inquiry in the moral sphere will force convergence of our various belief systems in the way that it has in every other science—that is, among those who are adequate to the task.[14] That so little convergence has been achieved in ethics can be ascribed to the fact that so few of the facts are in (indeed, we have yet to agree about the most basic criteria for deeming an ethical fact, *a fact*). So many conversations have not yet been had; so many intuitions have not yet been exercised; so many arguments have not yet been won. Our reliance upon religious dogma explains this. Most of our religions have been no more supportive of genuine moral inquiry than of scientific inquiry generally. This is a problem that only new rules of discourse can overcome. When was the last time that someone was criticized for not "respecting" another person's unfounded beliefs about physics or history? The same rules should apply to ethical, spiritual, and religious beliefs as well. Credit goes to Christopher Hitchens for distilling, in a single phrase, a principle of discourse that could well arrest our slide toward the abyss: "what can be asserted without evidence can also be dismissed without evidence."[15] Let us pray that billions of us soon agree with him.

Moral Communities

The notion of a moral community resolves many paradoxes of human behavior. How is it, after all, that a Nazi guard could return each day from his labors at the crematoria and be a loving father to his children? The answer is surprisingly straightforward: the Jews he spent the day torturing and killing were not objects of his moral concern. Not only were they outside his moral community; they were antithetical to it. His beliefs about Jews inured him to the natural human sympathies that might have otherwise prevented such behavior.

Unfortunately, religion casts more shadows than light on this terrain. Rather than find real reasons for human solidarity, faith offers us a solidarity born of tribal and tribalizing fictions. As we have seen, religion is one of the great limiters of moral identity, since most believers differentiate themselves, in moral terms, from those who do not share their faith. No other ideology is so eloquent on the subject of what divides one moral community from another. Once a person accepts the premises upon which most religious identities are built, the withdrawal of his moral concern from those who do not share these premises follows quite naturally. Needless to say, the suffering of those who are destined for hell can never be as problematic as the suffering of the righteous. If certain people can't see the unique wisdom and sanctity of my religion, if their hearts are so beclouded by sin, what concern is it of mine if others mistreat them? They have been cursed by the very God who made the world and all things in it. Their search for happiness was simply doomed from the start.

New problems arise once we commit ourselves to finding a rational foundation for our ethics. Indeed, we find that it is difficult to draw the boundaries of our moral concern in a principled way. It is clear, for instance, that susceptibility to pain cannot be our only criteria. As Richard Rorty observes, "If pain were all that mattered, it would be as important to protect the rabbits from the foxes as to protect the Jews from the Nazis."[16] In virtue of what have we convinced ourselves that we need not intercede on behalf of all rabbits? Most of us suspect rabbits are not capable of experiencing happiness or suffering on a human scale. Admittedly we could be wrong about this. And if it ever seems that we have underestimated the subjectivity of rabbits, our ethical stance toward them would no doubt change. Incidentally, here is where a rational answer to the abortion debate is lurking. Many of us consider human fetuses in the first trimester to be more or less like rabbits: having imputed to them a range of happiness and suffering that does not grant them full status in our moral community. At present, this seems rather reasonable. Only future scientific insights could refute this intuition.

The problem of specifying the criteria for inclusion in our moral community is one for which I do not have a detailed answer—other than to say that whatever answer we give should reflect our sense of the possible subjectivity of the creatures in question. Some answers are clearly wrong. We cannot merely say, for instance, that all human beings are in, and all animals are out. What will be our criterion for humanness? DNA? Shall a single human cell take precedence over a herd of elephants? The problem is that whatever attribute we use to differentiate between humans and animals—intelligence, language use, moral sentiments, and so on—will equally differentiate between human beings themselves. If people are more important to us than orangutans because they can articulate their interests, why aren't more articulate people more important still? And what about those poor men and woman with aphasia? It would seem that we have just excluded them from our moral community. Find an orangutan that can complain about his family in Borneo, and he may well displace a person or two from our lifeboat.

The Demon of Relativism

We saw in chapter 2 that for our beliefs to function logically—indeed, for them to be *beliefs* at all—we must also believe that they faithfully represent states of the world. This suggests that some systems of belief will appear more faithful than others, in that they will account for more of the data of experience and make better predictions about future events. And yet, many intellectuals tend to speak as though something in the last century of ratiocination in the West has placed all worldviews more or less on an equal footing. No one is ever really *right* about what he believes; he can only point to a community of peers who believe likewise. Suicide bombing isn't really *wrong*, in any absolute sense; it just seems so from the parochial perspective of Western culture. Throw a dash of Thomas Kuhn into this pot, and everyone can agree that we never really know how the world is, because each new generation of scientists reinvents the laws of nature to suit its taste. Convictions of this sort generally go by the name of "relativism," and they seem to offer a rationale for not saying anything too critical about the beliefs of others. But most forms of relativism—including moral relativism, which seems especially well subscribed—are nonsensical. And dangerously so. Some may think that it is immaterial whether we think the Nazis were really *wrong* in ethical terms, or whether we just don't like their style of life. It seems to me, however, that the belief that some worldviews really are better than others taps a different set of intellectual and moral resources. These are resources we will desperately need if we are to oppose, and ultimately unseat, the regnant ignorance and tribalism of our world.

The general retort to relativism is simple, because most relativists contradict their thesis in the very act of stating it. Take the case of relativism with respect to morality: moral relativists generally believe that all cultural practices should be respected on their own terms, that the practitioners of the various barbarisms that persist around the globe cannot be judged by the standards of the West, nor can the people of the past be judged by the standards of the present. And yet, implicit in this approach to morality lurks a claim that is not relative but absolute. Most moral relativists believe that tolerance of cultural diversity is better, in some important sense, than outright bigotry. This may be perfectly reasonable, of course, but it amounts to an overarching claim about how all human beings should live. Moral relativism, when used as a rationale for tolerance of diversity, is self-contradictory.

There is, however, a more sophisticated version of this line of thinking that is not so easily dispatched. It generally goes by the name of "pragmatism," and its most articulate spokesmen is undoubtedly Richard Rorty.[17] While Rorty is not a household name, his work has had a great influence on our discourse, and it offers considerable shelter to the shades of relativism. If we ever hope to reach a global consensus on matters of ethics—if we would say, for instance, that stoning women for adultery is *really* wrong, in some absolute sense—we must find deep reasons to reject pragmatism. Doing so, we will discover that we are in a position to make strong cross-cultural claims about the reasonableness of various systems of belief and about good and evil.

The pragmatist's basic premise is that, try as we might, the currency of our ideas cannot be placed on the gold standard of correspondence with reality as it is. To call a statement "true" is merely to praise it for how it functions in some area of discourse; it is not to say anything about how it relates to the universe at large. From the point of view of pragmatism, the notion that our beliefs might "correspond with reality" is absurd. Beliefs are simply tools for making one's way in the world. Does a hammer correspond with reality? No. It has merely proven its usefulness for certain tasks. So it is, we are told, with the "truths" of biology, history, or any other field. For the pragmatist, the *utility* of a belief trumps all other concerns, even the concern for coherence.[18] If a literalist reading of the Bible works for you on Sundays, while agnosticism about God is better suited to Mondays at the office, there is no reason to worry about the resulting contradictions in your worldview. These are not so much incompatible claims about the way the world is as different styles of talking, each suited to a particular occasion.

If all of this seems rather academic, it might be interesting to note that Sayyid Qutb, Osama bin Laden's favorite philosopher, felt that pragmatism would spell the death of American civilization. He thought that it would, in Berman's phrase, "undermine America's ability to fend off its enemies."[19] There may be some truth to this assertion. Pragmatism, when civilizations come clashing, does not appear likely to be very pragmatic. To lose the conviction that you can actually be right—about *anything*—seems a recipe for the End of Days chaos envisioned by Yeats: when "the best lack all conviction, while the worst are full of passionate intensity." I believe that relativism and pragmatism have already done much to muddle our thinking on a variety of subjects, many of which have more than a passing relevance to the survival of civilization.

In philosophical terms, pragmatism can be directly opposed to *realism*. For the realist, our statements about the world will be "true" or "false" not merely in virtue of how they function amid the welter of our other beliefs, or with reference to any culture-bound criteria, but because reality simply *is* a certain way, independent of our thoughts.[20] Realists believe that there are truths about the world that may exceed our capacity to know them; there are facts of the matter whether or not we can bring such facts into view. To be an ethical realist is to believe that in ethics, as in physics, there are truths waiting to be *discovered*—and thus we can be right or wrong in our beliefs about them.[21]

According to pragmatists like Rorty, realism is doomed because there is no way to compare our description of reality with a piece of *undescribed* reality. As Jürgen Habermas says, "since the truth of beliefs or sentences can in turn be justified only with the help of other beliefs and sentences, we cannot break free from the magic circle of our language."[22] This is a clever thesis. But is it true? The fact that language is the medium in which our knowledge is represented and communicated says nothing at all about the possibilities of unmediated knowledge per se. The fact that no experience *when talked about* escapes being mediated by language (this is a tautology) does not mean that all cognition, and hence all knowing, is interpretative. If it were possible for any facet of reality to be known perfectly—if certain mystics, for instance, were right to think that they had enjoyed unmediated knowledge of transcendental truths—then pragmatism would be just plain wrong, *realistically*. The problem for the pragmatist is not that such a mystic stands a good chance of being right. The problem is that, whether the mystic is right or wrong, he must be right or wrong realistically. In opposing the idea that we can know reality directly, the pragmatist has made a covert, *realistic* claim about the limits of human knowledge. Pragmatism amounts to a *realistic* denial of the possibility of realism. And so, like the relativist, the pragmatist appears to reach a contradiction before he has even laced his shoes. A more thorough argument along these lines has been relegated to a long endnote, so as not to kill the general reader with boredom.[23]

Relativists and pragmatists believe that truth is just a matter of consensus. I think it is clear, however, that while consensus among like minds may be the final arbiter of truth, it cannot *constitute* it. It is quite conceivable that everyone might agree and yet be wrong about the way the world is. It is also conceivable that a single person might be right in the face of unanimous opposition. From a realist point of view, it is possible (though unlikely) for a single person, or culture, to have a monopoly on the truth.

It would seem, therefore, that nothing stands in the way of our presuming that our beliefs about the world can correspond, to a greater or lesser degree, to the way the world is—whether or not we will ever be in a position to finally authenticate such correspondence. Given that there are likely to be truths to be known about how members of our species can be made as happy as possible, there are almost certainly truths to be known about ethics. To say that we will never agree on every question of ethics is the same as saying that we will never agree on every question of physics. In neither case does the open-endedness of our inquiry suggest that there are no real facts to be known, or that some of the answers we have in hand are not really better than some others. Respect for *diversity* in our ethical views is, at best, an intellectual holding pattern until more of the facts are in.

Intuition

One cannot walk far in the company of moral theorists without hearing our faculty of "moral intuition" either exalted or scorned. The reason for the latter attitude is that the term "intuition" has always carried the scent of impropriety in philosophical and scientific discourse. Having been regularly disgraced by its appearance in colloquialisms like "woman's intuition" (meaning "psychic"), or otherwise directly contrasted with "reason," the word now seems to conjure up all that is cloying and irrational outside the university gates. The only striking exception to this rule is to be found among mathematicians, who apparently speak of their intuitions without the least embarrassment—rather like travelers to exotic places in the developing world who can often be heard discussing the misadventures of their colon over breakfast. But, as we know, mathematicians travel to very exotic places indeed. We might also note that many of them admit to being philosophical Platonists, without feeling any apparent need to consult a trained philosopher for an exorcism.

Whatever its stigma, "intuition" is a term that we simply cannot do without, because it denotes the most basic constituent of our faculty of understanding. While this is true in matters of ethics, it is no less true in science. When we can break our knowledge of a thing down no further, the irreducible leap that remains is intuitively taken. Thus, the traditional opposition between reason and intuition is a false one: reason is itself intuitive to the core, as any judgment that a proposition is "reasonable" or "logical" relies on intuition to find its feet. One often hears scientists and philosophers concede that something or other is a "brute fact"—that is, one that admits of no reduction. The question of why physical events have *causes*, say, is not one that scientists feel the slightest temptation to ponder. It is just so. To demand an accounting of so basic a fact is like asking how we know that two plus two equals four. Scientists presuppose the validity of such brutishness—as, indeed, they must.

The point, I trust, is obvious: we cannot step out of the darkness without taking a *first* step. And reason, without knowing how, understands this axiom if it would understand anything at all. The reliance on intuition, therefore, should be no more discomfiting for the ethicist than it has been for the physicist. We are all tugging at the same bootstraps.

It is also true that our intuitions have been known to fail. Indeed, many of the deliverances of reason do not seem reasonable at first glance. When asked how thick a piece of newspaper would be if one could fold it upon itself one hundred times in succession, most of us imagine something about the size of a brick. A little arithmetic reveals, however, that such an object would be as thick as the known universe. If we've learned anything in the last two thousand years, it is that a person's sense of what is reasonable sometimes needs a little help finding its feet.

Or consider the unreliable species of intuition that might be summed up in the statement "Like breeds like"—yielding sympathetic magic and other obvious affronts to reason. Is it reasonable to believe, as many Chinese apparently do, that tiger-bone wine leads to virility? No, it is not. Could it *become* reasonable? Indeed it could. We need only be confronted with a well-run, controlled study yielding a significant correlation between tiger bones and human prowess. Would a reasonable person expect to find such a correlation? It does not seem very likely. But if it came, reason would be forced to yield its present position, which is that the Chinese are destroying a wondrous species of animal for no reason at all.

But notice that the only manner in which we can criticize the intuitive content of magical thinking is by resort to the intuitive content of rational thinking. "Controlled study"? "Correlation"? Why do these criteria persuade us at all? Isn't it just "obvious" that if one doesn't exclude other possible causes of increased potency— the placebo effect, delusion, environmental factors, differences in health among the subjects, etc.—one will have failed to isolate the variable of tiger bone's effects on the human body? Yes, it's just as obvious as a poke in the eye. Why is it obvious? Once again, we hit bedrock. As Wittgenstein said, "Our spade is turned."

The fact that we must rely on certain intuitions to answer ethical questions does not in the least suggest that there is anything insubstantial, ambiguous, or culturally contingent about ethical truth. As in any other field, there will be room for intelligent dissent on questions of right and wrong, but intelligent dissent has its limits. People who believe that the earth is flat are not dissenting *geographers*; people who deny that the Holocaust ever occurred are not dissenting *historians*; people who think that God created the universe in 4004 BC are not dissenting *cosmologists*; and we will see that people who practice barbarisms like "honor killing" are not dissenting *ethicists*. The fact that good ideas are intuitively cashed does not make bad ideas any more respectable.

Ethics, Moral Identity, and Self-Interest

While our ethical concerns are necessarily bound up with the understanding that others experience happiness and suffering, there is more to ethics than the mere knowledge that we are not alone in the world. For ethics to matter to us, the happiness and suffering of others must matter to us. It does matter to us, but why?

Strict reductionism does not seem to offer us much hope of insight into ethics. The same, of course, can be said of most higher-level phenomena. Economic behavior necessarily supervenes upon the behavior of atoms, but we will not approach an understanding of economics through particle physics. Fields like game theory and evolutionary biology, for instance, have some plausible stories to tell about the roots of what is generally called "altruistic behavior" in the scientific literature, but we should not make too much of these stories. The finding that nature seems to have selected for our ethical intuitions is relevant only insofar as it gives the lie to the ubiquitous fallacy that these intuitions are somehow the product of religion. But nature has selected for many things that we would have done well to leave behind us in the jungles of Africa. The practice of rape may have once conferred an adaptive advantage on our species—and rapists of all shapes and sizes can indeed be found in the natural world (dolphins, orangutans, chimpanzees, etc.). Does this mean that rape is any less objectionable in human society? Even if we concede that some number of rapes are inevitable, given how human beings are wired, how is this different from saying that some number of cancers are inevitable? We will strive to cure cancer in any case.

To say that something is "natural," or that it has conferred an adaptive advantage upon our species, is not to say that it is "good" in the required sense of contributing to human happiness in the present.[24] Admittedly, the problem of adjudicating what counts as happiness, and which forms of happiness should supersede others, is difficult—but so is every other problem worth thinking about. We need only admit that the happiness and suffering of sentient beings (including ourselves) concerns us, and the domain of such concerns is the domain of ethics, to see the possibility that much that is "natural" in human nature will be at odds with what is "good." Appeals to genetics and natural selection can take us only so far, because nature has not adapted us to do anything more than breed. From the point of view of evolution, the best thing a person can do with his life is have as many children as possible. As Steven Pinker observes, if we really took a gene's eye view of the world "men would line up outside sperm banks and women would pray to have their eggs harvested and given away to infertile couples."[25] After all, from my genome's point of view, nothing could be more gratifying than the knowledge that I have fathered thousands of children for whom I now bear no financial responsibility. This, needless to say, is not how most of us seek happiness in this world.

Nor are most of us resolutely selfish, in the narrowest sense of the term. Our selfishness extends to those with whom we are morally identified: to friends and family, to coworkers and teammates, and—if we are in an expansive mood—to humans and animals in general. As Jonathan Glover writes: "Our entanglements with people close to us erode simple self-interest. Husbands, wives, lovers, parents, children and friends all blur the boundaries of selfish concern. Francis Bacon rightly said that people with children have given hostages to fortune. Inescapably, other forms of friendship and love hold us hostage too. . . . Narrow self-interest is destabilized."[26]

To treat others ethically is to act out of concern for their happiness and suffering. It is, as Kant observed, to treat them as ends in themselves rather than as a means to some further end. Many ethical injunctions converge here—Kant's categorical imperative, Jesus' golden rule—but the basic facts are these: we experience happiness and suffering ourselves; we encounter others in the world and recognize that they experience happiness and suffering as well; we soon discover that "love" is largely a matter of wishing that others experience happiness rather than suffering; and most of us come to feel that love is more conducive to happiness, both our own and that of others, than hate. There is a circle here that links us to one another: we each want to be happy; the social feeling of love is one of our greatest sources of happiness; and love entails that we be concerned for the happiness of others. We discover that we can be selfish together.

This is just a sketch, but it suggests a clear link between ethics and positive human emotions. The fact that we want the people we love to be happy, and are made happy by love in turn, is an empirical observation. But such observations are the stuff of nascent science. What about people who do not love others, who see no value in it, and yet claim to be perfectly happy? Do such people even exist? Perhaps they do. Does this play havoc with a realistic account of ethics? No more so than an inability to understand the special theory of relativity would cast doubt upon modern physics. Some people can't make heads or tails of the assertion that the passage of time might be relative to one's frame of reference. This prevents them from taking part in any serious discussion of physics. People who can see no link between love and happiness may find themselves in the same position with respect to ethics. Differences of opinion do not pose a problem for ethical realism.

CONSIDER the practice of "honor killing" that persists throughout much of Africa, the Middle East, and Southeast Asia. We live in a world in which women and girls are regularly murdered by their male relatives for perceived sexual indiscretions—ranging from merely speaking to a man without permission to falling victim of rape. Coverage of these atrocities in the Western media generally refers to them as a "tribal" practice, although they almost invariably occur in a Muslim context. Whether we call the beliefs that inspire this behavior "tribal" or "religious" is immaterial; the problem is clearly a product of what men in these societies believe about shame and honor, about the role of women, and about female sexuality.

One consequence of these beliefs has been to promote rape as a weapon of war. No doubt there are more creaturely, and less calculating, motives for soldiers to commit rape on a massive scale, but it cannot be denied that male beliefs about "honor" have made it a brilliant instrument of psychological and cultural oppression. Rape has become a means through which the taboos of a community can be used to rend it from within. Consider the Bosnian women systematically raped by Serbs: one might have thought that since many of their male relatives could not escape getting killed, it would be only reasonable to concede that the women themselves could not escape getting raped. But such flights of ethical intelligence cannot be made with a sufficient payload of unjustified belief—in this case, belief in the intrinsic sinfulness of women, in the importance of virginity prior to marriage, and in the shamefulness of being raped. Needless to say, similar failures of compassion have a venerable pedigree in the Christian West. Augustine, for instance, when considering the moral stature of virgins who had been raped by the Goths, wondered whether they had not been "unduly puffed up by [their] integrity, continence and chastity." Perhaps they suffered "some lurking infirmity which might have betrayed them into proud and contemptuous bearing, had they not been subjected to the humiliation that befell them."[27] Perhaps, in other words, they deserved it.[28]

Given the requisite beliefs about "honor," a man will be desperate to kill his daughter upon learning that she was raped. The same angel of compassion can be expected to visit her brothers as well. Such killings are not at all uncommon in places like Jordan, Egypt, Lebanon, Pakistan, Iraq, the Gaza Strip, and the West Bank.[29] In these parts of the world, a girl of any age who gets raped has brought shame upon her family. Luckily, this shame is not indelible and can be readily expunged with her blood. The subsequent ritual is inevitably a low-tech affair, as none of these societies have devised a system for administering lethal injections for the crime of bringing shame upon one's family. The girl either has her throat cut, or she is dowsed with gasoline and set on fire, or she is shot. The jail sentences for these men, if they are prosecuted at all, are invariably short. Many are considered heroes in their communities.

What can we say about this behavior? Can we say that Middle Eastern men who are murderously obsessed with female sexual purity actually love their wives, daughters, and sisters *less* than American or European men do? Of course, we can. And what is truly incredible about the state of our discourse is that such a claim is not only controversial but actually *unutterable* in most contexts.

Where's the proof that these men are less capable of love than the rest of us? Well, where would the proof be if a person behaved this way in our own society? Where's the proof that the person who shot JFK didn't really love him? All the proof we need came from the book depository. We know how the word "love" functions in our discourse. We have all felt love, have failed to feel it, and have occasionally felt its antithesis. Even if we don't harbor the slightest sympathy for their notion of "honor," we know what these honor killers are up to—and it is not a matter of expressing their love for the women in their lives. Of course, honor killing is merely one facet in that terrible kaleidoscope that is the untutored, male imagination: dowry deaths and bride burnings, female infanticide, acid attacks, female genital mutilation, sexual slavery—these and other joys await unlucky women throughout much of the world. There is no doubt that certain beliefs are incompatible with love, and this notion of "honor" is among them.

What is love? Few of us will be tempted to consult a dictionary on the subject. We know that we want those we love to be happy. We feel compassion for their suffering. When love is really effective— that is, really *felt*, rather than merely imagined—we cannot help sharing in the joy of those we love, and in their anguish as well. The disposition of love entails the loss, at least to some degree, of our utter self-absorption—and this is surely one of the clues as to why this state of mind is so pleasurable. Most of us will find that cutting a little girl's head off after she has been raped just doesn't capture these sentiments very well.

At this point, many anthropologists will want to argue for the importance of cultural context. These murderers are not murderers in the usual sense. They are ordinary, even loving gentlemen who have become the pawns of tribal custom. Taken to its logical conclusion, this view suggests that any behavior is compatible with any mental state. Perhaps there is a culture in which you are expected to flay your firstborn child alive as an expression of "love." But unless everyone in such a culture wants to be flayed alive, this behavior is simply incompatible with love as we know it. The Golden Rule really does capture many of our intuitions here. We treat those we love more or less the way we would like to be treated ourselves. Honor killers do not seem to be in the habit of asking others to drench them in gasoline and immolate them in turn.

Any culture that raises men and boys to kill unlucky girls, rather than comfort them, is a culture that has managed to retard the growth of love. Such societies, of course, regularly fail to teach their inhabitants many other things—like how to read. Not learning how to read is not another *style* of literacy, and not learning to see others as ends in themselves is not another style of ethics. It is a *failure* of ethics.

How can we encourage other human beings to extend their moral sympathies beyond a narrow locus? How can we learn to be mere human beings, shorn of any more compelling national, ethnic, or religious identity? We can be reasonable. It is in the very nature of reason to fuse cognitive and moral horizons. Reason is nothing less than the guardian of love.

Morality and Happiness

The link between morality and happiness appears straightforward, though there is clearly more to being happy than merely being moral. There is no reason to think that a person who never lies, cheats, or steals is *guaranteed* to be happier than a person who commits each of these sins with abandon. As we all know, a kind and compassionate person can still be horribly unlucky, and many a brute appears to have seized Fortune herself by the skirts. Children born without a functioning copy of the gene that produces the enzyme hypoxanthine-guanine phosphoribosyltransferase will have a constellation of ailments and incapacities known as Lesch-Nyhan syndrome. They will also compulsively mutilate themselves, possibly as a result of the build-up of uric acid in their tissues. If left unrestrained, such children helplessly gnaw their lips and fingers and even thrust pointed objects into their eyes. It is difficult to see how instruction in morality will contribute meaningfully to their happiness. What these children need is not better moral instruction, or even more parental love. They need hypoxanthine-guanine phosphoribosyltransferase.

Without denying that happiness has many requisites—good genes, a nervous system that does not entirely misbehave, etc.—we can hypothesize that whatever a person's current level of happiness is, his condition will be generally improved by his becoming yet more loving and compassionate, and hence more ethical. This is a strictly empirical claim—one that has been tested for millennia by contemplatives in a variety of spiritual traditions, especially within Buddhism. We might wonder whether, in the limit, the unchecked growth of love and compassion might lead to the diminution of a person's sense of well-being, as the suffering of others becomes increasingly his own. Only people who have cultivated these states of mind to an extraordinary degree will be in a position to decide this question, but in the general case there seems to be no doubt that love and compassion are good, in that they connect us more deeply to others.[30]

Given this situation, we can see that one could desire to become more loving and compassionate for purely *selfish* reasons. This is a paradox, of sorts, because these attitudes undermine selfishness, by definition. They also inspire behavior that tends to contribute to the happiness of other human beings. These states of mind not only *feel* good; they ramify social relationships that lead one to feel good *with others*, leading others to feel good with oneself. Hate, envy, spite, disgust, shame—these are not sources of happiness, personally or socially. Love and compassion are. Like so much that we know about ourselves, claims of this sort need not be validated by a controlled study. We can easily imagine evolutionary reasons for why positive social emotions make us feel good, while negative ones do not, but they would be beside the point. The point is that the disposition to take the happiness of others into account—to be *ethical*—seems to be a rational way to augment one's own happiness. As we will see in the next chapter, the linkage here becomes increasingly relevant the more rarefied one's happiness becomes. The connection between spirituality—the cultivation of happiness directly, through precise refinements of attention—and ethics is well attested. Certain attitudes and behaviors seem to be conducive to contemplative insight, while others are not. This is not a proposition to be merely believed. It is, rather, a hypothesis to be tested in the laboratory of one's life.[31]

A Loophole for Torquemada?

Casting questions about ethics in terms of happiness and suffering can quickly lead us into unfamiliar territory. Consider the case of judicial torture. It would seem, at first glance, to be unambiguously evil. And yet, for the first time in living memory, reasonable men and women in our country have begun to reconsider it publicly. Interest in the subject appears to have been provoked by an interview given by Alan Dershowitz, an erstwhile champion of the rights of the innocent-until-proven-guilty, on CBS's *60 Minutes*.[32] There, before millions who would have thought the concept of torture impossible to rehabilitate, Dershowitz laid out the paradigmatic ticking-bomb case.

Imagine that a known terrorist has planted a large bomb in the heart of a nearby city. This man now sits in your custody. As to the bomb's location, he will say nothing except that the site was chosen to produce the maximum loss of life. Given this state of affairs—in particular, given that there is still time to prevent an imminent atrocity—it seems there would be no harm in dusting off the *strappado* and exposing this unpleasant fellow to a suasion of bygone times.

Dershowitz has argued that this situation can be cast in terms that will awaken the Grand Inquisitor in all of us. If a ticking bomb doesn't move you, picture your seven-year-old daughter being slowly asphyxiated in a warehouse just five minutes away, while the man in your custody holds the keys to her release. If your daughter won't tip the scales, then add the daughters of every couple for a thousand miles—millions of little girls have, by some perverse negligence on the part of our government, come under the control of an evil genius who now sits before you in shackles. Clearly, the consequences of one man's uncooperativeness can be made so grave, and his malevolence and culpability so transparent, as to stir even the most self-hating moral relativist from his dogmatic slumbers.

It is generally thought that the gravest ethical problem we face in resorting to torture is that we would be bound to torture some number of innocent men and women. Most of us who were eager to don the Inquisitor's cap in the case above begin to falter in more realistic scenarios, as a person's guilt becomes a matter of some uncertainty. And this is long before other concerns even attract our notice. What, for instance, is the *reliability* of testimony elicited under torture? We need not even pose questions of this sort yet, since we have already balked at the knowledge that, in the real world, we will not be able to tell the guilty from the innocent just by looking.

So it seems that we have two situations that will strike most sane and decent people as ethically distinct: in the first case, as envisioned by Dershowitz, it seems perverse to worry about the rights of an admitted terrorist when so many innocent lives are at stake; while under more realistic conditions, uncertainty about a person's guilt will generally preclude the use of torture. Is this how the matter really sits with us? Probably not.

It appears that such restraint in the use of torture cannot be reconciled with our willingness to wage war in the first place. What, after all, is "collateral damage" but the inadvertent torture of inno-cent men, women, and children? Whenever we consent to drop bombs, we do so with the knowledge that some number of children will be blinded, disemboweled, paralyzed, orphaned, and killed by them. It is curious that while the torture of Osama bin Laden him-self could be expected to provoke convulsions of conscience among our leaders, the unintended (though perfectly foreseeable, and therefore accepted) slaughter of children does not.

So we can now ask, if we are willing to act in a way that guaran-tees the misery and death of some considerable number of innocent children, why spare the rod with suspected terrorists? What is the difference between pursuing a course of action where we run the risk of inadvertently subjecting some innocent men to torture, and pursuing one in which we will inadvertently kill far greater num-bers of innocent men, women, and children? Rather, it seems obvi-ous that the misapplication of torture should be far *less* troubling to us than collateral damage: there are, after all, no *infants* interned at Guantanamo Bay, just rather scrofulous young men, many of whom were caught in the very act of trying to kill our soldiers.[33] Torture need not even impose a significant risk of death or permanent injury on its victims; while the collaterally damaged are, almost by defini-tion, crippled or killed. The ethical divide that seems to be opening up here suggests that those who are willing to drop bombs might want to abduct the nearest and dearest of suspected terrorists—their wives, mothers, and daughters—and torture *them* as well, assuming anything profitable to our side might come of it. Admittedly, this would be a ghastly result to have reached by logical argument, and we will want to find some way of escaping it.[34]

In this context, we should note that many variables influence our feelings about an act of physical violence, as well as our intuitions about its ethical status. As Glover points out, "in modern war, what is most shocking is a poor guide to what is most harmful." To learn that one's grandfather flew a bombing mission over Dresden in the Second World War is one thing; to hear that he killed five little girls and their mother with a shovel is another. We can be sure that he would have killed more women and girls by dropping bombs from pristine heights, and they are likely to have died equally horrible deaths, but his culpability would not appear the same. Indeed, we seem to know, intuitively, that it would take a different kind of person to perpetrate violence of the latter sort. And, as we might expect, the psychological effects of participating in these types of violence are generally distinct. Consider the following account of a Soviet soldier in Afghanistan: "It's frightening and unpleasant to have to kill, you think, but you soon realize that what you really find objectionable is shooting someone point-blank. Killing *en masse*, in a group, is exciting, even—and I've seen this myself—fun."[35] This is not to say that no one has ever enjoyed killing people up close; it is just that we all recognize that such enjoyment requires an unusual degree of callousness to the suffering of others.

It is possible that we are simply unequipped to rectify this disparity—to be, in Glover's terms, most shocked by what is most harmful. A biological rationale is not hard to find, as millions of years on the African veldt could not possibly have selected for an ability to make emotional sense of twenty-first-century horror. That our Paleolithic genes now have chemical, biological, and nuclear weapons at their disposal is, from the point of view of our evolution, little different from our having delivered this technology into the hands of chimps. The difference between killing one man and killing a thousand just doesn't seem as salient to us as it should. And, as Glover observes, in many cases we will find the former far more disturbing. Three million souls can be starved and murdered in the Congo, and our Argus-eyed media scarcely blink. When a princess dies in a car accident, however, a quarter of the earth's population falls prostrate with grief. Perhaps we are unable to feel what we must feel in order to change our world.

What does it feel like to see three thousand men, women, and children incinerated and crushed to ash in the span of a few seconds? Anyone who owned a television on September 11, 2001, now knows. But most of us know nothing of the sort. To have watched the World Trade Center absorbing two jet planes, along with the lives of thousands, and to have felt, above all things, *disbelief*, suggests some form of neurological impairment. Clearly, there are limits to what the human mind can make of the deliverances of its senses—of the mere sight of an office building, known to be full of people, dissolving into rubble. Perhaps this will change.

In any case, if you think the equivalence between torture and collateral damage does not hold, because torture is up close and personal while stray bombs aren't, you stand convicted of a failure of imagination on at least two counts: first, a moment's reflection on the horrors that must have been visited upon innocent Afghanis and Iraqis by our bombs will reveal that they are on par with those of any dungeon. That such an exercise of the imagination is required to bring torture and collateral damage to parity accounts for the dissociation between what is most shocking and what is most harmful that Glover notes. It also demonstrates the degree to which we have been bewitched by our own euphemisms. Killing people at a distance is easier, but perhaps it should not be *that* much easier.

Second, if our intuition about the wrongness of torture is born of an aversion to how people generally behave while being tortured, we should note that this particular infelicity could be circumvented pharmacologically, because paralytic drugs make it unnecessary for screaming ever to be heard or writhing seen. We could easily devise methods of torture that would render a torturer as blind to the plight of his victims as a bomber pilot is at thirty thousand feet. Consequently, our natural aversion to the sights and sounds of the dungeon provide no foothold for those who would argue against the use of torture. To demonstrate just how abstract the torments of the tortured can be made to seem, we need only imagine an ideal "torture pill"—a drug that would deliver both the instruments of torture and the instrument of their utter concealment. The action of the pill would be to produce transitory paralysis and transitory misery of a kind that no human being would willingly submit to a second time. Imagine how we torturers would feel if, after giving this pill to captive terrorists, each lay down for what appeared to be an hour's nap only to arise and immediately confess everything he knows about the workings of his organization. Might we not be tempted to call it a "truth pill" in the end?

No, there is no ethical difference to be found in how the suffering of the tortured or the collaterally damaged *appears*.

WHICH way should the balance swing? Assuming that we want to maintain a coherent ethical position on these matters, this appears to be a circumstance of forced choice: if we are willing to drop bombs, or even risk that pistol rounds might go astray, we should be willing to torture a certain class of criminal suspects and military prisoners; if we are unwilling to torture, we should be unwilling to wage modern war.

Opponents of torture will be quick to argue that confessions elicited by torture are notoriously unreliable. Given the foregoing, however, this objection seems to lack its usual force. Make these confessions as unreliable as you like—the chance that our interests will be advanced in any instance of torture need only equal the chance of such occasioned by the dropping of a single bomb. What was the chance that the dropping of bomb number 117 on Kandahar would effect the demise of Al Qaeda? It had to be pretty slim. Enter Khalid Sheikh Mohammed: our most valuable capture in our war on terror. Here is a character who actually seems cut from Dershowitzian cloth. U.S. officials now believe that his was the hand that decapitated the *Wall Street Journal* reporter Daniel Pearl. Whether or not this is true, his membership in Al Qaeda more or less rules out his "innocence" in any important sense, and his rank in the organization suggests that his knowledge of planned atrocities must be extensive. The bomb is ticking. Given the damage we were willing to cause to the bodies and minds of innocent children in Afghanistan and Iraq, our disavowal of torture in the case of Khalid Sheikh Mohammed seems perverse. If there is even one chance in a million that he will tell us something under torture that will lead to the further dismantling of Al Qaeda, it seems that we should use every means at our disposal to get him talking.

IN ALL likelihood you began reading this chapter, much as I began writing it, convinced that torture is a very bad thing and that we are wise not to practice it—indeed that we are civilized, in large measure, *because* we do not practice it. Most of us feel, intuitively at least, that if we can't quite muster a retort to Dershowitz and his ticking bomb, we can take refuge in the fact that the paradigmatic case will almost never arise. From this perspective, adorning the machinery of our justice system with a torture provision seems both unnecessary and dangerous, as the law of unintended consequences may one day find it throwing the whole works into disarray. Because I believe the account offered above is basically sound, I believe that I have successfully argued for the use of torture in any circumstance in which we would be willing to cause collateral damage.[36] Paradoxically, this equivalence has not made the practice of torture seem any more acceptable to me; nor has it, I trust, for most readers. I believe that here we come upon an ethical illusion of sorts—analogous to the perceptual illusions that are of such abiding interest to scientists who study the visual pathways in the brain. The full moon appearing on the horizon is no bigger than the full moon when it appears overhead, but it *looks* bigger, for reasons that are still obscure to neuroscientists. A ruler held up to the sky reveals something that we are otherwise incapable of seeing, even when we understand that our eyes are deceiving us. Given a choice between acting on the basis of the way things seem in this instance, or on the deliverances of our ruler, most of us will be willing to dispense with appearances—particularly if our lives or the lives of others depended on it. I believe that most readers who have followed me this far will find themselves in substantially the same position with respect to the ethics of torture. Given what many of us believe about the exigencies of our war on terrorism, the practice of torture, in certain circumstances, would seem to be not only permissible but necessary. Still, it does not seem any more acceptable, in ethical terms, than it did before. The reasons for this are, I trust, every bit as neurological as those that give rise to the moon illusion. In fact, there is already some scientific evidence that our ethical intuitions are driven by considerations of proximity and emotional salience of the sort I addressed above.[37] Clearly, these intuitions are fallible. In the present case, many innocent lives could well be lost as a result of our inability to feel a moral equivalence where a moral equivalence seems to exist. It may be time to take out our rulers and hold them up to the sky.[38]

The False Choice of Pacifism

Pacifism[39] is generally considered to be a morally unassailable position to take with respect to human violence. The worst that is said of it, generally, is that it is a difficult position to maintain in practice. It is almost never branded as flagrantly immoral, which I believe it is. While it can seem noble enough when the stakes are low, pacifism is ultimately nothing more than a willingness to die, and to let others die, at the pleasure of the world's thugs. It should be enough to note that a single sociopath, armed with nothing more than a knife, could exterminate a city full of pacifists. There is no doubt that such sociopaths exist, and they are generally better armed. Fearing that the above reflections on torture may offer a potent argument for pacifism, I would like to briefly state why I believe we must accept the fact that violence (or its threat) is often an ethical necessity.

I WAS once walking the streets of Prague late at night and came upon a man and a young woman in the midst of a struggle. As I drew nearer, it became obvious that the man, who appeared to be both drunk and enraged, was attempting to pull the woman into a car against her will. She was making a forceful show of resistance, but he had seized her arm with one hand and was threatening to strike her in the face with the other—which he had done at least once, it seemed, before I arrived on the scene. The rear door of the car was open, and an accomplice had taken a seat behind the wheel. Several other men were milling about, and from the looks of them, they appeared to approve of the abduction in progress.

Without knowing how I would proceed, I at once found myself interceding on the woman's behalf. As my adrenaline rose, and her assailant's attention turned my way, it occurred to me that his English might be terrible or nonexistent. The mere effort to understand me could be made so costly that it might prove a near-total diversion. The inability to make my intentions clear would also serve to forestall actual conflict. Had we shared a common language our encounter would have almost certainly come to blows within moments, as I would have thought of nothing more clever than to demand that he let the woman go, and he, to save face, would have demanded that I make him. Since he had at least two friends that I could see (and several fans), my evening would probably have ended very badly. Thus, my goal, as I saw it, was to remain unintelligible, without antagonizing any of the assembled hooligans, long enough for the young woman to get away.

"Excuse me," I said. "I seem to have lost my hotel, my lodging, my place of residence, where I lie supine, not prone. Can you help me? Where is it? Where is it?"

"*Sex?*" The man asked with obvious outrage, as though I had declared myself a rival for his prisoner's affections. It now occurred to me that the woman might be a prostitute, and he an unruly customer.

"No! Not *sex*. I am looking for a specific building. It has no aluminum siding or stained glass. It could be filled with marzipan. Do you know where it is? This is an emergency."

In an instant, the man's face underwent a remarkable transformation, changing from a mask of rage, to a vision of perplexity itself. While he attempted to decipher my request, I threw a conspiratorial glance at the woman—who, it must be said, seemed rather slow to appreciate that the moment of her emancipation was at hand.

The man began to discuss my case in fluent Czech with one of his friends. I continued to rave. The woman, for her part, glared at me as though I were an idiot. Then, realizing her opportunity for the first time, like a bird that had long sat within an open cage, she suddenly broke free and fled down the street. Her erstwhile attacker was too engrossed by his reflections even to notice that she had left.

Mission accomplished, I at once thanked the group and moved on.

While my conduct in the above incident seems to meet with the approval of almost everyone, I relate it here because I consider it an example of a moral failure. First, I was lying, and lying out of fear. I was not lost, and I needed no assistance of any kind. I resorted to this tactic because, quite frankly, I was afraid to openly challenge an indeterminate number of drunks to a brawl. Some may call this wisdom, but it seemed to me to be nothing more than cowardice at the time. I made no effort to communicate with these men, to appeal to their ethical scruples, however inchoate, or to make any impression upon them whatsoever. I perceived them not as ends in themselves, as sentient creatures capable of dialogue, appeasement, or instruction, but as a threat in its purest form. My ethical failure, as I see it, is that I never actually *opposed* their actions—hence they never received any correction from the world. They were merely diverted for a time, and to only a single woman's advantage. The next woman who became the object of their predations will have little cause to thank me. Even if a frank intercession on the woman's behalf would have guaranteed my own injury, a clear message would have been sent: not all strangers will stand idly by as you beat and abduct a woman in the street. The action I took sent no such message. Indeed,

I suspect that even the woman herself never knew that I had come to her aid.[40]

GANDHI was undoubtedly the twentieth century's most influential pacifist. The success he enjoyed in forcing the British Empire to withdraw from the Indian subcontinent brought pacifism down from the ethers of religious precept and gave it new political relevance. Pacifism in this form no doubt required considerable bravery from its practitioners and constituted a direct confrontation with injustice. As such, it had far more moral integrity than did my stratagem above. It is clear, however, that Gandhi's nonviolence can be applied to only a limited range of human conflict. We would do well to reflect on Gandhi's remedy for the Holocaust: he believed that the Jews should have committed mass suicide, because this "would have aroused the world and the people of Germany to Hitler's violence."[41] We might wonder what a world full of pacifists would have done once it had grown "aroused"—commit suicide as well?

Gandhi was a religious dogmatist, of course, but his remedy for the Holocaust seems ethically suspect even if one accepts the metaphysical premises upon which it was based. If we grant the law of karma and rebirth to which Gandhi subscribed, his pacifism still seems highly immoral. Why should it be thought ethical to safeguard one's own happiness (or even the happiness of others) in the next life at the expense of the manifest agony of children in this one? Gandhi's was a world in which millions more would have died in the hopes that the Nazis would have one day doubted the goodness of their Thousand Year Reich. Ours is a world in which bombs must occasionally fall where such doubts are in short supply. Here we come upon a terrible facet of ethically asymmetric warfare: when your enemy has no scruples, your own scruples become another weapon in his hand.

It is, as yet, unclear what it will mean to win our war on "terrorism"—or whether the religious barbarism that animates our enemies can ever be finally purged from our world—but it is all too obvious what it would mean to lose it. Life under the Taliban is, to a first approximation, what millions of Muslims around the world want to impose on the rest of us. They long to establish a society in which—when times are *good*—women will remain vanquished and invisible, and anyone given to spiritual, intellectual, or sexual freedom will be slaughtered before crowds of sullen, uneducated men. This, needless to say, is a vision of life worth resisting. We cannot let our qualms over collateral damage paralyze us because our enemies know no such qualms. Theirs is a kill-the-children-first approach to war, and we ignore the fundamental difference between their violence and our own at our peril. Given the proliferation of weaponry in our world, we no longer have the option of waging this war with swords. It seems certain that collateral damage, of various sorts, will be a part of our future for many years to come.

7

Experiments in Consciousness

●

At the core of every religion lies an undeniable claim about the human condition: it is possible to have one's experience of the world radically transformed. Although we generally live within the limits imposed by our ordinary uses of attention—we wake, we work, we eat, we watch television, we converse with others, we sleep, we dream—most of us know, however dimly, that extraordinary experiences are possible.

The problem with religion is that it blends this truth so thoroughly with the venom of unreason. Take Christianity as an example: it is not enough that Jesus was a man who transformed himself to such a degree that the Sermon on the Mount could be his heart's confession. He also had to be the Son of God, born of a virgin, and destined to return to earth trailing clouds of glory. The effect of such dogma is to place the example of Jesus forever out of reach. His teaching ceases to be a set of empirical claims about the linkage between ethics and spiritual insight and instead becomes a gratuitous, and rather gruesome, fairy tale. According to the dogma of Christianity, becoming just like Jesus is impossible. One can only enumerate one's sins, believe the unbelievable, and await the end of the world.

But a more profound response to existence is possible for us, and the testimony of Jesus, as well as that of countless other men and women over the ages, attests to this. The challenge for us is to begin talking about this possibility in rational terms.

The Search for Happiness

Though the lilies of the field are admirably clothed, you and I were driven from the womb naked and squalling. What do we need to be happy? Almost everything we do can be viewed as a reply to this question. We need food, shelter, and clothing. We need the company of others. Then we need to learn countless things to make the most of this company. We need to find work that we enjoy, and we need time for leisure. We need so many things, and there seems no alternative but to seek and maintain them, one after the next, hour after hour.

But are such things *sufficient* for happiness? Is a person guaranteed to be happy merely by virtue of having health, wealth, and good company? Apparently not. Are such things even *necessary* for happiness? If so, what can we make of those Indian yogis who renounce all material and familial attachments only to spend decades alone in caves practicing meditation? It seems that such people can be happy as well. Indeed, some of them claim to be perfectly so.

It is difficult to find a word for that human enterprise which aims at happiness directly—at happiness of a sort that can survive the frustration of all conventional desires. The term "spirituality" seems unavoidable here—and I have used it several times in this book already—but it has many connotations that are, frankly, embarrassing. "Mysticism" has more gravitas, perhaps, but it has unfortunate associations of its own. Neither word captures the reasonableness and profundity of the possibility that we must now consider: that there is a form of well-being that supersedes all others, indeed, that transcends the vagaries of experience itself. I will use both "spirituality" and "mysticism" interchangeably here, because there are no alternatives, but the reader should remember that I am using them in a restricted sense. While a visit to any New Age bookstore will reveal that modern man has embraced a daunting range of "spiritual" preoccupations—ranging from the healing power of crystals and colonic irrigation to the ardors of alien abduction—our discussion will focus on a specific insight that seems to have special relevance to our pursuit of happiness.

Most spiritual teachings agree that there is more to happiness than becoming a productive member of society, a cheerful consumer of every licit pleasure, and an enthusiastic bearer of children disposed to do the same. Indeed, many suggest that it is our *search* for happiness—our craving for knowledge and new experience, our desire for recognition, our efforts to find the right romantic partner, even our yearning for spiritual experience itself—that causes us to overlook a form of well-being that is intrinsic to consciousness in every present moment. Some version of this insight seems to lie at the core of many of our religions, and yet it is by no means always easy to discern among the articles of faith.

While many of us go for decades without experiencing a full day of solitude, we live every moment in the solitude of our own minds. However close we may be to others, our pleasures and pains are ours alone. Spiritual practice is often recommended as the most rational response to this situation. The underlying claim here is that we can realize something about the nature of consciousness in this moment that will improve our lives. The experience of countless contemplatives suggests that consciousness—being merely the condition in which thought, emotion, and even our sense of self arises—is never actually changed by what it knows. That which is aware of joy does not become joyful; that which is aware of sadness does not become sad. From the point of view of consciousness, we are merely aware *of* sights, sounds, sensations, moods, and thoughts. Many spiritual teachings allege that if we can recognize our identity as consciousness itself, as the mere witness of appearances, we will realize that we stand perpetually free of the vicissitudes of experience.

This is not to deny that suffering has a physical dimension. The fact that a drug like Prozac can relieve many of the symptoms of depression suggests that mental suffering can be no more ethereal than a little green pill. But the arrow of influence clearly flies both ways. We know that ideas themselves have the power to utterly define a person's experience of the world.[1] Even the significance of intense physical pain is open to subjective interpretation. Consider the pain of labor: How many women come away from the experience traumatized? The occasion itself is generally a happy one, assuming all goes well with the birth. Imagine how different it would be for a woman to be tortured by having the sensations of a normal labor inflicted upon her by a mad scientist. The sensations might be identical, and yet this would certainly be among the worst experiences of her life. There is clearly more to suffering even physical pain than painful sensation alone.

Our spiritual traditions suggest that we have considerable room here to change our relationship to the contents of consciousness, and thereby to transform our experience of the world. Indeed, a vast literature on human spirituality attests to this.[2] It is also clear that nothing need be believed on insufficient evidence for us to look into this possibility with an open mind.

Consciousness

Like Descartes, most of us begin these inquiries as *thinkers*, condemned by the terms of our subjectivity to maneuver in a world that appears to be other than what we are. Descartes accentuated this dichotomy by declaring that two substances were to be found in God's universe: matter and spirit. For most of us, a dualism of this sort is more or less a matter of common sense (though the term "spirit" seems rather majestic, given how our minds generally comport themselves). As science has turned its reifying light upon the mysteries of the human mind, however, Descartes' dualism (along with our own "folk psychology") has come in for some rough treatment. Bolstered by the undeniable successes of three centuries of purely physical research, many philosophers and scientists now reject Descartes' separation of mind and body, spirit and matter, as the concession to Christian piety that it surely was, and imagine that they have thereby erased the conceptual gulf between consciousness and the physical world.

In the last chapter we saw that our beliefs about consciousness are intimately linked to our ethics. They also happen to have a direct bearing upon our view of death. Most scientists consider themselves *physicalists*; this means, among other things, that they believe that our mental and spiritual lives are wholly dependent upon the work-ings of our brains. On this account, when the brain dies, the stream of our being must come to an end. Once the lamps of neural activ-ity have been extinguished, there will be nothing left to survive. Indeed, many scientists purvey this conviction as though it were itself a special sacrament, conferring intellectual integrity upon any man, woman, or child who is man enough to swallow it.

But the truth is that we simply do not know what happens after death. While there is much to be said against a naïve conception of a soul that is independent of the brain,[3] the place of consciousness in the natural world is very much an open question. The idea that brains *produce* consciousness is little more than an article of faith among scientists at present, and there are many reasons to believe that the methods of science will be insufficient to either prove or dis-prove it.

Inevitably, scientists treat consciousness as a mere *attribute* of certain large-brained animals. The problem, however, is that nothing about a brain, when surveyed as a physical system, declares it to be a bearer of that peculiar, interior dimension that each of us experi-ences as consciousness in his own case. Every paradigm that attempts to shed light upon the frontier between consciousness and unconsciousness, searching for the physical difference that makes the phenomenal one, relies upon subjective reports to signal that an experimental stimulus has been observed.[4] The operational defini-tion of consciousness, therefore, is *reportability*. But consciousness and reportability are not the same. Is a starfish conscious? No sci-ence that conflates consciousness with reportability will deliver an answer to this question. To look for consciousness in the world on the basis of its outward signs is the only thing that we can do. To *define* consciousness in terms of its outward signs, however, is a fallacy. Computers of the future, sufficiently advanced to pass the Turing test,* will offer up a wealth of self-report—but will they be conscious? If we don't already know, their eloquence on the matter will not decide the issue. Consciousness may be a far more rudimentary phenomenon than are living creatures and their brains. And there appears to be no obvious way of ruling out such a thesis experimentally.[5]

And so, while we know many things about ourselves in anatomical, physiological, and evolutionary terms, we currently have no idea why it is "like something" to be what we are. The fact that the universe is illuminated where you stand, the fact that your thoughts and moods and sensations have a qualitative character, is an absolute mystery—rivaled only by the mystery, famously articulated by the philosopher Schelling, that there should be anything at all in this universe rather than nothing. The problem is that our experience *of* brains, as objects in the world, leaves us perfectly insensible to the reality of consciousness, while our experience *as* brains grants us knowledge of nothing else. Given this situation, it is reasonable to conclude that the domain of our subjectivity constitutes a proper (and essential) sphere of investigation into the nature of the universe: as some facts will be discovered only in consciousness, in first-person terms, or not discovered at all.

Investigating the nature of consciousness directly, through sustained introspection, is simply another name for spiritual practice. It should be clear that whatever transformations of your experience are possible—after forty days and forty nights in the desert, after

---

* The mathematician Alan Turing once proposed a test for the adequacy of a computer simulation of the human mind (and this has since been promoted in the literature to a test for computer "consciousness"). The proposed test requires that a human subject interrogate another person and a computer by turns, without knowing which is which. If, at the end of the experiment, he cannot identify the computer with any confidence, it is said to have "passed" the Turing test.

twenty years in a cave, or after some new serotonin agonist has been delivered to your synapses—these will be a matter of changes occurring in the contents of your consciousness. Whatever Jesus experienced, he experienced as consciousness. If he loved his neighbor as himself, this is a description of what it felt like to be Jesus while in the presence of other human beings. The history of human spirituality is the history of our attempts to explore and modify the deliverances of consciousness through methods like fasting, chanting, sensory deprivation, prayer, meditation, and the use of psychotropic plants. There is no question that experiments of this sort can be conducted in a rational manner. Indeed, they are some of our only means of determining to what extent the human condition can be deliberately transformed. Such an enterprise becomes irrational only when people begin making claims about the world that cannot be supported by empirical evidence.

What Are We Calling "I"?

Our spiritual possibilities will largely depend on what we are as *selves*. In physical terms, each of us is a system, locked in an uninterrupted exchange of matter and energy with the larger system of the earth. The life of your very cells is built upon a network of barter and exchange over which you can exercise only the crudest conscious influence—in the form of deciding whether to hold your breath or take another slice of pizza out of the fridge. As a physical system, you are no more independent of nature at this moment than your liver is of the rest of your body. As a collection of self-regulating and continually dividing cells, you are also continuous with your genetic precursors: your parents, their parents, and backward through tens of millions of generations—at which point your ancestors begin looking less like men and women with bad teeth and more like pond scum. It is true enough to say that, in physical terms, you are little more than an eddy in a great river of life.

But, of course, your body is itself an environment teeming with creatures, in relation to which you are sovereign in name alone. To examine the body of a person, its organs and tissues, cells and intestinal flora (sometimes fauna, alas), is to be confronted by a world that bears no more evidence of an overriding conscious intelligence than does the world at large. Is there any reason to suspect, when observing the function of mitochondria within a cell, or the twitching of muscle fibers in the hand, that there is a mind, above and beyond such processes, thinking, "L'état c'est moi"? Indeed, any privilege we might be tempted to accord the boundary of the skin in our search for the physical self seems profoundly arbitrary.

The frontiers of the mental self are no easier to discern: memes, taboos, norms of decorum, linguistic conventions, prejudices, ideals, aesthetic biases, commercial jingles—the phenomena that populate the landscape of our minds are immigrants from the world at large. Is your desire to be physically fit—or your taste in clothing, your sense of community, your expectation of reciprocal kindness, your shyness, your affability, your sexual quirks, etc.—something that originates with you? Is it something best thought of as residing *in* you? These phenomena are the direct result of your embeddedness in a world of social relationships and culture (as well as a product of your genes). Many of them seem to be no more "you," ultimately, than the rules of English grammar are.

And yet, this feeling of being a self persists. If the term "I" refers to anything at all, it does not refer simply to the *body*. After all, most of us feel individuated as a self *within* the body. I speak of "my" body more or less as I speak of "my" car, for the simple reason that every act of perception or cognition conveys the tacit sense that the knower is something other than the thing known. Just as my awareness *of* my car demonstrates that I, as a subject, am something other than it, as an object, I can be aware of my hand, or an emotion, and experience the same cleavage between subject and object. For this reason, the self cannot simply be equated with the totality of a person's mental life or with his personality as a whole.[6] Rather, it is the point of view around which the changing states of his mind and body appear to be constellated. Whatever the relationship between consciousness and the body actually is, in experiential terms the body is something to which the conscious self, if such there be, stands *in relation*. Exactly when, in evolutionary or developmental terms, this point of view emerges is not known, but one thing is clear: at some point in the first years of life most human beings are christened as "I," the perennial subject, for whom all appearances, inside and out, become objects of a kind, waiting to be known. And it is as "I" that every scientist begins his inquiry into the nature of the world and every pious man folds his hands in prayer.[7]

THE sense of self seems to be the product of the brain's representing its own acts of representation; its seeing of the world begets an image of a *one who sees*. It is important to realize that this feeling— the sense that each of us has of *appropriating*, rather than merely *being*, a sphere of experience—is not a necessary feature of consciousness. It is, after all, conceivable that a creature could form a representation of the world without forming a representation of *itself* in the world. And, indeed, many spiritual practitioners claim to experience the world in just this way, perfectly shorn of self.

A basic finding of neurophysiology lends credence to such claims. It is not so much what they *are* but what they *do* that makes neurons see, hear, smell, taste, touch, think, and feel. Like any other function that emerges from the activity of the brain, the feeling of self is best thought of as a *process*. It is not very surprising, therefore, that we can lose this feeling, because processes, by their very nature, can be interrupted. While the experience of selflessness does not indicate anything about the relationship between consciousness and the physical world (and is thus mute on the question of what happens after death), it has broad implications for the sciences of mind, for our approach to spirituality, and for our conception of human happiness.

As a mental phenomenon, loss of self is not as rare as our scholarly neglect of it suggests. This experience is characterized by a sudden loss of subject/object perception: the continuum of experience remains, but one no longer feels that there is a knower standing apart from the known. Thoughts may arise, but the feeling that one is the thinker of these thoughts has vanished. Something has definitely changed at the level of one's moment-to-moment experience, and this change—the disappearance of anything to which the pronoun "I" can be faithfully attached—signals that there had been a conscious experience of selfhood all the while, however difficult it may be to characterize.

Look at this book as a physical object. You are aware *of* it as an appearance in consciousness. You may feel that your consciousness is one thing—it is whatever illuminates your world from some point behind your eyes, perhaps—and the book is another. This is the kind of dualistic (subject/object) perception that characterizes our normal experience of life. It is possible, however, to look for your self in such a way as to put this subject/object dichotomy in doubt—and even to banish it altogether.

The contents of consciousness—sights, sounds, sensations, thoughts, moods, etc.—whatever they are at the level of the brain, are merely *expressions* of consciousness at the level of our experience. Unrecognized as such, many of these appearances seem to impinge upon consciousness from without, and the sense of self emerges, and grows entrenched, as the feeling that *that which knows* is circumscribed, modified, and often oppressed by *that which is known*. Indeed, it is likely that our parents found us in our cribs long before we found ourselves there, and that we were merely led by their gaze, and their pointing fingers, to coalesce around an implied center of cognition that does not, in fact, exist.[8] Thereafter, every maternal caress, every satisfaction of hunger or thirst, as well as the diverse forms of approval and rebuke that came in reply to the actions of our embodied minds, seemed to confirm a self-sense that we, by example, finally learned to call "I"—and thus we became the narrow locus around which all things and events, pleasant and unpleasant, continue to swirl.

In subjective terms, the search for the self seems to entail a paradox: we are, after all, looking for the very thing that is doing the looking. Thousands of years of human experience suggests, however, that the paradox here is only apparent: it is not merely that the component of our experience that we call "I" cannot be found; it is that it actually disappears when looked for in a rigorous way.

THE foregoing is just a gloss on the phenomenology here, but it should be sufficient to get us started. The basic (and, I think, uncontestable) fact is that almost every human being experiences the duality of subject and object in some measure, and most of us feel it powerfully nearly every moment of our lives. It is scarcely an exaggeration to say that the feeling that we call "I" is one of the most pervasive and salient features of human life: and its effects upon the world, as six billion "selves" pursue diverse and often incompatible ends, rival those that can be ascribed to almost any other phenomenon in nature. Clearly, there is nothing optimal—or even necessarily *viable*—about our present form of subjectivity. Almost every problem we have can be ascribed to the fact that human beings are utterly beguiled by their feelings of separateness. It would seem that a spirituality that undermined such dualism, through the mere contemplation of consciousness, could not help but improve our situation. Whether or not great numbers of human beings will ever be in a position to explore this terrain depends on how our discourse on religion proceeds. There is clearly no greater obstacle to a truly empirical approach to spiritual experience than our current beliefs about God.

The Wisdom of the East

Inevitably, the foregoing will strike certain readers as a confusing eruption of speculative philosophy. This is unfortunate, for none of it has been speculative or even particularly philosophical—at least not in the sense that this term has acquired in the West. Thousands of years have passed since any Western philosopher imagined that a person should be made happy, peaceful, or even wise, in the ordinary sense, by his search for truth.[9] Personal transformation, or indeed liberation from the illusion of the self, seems to have been thought too much to ask: or rather, not thought of at all. Consequently, many of us in the West are conceptually unequipped to understand empirical claims of the sort adduced above.

In fact, the spiritual differences between the East and the West are every bit as shocking as the material differences between the North and the South. Jared Diamond's fascinating thesis, to sum it up in a line, is that advanced civilization did not arise in sub-Saharan Africa, because one can't saddle a rhinoceros and ride it into battle.[10] If there is an equally arresting image that accounts for why nondualistic, empirical mysticism seems to have arisen only in Asia, I have yet to find it. But I suspect that the culprit has been the Christian, Jewish, and Muslim emphasis on faith itself. Faith is rather like a rhinoceros, in fact: it won't do much in the way of real work for you, and yet at close quarters it will make spectacular claims upon your attention.

This is not to say that spiritual realization has been a common attainment east of the Bosporus. Clearly, it has not. It must also be conceded that Asia has always had its fair share of false prophets and charlatan saints, while the West has not been entirely bereft of wisdom.[11] Nevertheless, when the great philosopher mystics of the East are weighed against the patriarchs of the Western philosophical and theological traditions, the difference is unmistakable: Buddha, Shankara, Padmasambhava, Nagarjuna, Longchenpa, and countless others down to the present have no equivalents in the West. In spiritual terms, we appear to have been standing on the shoulders of dwarfs. It is little wonder, therefore, that many Western scholars have found the view within rather unremarkable.[12]

While this is not a treatise on Eastern spirituality, it does not seem out of place to briefly examine the differences between the Eastern and the Western canons, for they are genuinely startling. To illustrate this point, I have selected a passage at random from a shelf of Buddhist literature. The following text was found with closed eyes, on the first attempt, from among scores of books. I invite the reader to find anything even remotely like this in the Bible or the Koran.

> [I]n the present moment, when (your mind) remains in its own condition without constructing anything,
> Awareness at that moment in itself is quite ordinary.
> And when you look into yourself in this way nakedly (without any discursive thoughts),
> Since there is only this pure observing, there will be found a lucid clarity without anyone being there who is the observer;
> Only a naked manifest awareness is present.
> (This awareness) is empty and immaculately pure, not being created by anything whatsoever.
> It is authentic and unadulterated, without any duality of clarity and emptiness.
> It is not permanent and yet it is not created by anything.
> However, it is not a mere nothingness or something annihilated because it is lucid and present.
> It does not exist as a single entity because it is present and clear in terms of being many.
> (On the other hand) it is not created as a multiplicity of things because it is inseparable and of a single flavor.
> This inherent self-awareness does not derive from anything outside itself.
> This is the real introduction to the actual condition of things.
>
> —*Padmasambhava*[13]

One could live an eon as a Christian, a Muslim, or a Jew and never encounter any teachings like this about the nature of consciousness. The comparison with Islam is especially invidious, because Padmasambhava was virtually Muhammad's contemporary.[14] While the meaning of the above passage might not be perfectly apparent to all readers—it is just a section of a longer teaching on the nature of mind and contains a fair amount of Buddhist jargon ("clarity," "emptiness," "single flavor," etc.)—it is a rigorously empirical document, not a statement of metaphysics. Even the contemporary literature on consciousness, which spans philosophy, cognitive science, psychology, and neuroscience, cannot match the kind of precise, phenomenological studies that can be found throughout the Buddhist canon. Although we have no reason to be dogmatically attached to any one tradition of spiritual instruction, we should not imagine that they are all equally wise or equally sophisticated. They are not. Mysticism, to be viable, requires *explicit* instructions, which need suffer no more ambiguity or artifice in their exposition than we find in a manual for operating a lawn mower.[15] Some traditions realized this millennia ago. Others did not.

Meditation

Most techniques of introspection that aim at uncovering the intrinsic properties of consciousness are referred to as methods of meditation. To be told that a person is "meditating," however, is to be given almost no information at all about the content of his experience. "Meditation," in the sense that I use it here, refers to any means whereby our sense of "self"—of subject/object dualism in perception and cognition—can be made to vanish, while consciousness remains vividly aware of the continuum of experience.[16]

Inevitably, the primary obstacle to meditation is *thinking*. This leads many people to assume that the goal of meditation is to produce a thought-free state. It is true that some experiences entail the temporary cessation of thought, but meditation is less a matter of suppressing thoughts than of breaking our identification with them, so that we can recognize the condition in which thoughts themselves arise. Western scientists and philosophers generally imagine that thinking is the epitome of conscious life and would no sooner have a mind without thoughts than hands without fingers. The fundamental insight of most Eastern schools of spirituality, however, is that while thinking is a practical necessity, the failure to recognize thoughts *as thoughts*, moment after moment, is what gives each of us the feeling that we call "I," and this is the string upon which all our states of suffering and dissatisfaction are strung.[17] This is an empirical claim, not a matter of philosophical speculation. Break the spell of thought, and the duality of subject and object will vanish— as will the fundamental difference between conventional states of happiness and suffering. This is a fact about the mind that few Western scholars have ever made it their business to understand.

It is on this front that the practice of meditation reveals itself to be both intellectually serious and indispensable. There is something to realize about the nature of consciousness, and its realization does not entail thinking new thoughts. Like any skill that requires refinements in perception or cognition, the task of recognizing consciousness prior to the subject/object dichotomy can be facilitated by an expert.[18] But it is, at least in principle, an experience that is available to anyone.

You are now seated, reading this book. Your past is a memory. Your future is a matter of mere expectation. Both memories and expectations can arise in consciousness only as thoughts in the present moment.

Of course, reading is itself a species of thinking. You can probably hear the sound of your own voice reading these words in your mind. These sentences do not feel like *your* thoughts, however. Your thoughts are the ones that arrive unannounced and steal you away from the text. They may have some relevance to what you are now reading—you may think, "Didn't he just contradict himself there?"—or they may have no relevance at all. You may suddenly find yourself thinking about tonight's dinner, or about an argument you had days ago, even while your eyes still blindly scan lines of text. We all know what it is like to read whole paragraphs, and even pages of a book without assimilating a word. Few of us realize that we spend most of our lives in such a state: perceiving the present— present sights, sounds, tastes, and sensations—only dimly, through a veil of thought. We spend our lives telling ourselves the story of past and future, while the reality of the present goes largely unexplored. Now we live in ignorance of the freedom and simplicity of consciousness, prior to the arising of thought.

Your consciousness, while still inscrutable in scientific terms, is an utter simplicity as a matter of experience. It merely stands before you, *as* you, and as everything else that appears to your notice. You see this book. You hear a variety of sounds. You feel the sensations of your body in space. And then thoughts of past and future arise, endure for a time, and pass away.

If you will persistently look for the subject of your experience, however, its absence may become apparent, if only for a moment. Everything will remain—this book, your hands—and yet the illusory divide that once separated knower from known, self from world, inside from outside, will have vanished. This experience has been at the core of human spirituality for millennia. There is nothing we need believe to actualize it. We need only look closely enough at what we are calling "I."

Once the selflessness of consciousness has been glimpsed, spiritual life can be viewed as a matter of freeing one's attention more and more so that this recognition can become stabilized. This is where the connection between spirituality and ethics becomes inescapable. A vast literature on meditation suggests that negative social emotions such as hatred, envy, and spite both proceed from and ramify our dualistic perception of the world. Emotions such as love and compassion, on the other hand, seem to make our minds very pliable in meditative terms, and it is increasingly easy to concentrate under their influences. It does not seem surprising that it would be easier to free one's attention from the contents of thought, and simply abide as consciousness, if one's basic attitude toward other human beings were positive and if one had established relationships on this basis. Lawsuits, feuds, intricate deceptions, and being shackled and brought to The Hague for crimes against humanity are not among the requisites for stability in meditation. It also seems a matter of common sense that the more the feeling of selfhood is relaxed, the less those states that are predicated upon it will arise—states like fear and anger. Scientists are making their first attempts to test claims of this sort, but every experienced meditator has tested them already.[19] While much of the scientific research done on meditation has approached it as little more than a tool for stress reduction, there is no question that the phenomenon of selflessness has begun to make its way into the charmed circle of third-person, experimental science.[20]

As in any other field, spiritual intuitions are amenable to intersubjective consensus, and refutation. Just as mathematicians can enjoy mutually intelligible dialogue on abstract ideas (though they will not always agree about what is intuitively "obvious"), just as athletes can communicate effectively about the pleasures of sport, mystics can consensually elucidate the data of their sphere. Thus, genuine mysticism can be "objective"—in the only normative sense of this word that is worth retaining—in that it need not be contaminated by dogma.[21] As a phenomenon to be studied, spiritual experience is no more refractory than dreams, emotions, perceptual illusions, or, indeed, thoughts themselves.[22]

A STRANGE future awaits us: mind-reading machines, genuine virtual reality, neural implants, and increasingly refined drugs may all have implications for our view of ourselves and of our spiritual possibilities. We have entered an era when our very humanness, in genetic terms, is no longer a necessary condition of our existence. The fusion of human and machine intelligence is also a serious possibility. What will such changes in the conventional boundaries between self and world mean for us? Do they have any relevance for a spirituality that is rooted in the recognition of the nonduality of consciousness?

It seems to me that the nature of consciousness will trump all these developments. Whatever experience awaits us—either with the help of technology or after death—experience itself is a matter of consciousness and its content. Discover that consciousness inherently transcends its contents, discover that it already enjoys the well-being that the self would otherwise seek, and you have transcended the logic of experience. No doubt experience will always have the potential to change us, but it appears these changes will still be a matter of what we can be conscious *of* in the next moment, not of what consciousness is in itself.[23]

MYSTICISM is a rational enterprise. Religion is not. The mystic has recognized something about the nature of consciousness prior to thought, and this recognition is susceptible to rational discussion. The mystic has reasons for what he believes, and these reasons are empirical. The roiling mystery of the world can be analyzed with concepts (this is science), or it can be experienced free of concepts (this is mysticism).[24] Religion is nothing more than bad concepts held in place of good ones for all time. It is the denial—at once full of hope and full of fear—of the vastitude of human ignorance.

A kernel of truth lurks at the heart of religion, because spiritual experience, ethical behavior, and strong communities are essential for human happiness. And yet our religious traditions are intellectually defunct and politically ruinous. While spiritual experience is clearly a natural propensity of the human mind, we need not believe anything on insufficient evidence to actualize it. Clearly, it must be possible to bring reason, spirituality, and ethics together in our thinking about the world. This would be the beginning of a rational approach to our deepest personal concerns. It would also be the end of faith.

Epilogue

MY GOAL in writing this book has been to help close the door to a certain style of irrationality. While religious faith is the one species of human ignorance that will not admit of even the *possibility* of correction, it is still sheltered from criticism in every corner of our culture. Forsaking all valid sources of information about this world (both spiritual and mundane), our religions have seized upon ancient taboos and prescientific fancies as though they held ultimate metaphysical significance. Books that embrace the narrowest spectrum of political, moral, scientific, and spiritual understanding—books that, by their antiquity alone, offer us the most dilute wisdom with respect to the present—are still dogmatically thrust upon us as the final word on matters of the greatest significance. In the best case, faith leaves otherwise well-intentioned people incapable of thinking rationally about many of their deepest concerns; at worst, it is a continuous source of human violence. Even now, many of us are motivated not by what we know but by what we are content merely to imagine. Many are still eager to sacrifice happiness, compassion, and justice in this world, for a fantasy of a world to come. These and other degradations await us along the well-worn path of piety. Whatever our religious differences may mean for the next life, they have only one terminus in this one—a future of ignorance and slaughter.

We live in societies that are still constrained by religious laws and threatened by religious violence. What is it about us, and specifically about our discourse with one another, that keeps these astonishing bits of evil loose in our world? We have seen that education and wealth are insufficient guarantors of rationality. Indeed, even in the West, educated men and women still cling to the blood-soaked heirlooms of a previous age. Mitigating this problem is not merely a matter of reining in a minority of religious extremists; it is a matter of finding approaches to ethics and to spiritual experience that make no appeal to faith, and broadcasting this knowledge to everyone.

Of course, one senses that the problem is simply hopeless. What could possibly cause billions of human beings to reconsider their religious beliefs? And yet, it is obvious that an utter revolution in our thinking could be accomplished in a single generation: if parents and teachers would merely give honest answers to the questions of every child. Our doubts about the feasibility of such a project should be tempered by an understanding of its necessity, for there is no reason whatsoever to think that we can survive our religious differences indefinitely.

Imagine what it would be like for our descendants to experience the fall of civilization. Imagine failures of reasonableness so total that our largest bombs finally fall upon our largest cities in defense of our religious differences. What would it be like for the unlucky survivors of such a holocaust to look back upon the hurtling career of human stupidity that led them over the precipice? A view from the end of the world would surely find that the six billion of us currently alive did much to pave the way to the Apocalypse.

THIS world is simply ablaze with bad ideas. There are still places where people are put to death for imaginary crimes—like blasphemy—and where the totality of a child's education consists of his learning to recite from an ancient book of religious fiction. There are countries where women are denied almost every human liberty, except the liberty to breed. And yet, these same societies are quickly acquiring terrifying arsenals of advanced weaponry. If we cannot inspire the developing world, and the Muslim world in particular, to pursue ends that are compatible with a global civilization, then a dark future awaits all of us.

The contest between our religions is zero-sum. Religious violence is still with us because our religions are *intrinsically* hostile to one another. Where they appear otherwise, it is because secular knowledge and secular interests are restraining the most lethal improprieties of faith. It is time we acknowledged that no real foundation exists within the canons of Christianity, Islam, Judaism, or any of our other faiths for religious tolerance and religious diversity.

If religious war is ever to become unthinkable for us, in the way that slavery and cannibalism seem poised to, it will be a matter of our having dispensed with the dogma of faith. If our tribalism is ever to give way to an extended moral identity, our religious beliefs can no longer be sheltered from the tides of genuine inquiry and genuine criticism. It is time we realized that to presume knowledge where one has only pious hope is a species of evil. Wherever conviction grows in inverse proportion to its justification, we have lost the very basis of human cooperation. Where we have reasons for what we believe, we have no need of faith; where we have no reasons, we have lost both our connection to the world and to one another. People who harbor strong convictions without evidence belong at the margins of our societies, not in our halls of power. The only thing we should respect in a person's faith is his desire for a better life in *this* world; we need never have respected his certainty that one awaits him in the next.

Nothing is more sacred than the facts. No one, therefore, should win any points in our discourse for deluding himself. The litmus test for reasonableness should be obvious: anyone who wants to know how the world is, whether in physical or spiritual terms, will be open to new evidence. We should take comfort in the fact that people tend to conform themselves to this principle whenever they are obliged to. This will remain a problem for religion. The very hands that prop up our faith will be the ones to shake it.

It is as yet undetermined what it means to be human, because every facet of our culture—and even our biology itself—remains open to innovation and insight. We do not know what we will be a thousand years from now—or indeed *that* we will be, given the lethal absurdity of many of our beliefs—but whatever changes await us, one thing seems unlikely to change: as long as experience endures, the difference between happiness and suffering will remain our paramount concern. We will therefore want to understand those processes—biochemical, behavioral, ethical, political, economic, and spiritual—that account for this difference. We do not yet have anything like a final understanding of such processes, but we know enough to rule out many false understandings. Indeed, we know enough at this moment to say that the God of Abraham is not only unworthy of the immensity of creation; he is unworthy even of man.

We do not know what awaits each of us after death, but we know that we will die. Clearly, it must be possible to live ethically—with a genuine concern for the happiness of other sentient beings—without presuming to know things about which we are patently ignorant. Consider it: every person you have ever met, every person you will pass in the street today, is going to die. Living long enough, each will suffer the loss of his friends and family. All are going to lose everything they love in this world. Why would one want to be anything but kind to them in the meantime?

We are bound to one another. The fact that our ethical intuitions must, in some way, supervene upon our biology does not make ethical truths reducible to biological ones. We are the final judges of what is good, just as we remain the final judges of what is logical. And on neither front has our conversation with one another reached an end. There need be no scheme of rewards and punishments transcending this life to justify our moral intuitions or to render them effective in guiding our behavior in the world. The only angels we need invoke are those of our better nature: reason, honesty, and love. The only demons we must fear are those that lurk inside every human mind: ignorance, hatred, greed, and *faith*, which is surely the devil's masterpiece.

Man is manifestly *not* the measure of all things. This universe is shot through with mystery. The very fact of its being, and of our own, is a mystery absolute, and the only miracle worthy of the name. The consciousness that animates us is itself central to this mystery and the ground for any experience we might wish to call "spiritual." No myths need be embraced for us to commune with the profundity of our circumstance. No personal God need be worshiped for us to live in awe at the beauty and immensity of creation. No tribal fictions need be rehearsed for us to realize, one fine day, that we do, in fact, love our neighbors, that our happiness is inextricable from their own, and that our interdependence demands that people everywhere be given the opportunity to flourish. The days of our religious identities are clearly numbered. Whether the days of civilization itself are numbered would seem to depend, rather too much, on how soon we realize this.

Afterword

●

The human psyche has two great sicknesses: the urge to carry
vendetta across generations, and the tendency to fasten group
labels on people rather than see them as individuals. Abrahamic
religion gives strong sanction to both—and mixes explosively
with both. Only the willfully blind could fail to implicate the divisive force of religion in most, if not all, of the violent enmities in
the world today. Without a doubt it is the prime aggravator of the
Middle East. Those of us who have for years politely concealed our
contempt for the dangerous collective delusion of religion need to
stand up and speak out. Things are different now. "All is changed,
changed utterly."   —RICHARD DAWKINS

IT HAS BEEN nearly a year since *The End of Faith* was first published
in the United States. In response, I have received a continuous correspondence from readers and nonreaders alike, expressing everything from ecstatic support to nearly homicidal condemnation.
Many thousands of people have apparently read the book, and millions more have heard its contents discussed in the media. In
response, letters and e-mails have come to me from scientists and
physicians at every stage of their careers, from soldiers fighting in
Iraq, from Christian ministers who have lost their faith (and from
those who haven't), from Muslims who agree with my general dis-
paragement of their religion, and from others who would have me
meet them at a local mosque so that I might better learn the will of
God. I have also heard from hundreds of embattled freethinkers liv-

ing in "red state" America. Judging from this last group of corre-
spondents, the American heartland is fast becoming as blinkered as
the wilds of Afghanistan. It may be too much to hope that the efforts
of reasonable people will yet turn the tide.

According to several recent polls, 22 percent of Americans are certain that Jesus will return to earth sometime in the next fifty years.
Another 22 percent believe that he will probably do so. This is likely
the same 44 percent who go to church once a week or more, who
believe that God literally promised the land of Israel to the Jews, and
who want to stop teaching children about the biological fact of evolution. Believers of this sort constitute the most cohesive and motivated segment of the American electorate. Consequently, their views
and prejudices now influence almost every decision of national
importance. Political liberals seem to have drawn the wrong lesson
from these developments and are now thumbing scripture, wonder-
ing how best to ingratiate themselves to the legions of men and
women in our country who vote mainly on the basis of religious
dogma. More than 50 percent of Americans have a "negative" or
"highly negative" view of people who do not believe in God; 70 percent think it important for presidential candidates to be "strongly
religious." Because it is taboo to criticize a person's religious beliefs,
political debate over questions of public policy (stem-cell research,
the ethics of assisted suicide and euthanasia, obscenity and free
speech, gay marriage, etc.) generally gets framed in terms appropriate to a theocracy. Unreason is now ascendant in the United States—
in our schools, in our courts, and in each branch of the federal
government. Only 28 percent of Americans believe in evolution; 72
percent believe in angels. Ignorance in this degree, concentrated in
both the head and the belly of a lumbering superpower, is now a
problem for the entire world.

HAVING seen my argument against faith discussed, attacked, celebrated, and misconstrued in blogs and book reviews throughout the

world, I would like to take the occasion of its release in paperback as an opportunity to respond to the most common criticisms and misconceptions. These are by no means straw-man arguments; these are what real people (and the occasional book reviewer) believe to be devastating retorts to my basic thesis:

1. *Yes, religion occasionally causes violence, but the greatest crimes of the twentieth century were perpetrated by atheists. Godlessness— as witnessed by the regimes of Hitler, Stalin, Mao, Pol Pot, and Kim Jong-Il—is the most dangerous condition of all.*

This is one of the most common criticisms I encounter. It is also the most depressing, as I anticipate and answer it early in the book (p. 79). While some of the most despicable political movements in human history have been explicitly irreligious, they were not especially rational. The public pronouncements of these regimes have been mere litanies of delusion—about race, economics, national identity, the march of history, or the moral dangers of intellectualism. Auschwitz, the gulag, and the killing fields are not examples of what happens when people become *too critical of unjustified beliefs*; to the contrary, these horrors testify to the dangers of not thinking critically enough about specific secular ideologies. Needless to say, my argument against religious faith is not an argument for the blind embrace of atheism as a *dogma*. The problem I raise in the book is none other than the problem of dogma itself—of which every religion has more than its fair share. I know of no society in human history that ever suffered because its people became too reasonable.

As I argue throughout the book, certainty without evidence is necessarily divisive and dehumanizing. In fact, respect for evidence and rational argument is what makes peaceful cooperation possible. As human beings, we live in a perpetual choice between conversation and violence; what, apart from a fundamental willingness to be reasonable, can guarantee that we will keep talking to one another?

2. We need faith to do almost anything. It is absurd to think that we could ever do without it.

One e-mail I received on this subject began: "I like your writing style but you are an idiot." Fair enough. My correspondent then went on to point out, as many have, that each of us has to get out of bed in the morning and live his life, and we do this in a context of uncertainty, and in the context of terrible certainties, like the certainty of death. This positive disposition, this willingness to set a course in life without any assurance that things will go one's way, is occasionally called "faith." Thus, one may prop up a disconsolate friend with the words "have faith in yourself." Such words are almost never facetious, even on the forked tongue of an atheist. Let me state for the record that I see nothing wrong with this kind of "faith."

But this is not the faith that has given us religion. It would be rather remarkable if a positive attitude in the face of uncertainty led inevitably to ludicrous convictions about the divine origin of certain books, to bizarre cultural taboos, to the abject hatred of homosexuals, and to the diminished status of women. Adopt too positive an outlook, and the next thing you know architects and engineers may start flying planes into buildings.

As I do my best to spell out over the course of the book, religious faith is the belief in historical and metaphysical propositions without sufficient evidence. When the evidence for a religious proposition is thin or nonexistent, or there is compelling evidence against it, people invoke faith. Otherwise, they simply cite the reasons for their beliefs (e.g., "the New Testament confirms Old Testament prophecy," "I saw the face of Jesus in a window," "We prayed, and our daughter's cancer went into remission"). Such reasons are generally inadequate, but they are better than no reasons at all. People of faith naturally recognize the primacy of reasons and resort to reasoning whenever they possibly can. Faith is simply the license they give themselves to *keep believing when reasons fail.* When rational inquiry supports the creed it is championed; when it poses a threat, it is derided; sometimes in the same sentence. Faith is the mortar that fills the cracks in the evidence and the gaps in the logic, and thus it is faith that keeps the whole terrible edifice of religious certainty still looming dangerously over our world.

3. *Islam is no more amenable to violence than any other religion is. The violence we see in the Muslim world is the product of politics and economics, not faith.*

The speciousness of this claim is best glimpsed by the bright light of bomb blasts. Where are the Palestinian *Christian* suicide bombers? They, too, suffer the daily indignity of the Israeli occupation. Where, for that matter, are the Tibetan Buddhist suicide bombers? The Tibetans have suffered an occupation far more cynical and repressive than any that the United States or Israel has ever imposed upon the Muslim world. Where are the throngs of Tibetans ready to perpetrate suicidal atrocities against Chinese noncombatants? They do not exist. What is the difference that makes the difference? The difference lies in the specific tenets of Islam. This is not to say that Buddhism could not help inspire suicidal violence. It can, and it has (Japan, World War II). But this concedes absolutely nothing to the apologists for Islam. As a Buddhist, one has to work extremely hard to justify such barbarism. One need not work nearly so hard as a Muslim.

Recent events in Iraq offer further corroboration on this point. It is true, of course, that the Iraqi people have been traumatized by decades of war and repression. But war and repression do not account for suicidal violence directed against the Red Cross, the United Nations, foreign workers, and Iraqi innocents. War and repression would not have attracted an influx of foreign fighters willing to sacrifice their lives merely to sow chaos. The Iraqi insurgents have not been motivated principally by political or economic grievances. They have such grievances, of course, but politics and economics do not get a man to intentionally blow himself up in a crowd of children, or get his mother to sing his praises for it. Miracles of this order generally require religious faith.

There are other confounding variables here, of course—state sponsorship of terrorism, the occasional coercion of reluctant suicide bombers—but we cannot let them blind us to the pervasive and lunatic influence of religious belief. The truth that we must finally confront is that Islam contains specific doctrines about martyrdom and jihad that now directly inspire Muslim terrorism. Unless the world's Muslims can find some way of expunging a theology that is fast turning their religion into a cult of death, we will ultimately face the same perversely destructive behavior throughout much of the world. Wherever these events occur, we will find Muslims tending to side with other Muslims, no matter how sociopathic their behavior. This is the malignant solidarity that religion breeds. It is time that sane human beings stopped making apologies for it. And it is time for Muslims—especially Muslim women—to realize that nobody suffers the consequences of Islam more than they do.

4. The End of Faith is not a truly atheistic book. It is really a stalking horse for Buddhism, New-Age mysticism, or some other form of irrationality.

As almost every page of my book is dedicated to exposing the problems of religious faith, it is ironic that some of the harshest criticism has come from atheists who feel that I have betrayed their cause on peripheral issues. If there is a book that takes a harder swing at religion, I'm not aware of it. This is not to say that my book does not have many shortcomings—but appeasing religious irrationality is not among them.

Nevertheless, atheists have found much to complain about in the book, especially in the last chapter where I attempt to put meditation and "spirituality" on a rational footing. "Meditation," in the sense that I use the term, merely requires that a person pay extraordinarily close attention to his moment-by-moment experience of the world. There is nothing irrational about doing this. In fact, it constitutes the only rational basis for making detailed claims about the nature of our subjectivity.

Through meditation, a person can come to observe the flow of his experience with remarkable clarity, and this sometimes results in a variety of insights that people tend to find both intellectually credible and personally transformative. As I discuss in the final chapter of the book, one of these insights is that the feeling we call "I"—the sense that we are the thinker of our thoughts, the experiencer of our experiences—can disappear when looked for in a rigorous way. This is not a proposition to be accepted on faith; it is an empirical observation, analogous to the discovery of one's optic blind spots. Most people never notice their blind spots (caused by the transit of the optic nerve through the retina of each eye), but they can be pointed out to almost anyone with a little effort. The absence of the "self" can also be pointed out with some effort, though this discovery tends to require considerably more training on the part of both teacher and student. The only faith required to get such a project off the ground is the faith of scientific hypothesis. The hypothesis is this: If I use my attention in a certain way, it may have a specific, reproducible effect. Needless to say, what happens (or fails to happen) along any path of "spiritual" practice must be interpreted in light of some conceptual scheme, and everything should be open to rational argument.

I have also taken considerable heat from atheists for a few remarks I made about the nature of consciousness. Most atheists appear to be certain that consciousness is entirely dependent on (and reducible to) the workings of the brain. In the last chapter of the book, I briefly argue that this certainty is unwarranted. The fact is that scientists still do not know what the relationship between consciousness and matter actually is. I am not suggesting that we make a religion out of this uncertainty, or do anything else with it. And, needless to say, the mysteriousness of consciousness does nothing to make conventional religious notions about God and paradise any more plausible.

SINCE *The End of Faith* was first published, current events have remained a running confirmation of its central thesis. There are days when almost every headline in the morning paper attests to the social costs of religious faith, and the nightly news seems miraculously broadcast from the fourteenth century. One spectacle of religious hysteria follows fast upon the next. Sanctimonious eruptions announcing the death of the pope (a man who actively opposed condom use in sub-Saharan Africa and shielded frocked child molesters from secular justice) are soon followed by other outbursts of religious lunacy. At the time of this writing, Muslims in several countries are rioting over a report that U.S. interrogators desecrated a copy of the Koran. Seventeen people are dead and hundreds injured. The response of the U.S. government has been to offer up some lunacy of its own. No less a spokeswoman than the Secretary of State has assured the righteous hordes that "the United States government will not tolerate any disrespect for the holy Koran." What form our government's intolerance will take remains unspecified. I await a knock on the door.

Such perfect visions of unreason have been punctuated by the more ordinary trespasses of faith: daily reports of pious massacres in Iraq, of evangelical ravings against the evils of a secular judiciary, of widespread religious coercion in the U.S. Air Force, of efforts in at least twenty states to redefine science to include supernatural explanations of the origin of life, of devout pharmacists refusing to fill prescriptions for birth control, of movie theaters refusing to show documentaries that report the actual age of the earth, and on and on and onward . . . to the fifteenth century.

For anyone with eyes to see, there can be no doubt that religious faith remains a perpetual source of human conflict. Religion persuades otherwise intelligent men and women to not think, or to think badly, about questions of civilizational importance. And yet it remains taboo to criticize religious faith in our society, or to even observe that some religions are less compassionate and less tolerant than others. What is worst in us (outright delusion) has been elevated beyond the reach of criticism, while what is best (reason and intellectual honesty) must remain hidden, for fear of giving offense. *The End of Faith* represents my first attempt to call attention to the dangers and absurdities inherent in this situation. I sincerely hope that readers will continue to find the book useful.

Sam Harris
New York
May 2005

Notes

1 Reason in Exile

1 As we will see in chapter 4, the chances are decidedly *against* the possibility that he comes from the lowest strata of society.

2 Some readers may object that the bomber in question is most likely to be a member of the Liberations Tigers of Tamil Eelam—the Sri Lankan separatist organization that has perpetrated more acts of suicidal terrororism than any other group. Indeed, the "Tamil Tigers" are often offered as a counterexample to any claim that suicidal terrorism is a product of religion. But to describe the Tamil Tigers as "secular"—as R. A. Pape, "The Strategic Logic of Suicide Terrorism," *American Political Science Review* 97, no. 3 (2003): 20–32, and others have—is misleading. While the motivations of the Tigers are not explicitly religious, they are Hindus who undoubtedly believe many improbable things about the nature of life and death. The cult of martyr worship that they have nurtured for decades has many of the features of religiosity that one would expect in people who give their lives so easily for a cause. Secular Westerners often underestimate the degree to which certain cultures, steeped as they are in otherworldliness, look upon death with less alarm than seems strictly rational. I was once traveling in India when the government rescheduled the exams for students who were preparing to enter the civil service: what appeared to me to be the least of bureaucratic inconveniences precipitated a wave of teenage *self-immolations* in protest. Hindus, even those whose preoccupations appear to be basically secular, often harbor potent religious beliefs.

3 I am speaking here of "alchemy" as that body of ancient and ultimately fanciful metallurgic and chemical techniques whose purpose was to transmute base metals into gold and mundane materials into an "elixir of life." It is true that there are people who claim to find the alchemical lit-

erature prescient with the most contemporary truths of pharmacology, solid-state physics, and a variety of other disciplines. I find the results of such Rorschach readings less than inspiring, however. See T. McKenna, *The Archaic Revival* ([San Francisco]: Harper San Francisco, 1991), *Food of the Gods: The Search for the Original Tree of Knowledge* (New York: Bantam Books, 1992), and *True Hallucinations* ([San Francisco]: Harper San Francisco, 1993), for an example of a bright and beautiful mind that takes such revaluations of alchemy seriously, however.

4 S. J. Gould, "Nonoverlapping Magisteria," *Natural History*, March 1997.

5 G. H. Gallup Jr., *Religion in America 1996* (Princeton: Princeton Religion Research Center, 1996).

6 This is not to deny that there are problems with democracy, particularly when it is imposed prematurely on societies that have high birthrates, low levels of literacy, profound ethnic and religious factionalism, and unstable economies. There is clearly such a thing as a benevolent despotism, and it may be a necessary stage in the political development of many societies. See R. D. Kaplan, "Was Democracy Just a Moment?," *Atlantic Monthly*, Dec. 1997, pp. 55–80, and F. Zakaria, *The Future of Freedom: Illiberal Democracy at Home and Abroad* (New York: W. W. Norton, 2003).

7 Bernard Lewis, in "The Revolt of Islam," *New Yorker*, Nov. 19, 2001, pp. 50–63, and *The Crisis of Islam: Holy War and Unholy Terror* (New York: Modern Library, 2003), has pointed out that the term "fundamentalist" was coined by American Protestants and can be misleading when applied to other faiths. It seems to me that the term has escaped into general usage, however, and that it now signifies any sort of scriptural literalism. I use it only in this general sense. The problems of applying the phrase to Islam in particular will be addressed in chapter 4.

8 C. W. Dugger, "Religious Riots Loom over Indian Politics," *New York Times*, July 27, 2002. See also P. Mishra, "The Other Face of Fanaticism," *New York Times Magazine*, Feb. 2, 2003, pp. 42–46.

9 A. Roy, *War Talk* (Cambridge, Mass.: South End Press, 2003), 1.

10 As Lewis, *Crisis of Islam*, 57–58, notes, we have caused far more chaos in Central America, Southeast Asia, and southern Africa. Those Muslim countries which have been occupied by foreign powers (like Egypt) are in many ways much better off than countries (like Saudi Arabia) which have not. Taking Saudia Arabia as an example, despite its relative wealth —which is due to nothing more than an accident of nature—this country lags behind its neighbors in many respects. The Saudis have only

eight universities to serve 21 million people, and they did not abolish slavery until 1962. P. Berman, *Terror and Liberalism* (New York: W. W. Norton, 2003), 16, also points out that most of our conflicts of recent years have been fought in *defense* of various Muslim populations: the first Gulf War was fought in defense of Kuwait and Saudi Arabia, and was followed by a decade of air protection for the Iraqi Kurds in the north and the Iraqi Shia in the south; the intervention in Somalia was designed to relieve famine there; and our intervention in the Balkans was for the purpose of defending Bosnians and Kosovars from marauding Christian Serbs. Our original support of the mujahideen in Afghanistan belongs in this category as well. As Berman says, "In all of recent history, no country on earth has fought so hard and consistently as the United States on behalf of Muslim populations." This is true. And yet the Muslim worldview is such that this fact, if acknowledged at all, is generally counted as a further grievance against us; it is yet another source of Muslim "humiliation."

[11] Of course, the Sunnis would still hate the Shiites, but this is also an expression of their faith.

[12] J. Bennet, "In Israeli Hospital, Bomber Tells of Trying to Kill Israelis," *New York Times*, June 8, 2002.

[13] "[I]n 1994, at a village south of Islamabad, police charged a doctor with setting fire to the sacred Koran, a blasphemous crime punishable by death. Before he could be tried, an enraged mob dragged him from the police station, doused him with kerosene, and burned him alive." J. A. Haught, *Holy Hatred: Religious Conflicts of the '90s* (Amherst, Mass.: Prometheus Books, 1995), 179.

[14] S. P. Huntington, *The Clash of Civilizations and the Remaking of World Order* (New York: Simon and Schuster, 1996).

[15] As many commentators have observed, there is no Koranic equivalent of the New Testament line "Render unto Caesar those things that are Caesar's, and render unto God those things that are God's" (Matt. 22:21). As a result, there appears to be no Islamic basis for the separation of the powers of the church and state. This, needless to say, is a problem.

[16] Lewis, *Crisis of Islam*, 20.

[17] Just consider what would fill our newspapers if there were no conflict between Israel and the Palestinians, the Indians and the Pakistanis, the Russians and the Chechens, Muslim militants and the West, etc. Problems between the West and countries like China and North Korea would remain—but they, too, are often the result of an uncritical acceptance of

a variety of dogmas. While our differences with North Korea, for instance, are not explicitly religious, they are a direct consequence of the North Koreans' having grown utterly deranged by their political ideology, their abject worship of their leaders, and their lack of information about the outside world. They are now like a cargo cult armed with nuclear weapons. If the 29 million inhabitants of North Korea knew that they were unique among the world's basket cases, they might behave rather differently. The problem of North Korea is, first and foremost, a problem of the unjustified (and unjustifiable) beliefs of North Koreans. See P. Gourevitch, "Letter from Korea: Alone in the Dark," *New Yorker*, Sept. 8, 2003, pp. 55–75.

[18] See, e.g., D. Radin, *The Conscious Universe: The Scientific Truth of Psychic Phenomena* (New York: HarperCollins, 1997), R. Sheldrake, *The Sense of Being Stared At: And Other Aspects of the Extended Mind* (New York: Crown, 2003), and R. S. Bobrow, "Paranormal Phenomena in the Medical Literature Sufficient Smoke to Warrant a Search for Fire," *Medical Hypotheses* 60 (2003): 864–68. There may even be some credible evidence for reincarnation. See I. Stevenson, *Twenty Cases Suggestive of Reincarnation* (Charlottesville: Univ. Press of Virginia, 1974), *Unlearned Language: New Studies in Xenoglossy* (Charlottesville: Univ. Press of Virginia, 1984), and *Where Reincarnation and Biology Intersect* (Westport, Conn.: Praeger, 1997).

[19] Yes, human beings can echolocate. We're just not very good at it. To demonstrate this, simply close your eyes, hum loudly, and pass your hand back and forth in front of your face. The sound reflecting off your hand indicates its position.

[20] Witness John von Neumann—mathematician, game theorist, savant of national defense, and agnostic—converting to Catholicism while in the throes of cancer. See W. Poundstone, *Prisoner's Dilemma* (New York: Doubleday, 1992).

[21] The Nazis disparaged the "Jewish physics" of Einstein, and the communists rejected the "capitalist biology" of Mendel and Darwin. But these were not rational criticisms—as witnessed by the fact that dissenting scientists were often imprisoned or killed.

These facts notwithstanding, K. Peng and R. E. Nisbett, "Culture, Dialectics, and Reasoning about Contradiction," *American Psychologist* 54 (1999): 741–54, have argued that significant differences in reasoning styles exist across cultures. While the data appear to me to be inconclusive, even if Eastern and Western minds address problems differently, there is no reason why we cannot, in principle, agree about what it is ultimately rational to believe.

[22] The emergence in 2003 of severe acute respiratory syndrome (SARS) in southern China is a recent example of the global implications of local health practices. China's mishandling of the epidemic was born not of irrational medical beliefs but of irrational political ones—and the consequences, at the time of this writing, have not been catastrophic. But it is not difficult to imagine a culture whose beliefs relative to epidemiology could systematically impose unacceptable risks on the rest of us. There is little doubt that we would ultimately quarantine, invade, or otherwise subjugate such a society.

[23] *Los Angeles Times*, March 18, 2002.

[24] G. Wills, "With God on His Side," *New York Times Magazine*, March 30, 2003.

[25] M. Rees, *Our Final Hour* (New York: Basic Books, 2003), 61.

[26] Questions of their plausibility aside, the mutual incompatibility of our religious beliefs renders them suspect *in principle*. As Bertrand Russell observed, even if we were to grant that one of our religions must be correct in its every particular, given the number of conflicting views on offer, every believer should expect damnation on mere probabilistic grounds.

[27] Rees, *Our Final Hour*, has given our species no better than a 50 percent chance of surviving this century. While his prognostications are nothing more than educated guesswork, they are worth taking seriously. The man is not a crank.

2 *The Nature of Belief*

[1] Proof of this fact is never so eloquent as when injury to the brain destroys one facet of a person's memory while sparing the others—and indeed, it is largely upon such clinical case histories (like W. B. Scoville and B. Milner, "Loss of Recent Memory after Bilateral Hippocampal Lesions," *Journal of Neurology, Neurosurgery and Psychiatry* 20 (1957): 11–21) that our understanding of human memory depends. Long-term memory has since fragmented into *semantic, episodic, procedural,* and other forms of information processing; and short-term memory (generally called "working memory") is now subdivided into *phonological, visual, spatial, conceptual, echoic,* and *central executive* components. Our analysis of both forms of memory is surely incomplete. The distinction

between semantic and episodic memory, for instance, doesn't seem to hold for topographical recall (E. A. Maguire et al., "Recalling Routes around London: Activation of the Right Hippocampus in Taxi Drivers," *Journal of Neuroscience* 17 [1997]: 7103–10); and semantic memory seems susceptible to further division into category-specific subtypes, as in memory for living v. nonliving things (S. L. Thompson-Schill et al., "A Neural Basis for Category and Modality Specificity of Semantic Knowledge," *Neuropsychologia* 37 [1999]: 671–76; J. R. Hart et al., "Category-Specific Naming Deficit following Cerebral Infarction," *Nature* 316 [Aug. 1, 1985]: 439–40).

[2] There are ways of construing the concept of "belief" that make it appear equally disjoint. If we use the term too loosely, it can seem that the entire brain is intimately involved in "belief" formation. Imagine, for instance, that a man has come to your door claiming to represent the "Publishers Clearing House Sweepstakes":

1. You see the man's face, recognize it, and therefore "believe" that you know who this person is. Activity in your fusiform cortex, especially in the right hemisphere, is crucial for such recognition to occur, and a lesion here will lead to *prosopagnosia* (the inability to recognize familiar faces, or indeed to see faces as *faces* at all). Using "belief" in this context, it is tempting to say that prosopagnosics have lost certain "beliefs" about what other people look like.

2. Having recognized the man's face, you form the "belief," based on your long-term memory for both faces and facts that he is Ed McMahon, the famous spokesman for Publishers Clearing House. Damage to your perirhinal and perihippocampal cortices would have prevented this "belief" from forming. See R. R. Davies et al., "The Human Perirhinal Cortex in Semantic Memory: An in Vivo and Postmortem Volumetric Magnetic Resonance Imaging Study in Semantic Dementia, Alzheimer's Disease and Matched Controls," *Neuropathology and Applied Neurobiology* 28, no. 2 (2002): 167–78 [abstract], and A. R. Giovagnoli et al., "Preserved Semantic Access in Global Amnesia and Hippocampal Damage," *Clinical Neuropsychology* 15 (2001): 508–15 [abstract].

3. Not yet being sure whether this is a hoax of some sort (perhaps Mr. McMahon is now working for *Candid Camera*) you take another moment to study the man at your door. You form the "belief," based on his tone of voice, the look in his eye, and many other factors, that

he is trustworthy and therefore means what he says. Your ability to form such judgments reliably—in particular, your ability to detect *un*trustworthiness—requires that you have at least one functioning amygdala (R. Adolphs et al., "The Human Amygdala in Social Judgment," *Nature* 393 [June 4, 1998]: 470–74), a small, almond-shaped nucleus in your medial temporal lobe.

4. Mr. McMahon then informs you that you are the lucky winner of a "big jackpot." Your memory for words (requiring different processing from your memory for faces) leads you to "believe" that you have won some money, rather than a "pot" of some sort. Making sense of this phrase will require the work of your superior and middle temporal gyri, predominantly in your left hemisphere. See A. Ahmad et al., "Auditory Comprehension of Language in Young Children: Neural Networks Identified with fMRI," *Neurology* 60 (2003): 1598–605, and M. H. Davis and I. S. Johnsrude, "Hierarchical Processing in Spoken Language Comprehension," *Journal of Neuroscience* 23 (2003): 3423–31.

5. Ed then produces a piece of paper, which he invites you to read. He does this by pointing. Your "belief" that he wants you to read requires what has come to be called "theory of mind" processing on your part (D. Premack and G. Woodruff, "Does the Chimpanzee Have a Theory of Mind," *Behavioral and Brain Sciences* 1 (1978): 515–26)—if a tree limb had swayed in the direction of a piece of paper, you would not have understood it as "pointing" at all. The anatomy underlying theory of mind processing is not entirely clear at present, but it seems that the anterior cingulate cortex as well as regions of the frontal and temporal lobes enable to you to attribute mental states (including beliefs) to others. See K. Vogeley et al., "Mind Reading: Neural Mechanisms of Theory of Mind and Self-perspective," *NeuroImage* 14 (2001): 170–81; C. D. Frith and U. Frith, "Interacting Minds—A Biological Basis," *Science's Compass* 286 (1999): 1692–95; and P. C. Fletcher et al., "Other Mind in the Brain: A Functional Imaging Study of 'Theory of Mind' in Story Comprehension," *Cognition* 57 (1995): 109–28.

6. Scanning the paper with your eyes, you see the following symbols appended after your name: $10,000,000. Some processing relative to Arabic numerals (probably in your left parietal lobe—G. Denes and M. Signorini, "Door But Not Four and 4 a Category Specific Transcoding Deficit in a Pure Acalculic Patient," *Cortex* 37, no. 2 [2001]:

267–77) leads you to "believe" that this paper is actually a check for ten million dollars.

While many diverse streams of neural activity have conspired to make you believe that you have won a terrific sum of money, it is *this* idea—explicitly represented in language—that underwrites the sweeping changes that will take place in your nervous system, and in your life. Perhaps you will startle the benevolent Mr. McMahon by shrieking; you may even burst into tears; it is only a matter of hours before you begin shopping with an unusual degree of abandon. Your belief that you have just won ten million dollars will be the author of all these actions, both voluntary and involuntary. In particular, it will dictate the following behavior: to the question "Have you just won ten million dollars?" you will—if moved by the spirit of candor—reply yes.

3 Belief, in this sense, is what philosophers generally call a "propositional attitude." We have many such attitudes, in fact, and they are usually indicated by a clause containing the word "that"; we can *believe that, fear that, intend that, appreciate that, hope that,* etc.

4 The formation of certain primitive beliefs may be indistinguishable from the preparation of a motor plan. See J. I. Gold and M. N. Shadlen, "Representation of a Perceptual Decision in Developing Oculomotor Commands," *Nature* 404 (March 23, 2000): 390–94, and "Banburismus and the Brain: Decoding the Relationship between Sensory Stimuli, Decisions, and Reward," *Neuron* 36, no. 2 (2002): 299–308, for a discussion of visual judgments and oculomotor response.

5 We do not have to bring the membership of Al Qaeda "to justice" merely because of what happened on Sept. 11, 2001. The thousands of men, women, and children who disappeared in the rubble of the World Trade Center are beyond our help—and successful acts of retribution, however satisfying they may be to some people, will not change this fact. Our subsequent actions in Afghanistan and elsewhere are justified because of what will happen to more innocent people if members of Al Qaeda are allowed to go on living by the light of their peculiar beliefs. The horror of Sept. 11 should motivate us, not because it provides us with a grievance that we now must avenge, but because it proves beyond any possibility of doubt that certain twenty-first-century Muslims actually believe the most dangerous and implausible tenets of their faith.

6 A consideration of the structure of our language reveals that this is not a

special case, since all words and their usages lead us in circles of mutual explanation.

7 The philosopher Donald Davidson has made this insight do some very heavy lifting in his work on "radical interpretation." One interesting consequence of the relationship between belief and meaning is that any attempt to understand a language user requires that we assume him to be basically rational (this is Davidson's "principle of charity").

8 At least at the "classical" scale at which we live. That the quantum world does not behave in this way accounts for why no one can claim to "understand" it in realistic terms.

9 D. Kahneman and A. Tversky, "On the Reality of Cognitive Illusions," *Psychological Review* 103 (1996): 582–91; G. Gigerenzer, "On Narrow Norms and Vague Heuristics: A Reply to Kahneman and Tversky," ibid., 592–96; K. J. Holyoak and P. C. Cheng, "Pragmatic Reasoning with a Point of View," *Thinking and Reasoning* 1 (1995): 289–313; J. R. Anderson, "The New Theoretical Framework," in *The Adaptive Character of Thought* (Hillsdale, N.J.: Erlbaum, 1990); K. Peng and R. E. Nisbett, "Culture, Dialectics, and Reasoning about Contradiction," American Psychologist 54 (1999): 741–54; K. E. Stanovich and R. F. West, "Individual Differences in Rational Thought," *Journal of Experimental Psychology: General* 127 (1998): 161.

10 A. R. Mele, "Real Self-Deception," *Behavioral and Brain Sciences* 20 (1997): 91–102, "Understanding and Explaining Real Self-Deception," ibid., 127–36, and *Self-Deception Unmasked* (Princeton: Princeton Univ. Press, 2001); H. Fingarette, *Self-Deception* (Berkeley: Univ. of California Press, 2000); J. P. Dupuy, ed., *Self-Deception and Paradoxes of Rationality* (Stanford: CSLI Publications, 1998); D. Davidson, "Who Is Fooled?" ibid.; G. Quattrone and A. Tversky, "Self-Deception and the Voter's Illusion," in *The Multiple Self*, ed. J. Elster (Cambridge: Cambridge Univ. Press, 1985), 35–57.

11 This assumes that many of the beliefs have common terms, as the beliefs of human beings invariably do.

12 This example is taken from W. Poundstone, *Labyrinths of Reason: Paradox, Puzzles, and the Frailty of Knowledge* (New York: Anchor Press, 1988), 183–88.

13 Recently, physical theories have been advanced that predict quantum computation across an infinite number of parallel universes (D. Deutsch, *The Fabric of Reality* [New York: Penguin, 1997]) or the possibility that all matter will one day be organized as an "omniscient" supercomputer

(F. Tipler, *The Physics of Immortality* [New York: Doubleday, 1995])
availing itself of a dilation of space-time resulting from the gravitational
collapse of the universe. I have excluded these and other theoretical
hierophanies from the present discussion.

14 Another way of getting at these logical and semantic constraints is to say
that our beliefs must be *systematic*. Systematicity is a property that
beliefs inherit from language, logic, and the world at large. Just as most
words derive their sense from the existence of other words, every belief
requires many others to situate it in a person's overall representation of
the world. How the loom of cognition first begins weaving is still a mystery, but there seems little doubt that we come hardwired with a variety
of proto-linguistic, proto-doxastic (from the Greek *doxa*, "belief") capacities that enable us to begin interpreting the tumult of the senses as regularities in the environment and in ourselves. We do not learn a language
by memorizing a list of unrelated phrases, and we do not form a view of
the world by adopting a string of unconnected beliefs. For a discussion of
the systematicity of language, see J. A. Fodor and Z. W. Pylyshyn, "Systematicity of Cognitive Representation," excerpt from "Connectionism
and Cognitive Architecture," in *Connections and Symbols*, ed. S. Pinker
and J. Mehler (Cambridge: MIT Press, 1988). A belief must be knitted
together with other beliefs for it to be a belief *about* anything at all. (I
have left aside, for the moment, whether there exist beliefs that do not
rely upon any others to derive their meaning. Whether or not such
atomic beliefs exist, it is clear that most of our beliefs are not of this sort.)

The systematicity of logic seems guaranteed by the following fact: if
a given proposition is "true," any proposition (or chain of reasoning) that
contradicts it must be "false." Such a requirement seems to mirror the
disposition of objects in the world, and therefore places logical constraints
upon our behavior. If a statement like "The cookies are in the cupboard"
is believed, it will become a principle of action—which is to say that when
I desire cookies, I will seek them in the cupboard. In the face of such a
belief, a contradictory claim like "The cupboard is bare" will be seen as
hostile to my forming a behavioral plan. Confident cookie-seeking
behavior requires that my beliefs have a certain logical relationship.

15 S. Pinker, *The Blank Slate* (New York: Viking, 2002), p. 33.

16 There is a point of contact between my remarks here and the "mental
models" account of reasoning developed by P. N. Johnson-Laird and R.
M. J. Byrne, *Deduction* (Hillsdale, N.J.: Erlbaum, 1991), chaps. 5–6. I
would note, however, that our mental models of objects in the world

behave as they do because objects do likewise. See L. Rips, "Deduction and Cognition," in *An Invitation to Cognitive Science: Thinking,* ed. E. E. Smith and D. N. Osherson (Cambridge: MIT Press, 1995), 297–343, for doubts about whether a concept like AND could be learned at all.

[17] Of course, we can think of examples where certain of our words run afoul of ordinary logic. For instance, one cannot put *the shadow of an apple* and *the shadow of an orange* in Jack's lunchbox, close the lid, and then expect to retrieve one or the other at the end of the day.

[18] Another property of belief follows directly from the nature of language: just as there is no limit to the number of sentences a person can potentially speak (language is often said to be "productive" in this sense), there is no limit to the number of beliefs he can potentially form about the world. Because I now believe that *there is no owl in my closet,* I also believe that there are not two owls there, or three . . . *ad infinitum.*

[19] Most neuroscientists believe that we have somewhere on the order of 10^{11}–10^{12} neurons, each of which makes an average of 10^4 connections with its neighbors. We therefore have something like 10^{15} or 10^{16} individual synapses. It's a big number, but it's still finite.

[20] Following N. Block, "The Mind as the Software of the Brain," in *An Invitation to Cognitive Science: Thinking,* ed. E. E. Smith and D. N. Osherson (Cambridge: MIT Press, 1995), 377–425.

[21] D. J. Simons et al., "Evidence for Preserved Representations in Change Blindness," *Consciousness and Cognition* 11, no. 1 (2002): 78–97; M. Niemeier et al., "A Bayesian Approach to Change Blindness," *Annals of the New York Academy of Sciences* 956 (2002): 474–75 [abstract].

[22] R. Kurzweil, *The Age of Spiritual Machines* (New York: Penguin, 1999).

[23] Consider a mathematical belief like $2 + 2 = 4$. Not only do most of us believe this proposition; this belief seems to be *antecedently* true of us in every present moment. We do not appear to construct it as the occasion warrants, rather it is by virtue of such rudimentary beliefs that we construct others. But what about a belief like $865762 + 2 = 865764$? Most of us will have never considered this sum before, and we will believe it only by virtue of constructing it according to the laws of arithmetic. And yet, doing so, we can cash it out just as we do the proposition $2 + 2 = 4$. Is there any difference between these two mathematical beliefs? In phenomenological terms there surely is. You will notice, for instance, that you cannot easily speak (or think) the longer sum, while *two plus two equals four* comes to mind almost reflexively. As far as our basic epistemic commitments are concerned, however, these beliefs are equally

"true." In fact, all of us stake our lives on the validity of far more complicated (and therefore less transparent) mathematical propositions every time we board an airplane or cross a bridge. At bottom, most of us believe that an operation like addition is *truth preserving*, in that it can be repeated over and over, and with arbitrarily large values, and still yield a true result. But the question remains, how can we know that our belief that $2 + 2 = 4$ isn't constructed anew each time we use it? How, in other words, do we know that we believe it *antecedently*? If we are tempted to say that this belief is always newly constructed, we must ask, constructed with *what*? The rules of addition? It seems doubtful that a person could know that he was successfully practicing addition unless he already believed that $2 + 2 = 4$. It seems just as certain, however, that you did not wake up this morning believing that *eight hundred and sixty-five thousand, seven hundred and sixty-two, plus two, equals eight hundred and sixty-five thousand, seven hundred and sixty-four*. To really exist inside your brain, this belief must be constructed, in the present moment, on the basis of your prior belief that *two plus two equals four*. Clearly, many beliefs are like this. We may not, in fact, believe most of what we believe about the world until we say we do.

24 See D. T. Gilbert et al., "Unbelieving the Unbelievable: Some Problems in the Rejection of False Information," *Journal of Personality and Social Psychology* 59 (1990): 601–13; D. T. Gilbert, "How Mental Systems Believe," *American Psychologist* 46, no. 2 (1991): 107–19.

25 This explains why beliefs that are *accidentally* true do not constitute knowledge, even when they are justified. As the philosopher Edmund Gettier observed long ago, we may believe something to be true (e.g., I may think the time is exactly 12:31 a.m.), we may believe it for good reasons (I am currently looking at a clock that reads 12:31 a.m.), and our belief may *be* true (it really is 12:31 a.m.), but we may not be in a state of knowledge about the world (because, in the present instance, the clock is broken and shows the correct time only by accident). While there are many philosophical niceties to be explored here, the basic fact is that for our beliefs to be truly *representative* of the world, they must stand in the right relationship *to* the world.

26 Questions of epistemology seem to be stirring here: How, after all, is it possible for us to have true knowledge of the world? Depending how one interprets words like "true" and "world," questions of this sort can seem either hopelessly difficult or trivial. As it turns out, a trivial reading will be good enough for our present purposes. Whatever reality is,

in ultimate terms, the world of our experience displays undeniable regularities. These regularities are of various kinds, of course, and some of them suggest lawful connections between certain events. There is a difference between mere *correlation*, and juxtapositions of the sort that we deem to be *causal*. As the Scottish philosopher David Hume famously noted, this presents an interesting puzzle, because we never encounter causes in the world, only reliable correlations. What, exactly, leads us to attribute causal power to certain events, while withholding it from others, is still a matter of debate. (See M. Wu and P. W. Cheng, "Why Causation Need Not Follow from Statistical Association: Boundary Conditions for the Evaluation of Generative and Preventative Causal Powers," *Psychological Science* 10 [1999]: 92–97.) And yet, once we have our beliefs about the world in hand, and they are guiding our behavior, there seems to be no mystery worth worrying about. It just so happens that certain regularities (those we deem to be causal), when adopted as guides to action, serve our purposes admirably; others that are equally regular (mere correlations, epiphenomena) do not. Surprises here simply lead to a reevaluation of causal roles and to the formation of new beliefs. We need not wrestle with Hume to know that if it is heat we want, it is better to seek fire than smoke; nor need we know all the criteria we employ in making causal judgments to appreciate the logical and behavioral implications of believing that A is the cause of B, while C is not. Once we find ourselves believing anything (whether for good or bad reasons), our words and actions demand that we rectify inconsistency wherever we find it.

[27] See H. Benson, with M. Stark, *Timeless Healing: The Power and Biology of Belief* (New York: Scribner, 1996).

[28] The shroud of Turin has been perhaps the most widely venerated relic of Christendom, for it is believed to be the very shroud in which the body of Jesus was wrapped for burial. In 1988 the Vatican allowed small sections of the shroud to be carbon-dated by three independent laboratories (Oxford University, University of Arizona, and the Federal Institute of Technology in Zurich) in a blind study coordinated by the British Museum. All three institutions concluded that the shroud was a medieval forgery dating from between 1260 and 1390.

[29] O. Friedrich, *The End of the World: A History* (New York: Coward, McCann & Geoghegan, 1982), 122–24.

[30] The quoted passage is found in *The Profession of Faith of the Roman Catholic Church*.

[31] This explicit belief has behavioral and neural underpinnings that are *implicit*, and clearly a matter of our genetic inheritance. Lower animals, it will be noted, are not in the habit of wandering off cliffs.

[32] K. Popper, *The Logic of Scientific Discovery* (1959; reprint, London: Routledge, 1972), and *Objective Knowledge* (1972; reprint, Oxford: Clarendon Press, 1995).

[33] T. Kuhn, *The Structure of Scientific Revolutions* (1962; reprint, Chicago: Univ. of Chicago Press, 1970).

[34] Popper and Kuhn both had some very interesting and useful things to say about the philosophy of science and about the problems we face in claiming to know how the world is, but one effect of their work, particularly on those who haven't read it, has been to engender the growth of ridiculous ideas across the quad. While there are genuine problems of epistemology to be thought about, there are gradations of reasonableness that can be appreciated by any sane person. Not all knowledge claims are on the same footing.

[35] B. Russell, *Why I Am Not a Christian*, ed. P. Edwards (New York: Simon and Schuster 1957), 35.

[36] J. Glover, *Humanity: A Moral History of the Twentieth Century* (New Haven: Yale Univ. Press, 1999), strikes the same note. See also A. N. Yakovlev, *A Century of Violence in Soviet Russia* (New Haven: Yale Univ. Press, 2002).

3   In the Shadow of God

[1] "As to squassation, it is thus performed: The prisoner hath his hands bound behind his back, and weights tied to his feet, and then is drawn up on high, till his head reaches the pulley. He is kept hanging in this manner for some time, that by the greatness of the weight hanging at his feet, all his joints and limbs may be dreadfully stretched, and on a sudden he is let down with a jerk, by the slackening of the rope, but is kept from coming quite to the ground, by which terrible shake, his arms and legs are disjointed, whereby he is put to the most exquisite pain; the shock which he receives by the sudden stop of his fall, and the weight at his feet stretching his whole body more intensely and cruelly." John Marchant, cited in J. Swain, *The Pleasures of the Torture Chamber* (New York: Dorset Press, 1931), 169.

[2] Ibid., 174–75, 178.

3 See Swain, *Pleasures*; O. Friedrich, *The End of the World: A History* (New York: Coward, McCann & Geoghegan, 1982); and L. George, *Crimes of Perception: An Encyclopedia of Heresies and Heretics* (New York: Paragon House, 1995).

4 For explicit mention of heresy in the New Testament, and of the natural intolerance of the faithful to dissent, see 1 Cor. 11:19; Gal. 5:20; 2 Pet. 2:1; Rom. 16:17; 1 Cor. 1:10, 3:3, 14:33; Phil. 4:2; and Jude 19.

5 We need only recall the fate of William Tyndale, which came as late as 1536, after he published his translation of the New Testament in English:

> Then, believing himself safe, he settled in Antwerp. However, he had underestimated the gravity of his offense and the persistence of his sovereign [Henry VIII, in a pious mood]. British agents had never ceased stalking him. Now they arrested him. At Henry's insistence he was imprisoned for sixteen months in the castle of Vilvorde, near Brussels, tried for heresy, and, after his conviction, publicly garrotted. His corpse was burned at the stake, an admonition for any who might have been tempted by his folly.

See W. Manchester, *A World Lit Only by Fire: The Medieval Mind and the Renaissance* (Boston: Little, Brown, 1992), 204.

6 The Bible, however, demands that there be at least two witnesses attesting that the accused has "served other gods," and that they be the first to stone him (Deut. 17:6–7). The Inquisition was forced, for the sake of efficiency, to relax this standard.

7 Matt. 5:18.

8 Friedrich, *End of the World*, 70.

9 The Franciscans, it is true, shouldered their share of the burden. As Russell wrote in *A History of Western Philosophy* (New York: Simon and Schuster, 1945), 450:

> If Satan existed, the future of the order founded by Saint Francis would afford him the most exquisite gratification. The saint's immediate successor as head of the order, Brother Elias, wallowed in luxury, and allowed complete abandonment of poverty. The chief work of the Franciscans in the years immediately following the death of their founder was as recruiting sergeants in the bitter and bloody wars of Guelfs and Ghibellines. The Inquisition, founded seven years after his death, was, in several countries, chiefly conducted by Franciscans. A small minority, called the Spirituals, remained true to his teaching;

many of these were burnt by the Inquisition for heresy. These men held that Christ and the Apostles owned no property, not even the clothes they wore; this opinion was condemned as heretical in 1323 by John XXII. The net result of Saint Francis' life was to create yet one more wealthy and corrupt order, to strengthen the hierarchy, and to facilitate the persecution of all who excelled in moral earnestness or freedom of thought. In view of his own aims and character, it is impossible to imagine any more bitterly ironical outcome.

10 Friedrich, *End of the World*, 74.

11 Ibid., 96.

12 Compare much of what Jesus taught with the above quotation from John 15:6, or with Matt. 10:34—"Think not that I am come to send peace on earth: I came not to send peace, but a sword." For a remarkably elegant demonstration of the incoherency of the Bible, I recommend Burr's *Self-contradictions of the Bible* (1860). In it, Burr presents 144 propositions— theological, moral, historical, and speculative—all neatly opposed by their antitheses, in the following manner: *God is seen and heard/God is invisible and cannot be heard; God is everywhere present, sees and knows all things/God is not everywhere present, neither sees nor knows all things; God is the author of evil/God is not the author of evil; Adultery forbidden/adultery allowed; The father of Joseph, Mary's husband, was Jacob/The father of Mary's husband was Heli; The infant Christ was taken into Egypt/The infant Christ was not taken into Egypt; John was in prison when Jesus went into Galilee/John was not in prison when Jesus went into Galilee; Jesus was crucified at the third hour/Jesus was crucified at the sixth hour; Christ is equal with God/Christ is not equal with God; It is impossible to fall from grace/It is possible to fall from grace;* etc.—all with supporting quotations from the Old and New Testaments. Many of these passages represent perfect contradictions (that is, one cannot affirm the truth of one without equally asserting the falsity of the other). There is, perhaps, no greater evidence for the imperfection of the Bible as an account of reality, divine or mundane, than such instances of self-refutation. Of course, once faith has begun its reign of folly, even perfect contradictions may be relished as heavenly rebukes to earthly logic. Martin Luther closed the door on reason with a single line: "The Holy Spirit has an eye only to substance and is not bound by words." The Holy Spirit, it seems, is happy to play tennis without the net.

13 It is true that Augustine was not a perfect sadist. He thought that

heretics should be examined "not by stretching them on the rack, not by scorching them with flames or furrowing their flesh with iron claws, but by beating them with rods." See P. Johnson, *A History of Christianity* (New York: Simon and Schuster, 1976), 116–17.

14 Voltaire, "Inquisition," *Philosophical Dictionary*, ed and trans. T. Bester-man (London: Penguin Books, 1972), 256.

15 From *The Percy Anecdotes*, cited in Swain, *Pleasures*, 181.

16 Manchester, *A World Lit Only by Fire*, 190–93.

17 W. Durant, *The Age of Faith* (1950; reprint, Norwalk, Conn.: Easton Press, 1992), 784.

18 The Christians, while they were still a lowly sect, had been accused of the same crime by pagan Romans. There were, in fact, many points of con-vergence between witches and Jews in the mind of medieval Christians. Jews were regularly accused of sorcery, and magical texts were often attributed (speciously) to Solomon and to a variety of kabbalistic sources.

19 R. Briggs, *Witches and Neighbors: The Social and Cultural Context of European Witchcraft* (New York: Viking, 1996), 8, has this to say on the subject:

> On the wilder shores of the feminist and witch-cult movements a potent myth has become established, to the effect that 9 million women were burned as witches in Europe; gendercide rather than genocide. This is an overestimate by a factor of up to 200, for the most reasonable modern estimates suggest perhaps 100,000 trials between 1450 and 1750, with something between 40,000 and 50,000 execu-tions, of which 20 to 25 per cent were men.

Such a revaluation of numbers does little to mitigate the horror and injustice of this period. Even to read of the Salem witch trials, which resulted in the hanging of "only" nineteen people, is to be brought face to face with the seemingly boundless evil that is apt to fill the voids in our understanding of the world.

20 C. Mackay, *Extraordinary Popular Delusions and the Madness of Crowds* (1841; reprint, New York: Barnes & Noble, 1993), 529.

21 R. Rhodes, *Deadly Feasts: Tracking the Secrets of a Terrifying New Plague* (New York: Simon and Schuster, 1997), 78.

22 There is some doubt as to whether the Fore, or any other people for that matter, ever practiced systematic cannibalism (see the entry "cannibal-ism" in *The Oxford Companion to the Body*). If these doubts are borne out, an alternative explanation for the transmission of kuru would have

to be found. But it should go without saying that its vector was not sorcery. Scholarly doubts about cannibalism seem somewhat far-fetched, however, given the widespread evidence of it among modern African militias in countries like Congo, Uganda, Liberia, Angola, and elsewhere. In such places, magical beliefs remain widespread—like the notion that eating your enemy's organs can make you immune to bullets. See D. Bergner, "The Most Unconventional Weapon," *New York Times Magazine*, March 26, 2003, pp. 48–53.

23 Friedrich Spee (1631), cited in Johnson, *History of Christianity*, 311.

24 Mackay, *Delusions*, 540–41.

25 B. Russell, *Religion and Science* (1935; reprint, Oxford: Oxford Univ. Press, 1997), 95.

26 Mackay, *Delusions*, 525–26.

27 "Anti-Semitism," like the term "Aryan," is a misnomer of nineteenth-century German pseudo-science. *Semitic* (derived from *Shem*, one of Noah's three sons) "designated a group of cognate languages that included Hebrew, Arabic, Aramaic, Babylonian, Assyrian and Ethiopic, not an ethnic or racial group." See R. S. Wistrich, *Anti-Semitism: The Longest Hatred* (New York: Schocken Books, 1991), xvi. "Anti-Semitism" should therefore denote a hatred of Arabs as well, which it does not. Despite its mistaken roots, "anti-Semitism" has become the only acceptable term for the hatred of Jews.

28 D. J. Wakin, "Anti-Semitic 'Elders of Zion' Gets New Life on Egypt TV," *New York Times*, Oct. 26, 2002. This spurious document is actually cited in the founding covenant of Hamas. See J. I. Kertzer, "The Modern Use of Ancient Lies," *New York Times*, May 9, 2002.

29 E. Goldberg, *The Executive Brain: Frontal Lobes and the Civilized Mind* (Oxford: Oxford Univ. Press, 2001).

30 This said, Judaism is a far less fertile source of militant extremism. Jews tend not to draw their identity as Jews exclusively from the contents of their beliefs about God. It is possible, for instance, to be a practicing Jew who does *not* believe in God. The same cannot be said for Christianity and Islam.

31 See B. M. Metzger and M. D. Coogan, eds., *The Oxford Companion to the Bible* (Oxford: Oxford Univ. Press, 1993), 789–90, and A. N. Wilson, *Jesus: A Life* (New York: W. W. Norton, 1992), 79. Many other uncouth pairings have been pointed out: Matt. 2:3–5 and Micah 5:2; Matt. 2:16–18 and Jer. 31:15/Gen. 35:19; Matt. 8:18 and Isa. 53:4; Matt. 12:18 and Isa. 42:1–4; Matt. 13:35 and Ps. 78:2; Matt. 21:5f. and Zech. 9:9/Isa. 62:11.

Matt. 27:9–10 claims to fulfill a saying that it erroneously attributes to Jeremiah, which actually appears in Zech. 11:12—providing further evidence of the text's "inerrancy."

[32] The stigma attached to illegitimacy among Jews in the first century CE was considerable. See S. Mitchell, *The Gospel According to Jesus* (New York: HarperCollins, 1991).

[33] See ibid., 78, and J. Pelikan, *Jesus through the Centuries* (New York: Harper and Row, 1987), 80.

[34] B. Pascal, *Pensées*, trans. A. J. Krailsheimer (Baltimore: Penguin Books, 1966), sec. 189.

[35] Nietzsche had it right when he wrote, "The most pitiful example: the corruption of Pascal, who believed in the corruption of his reason through original sin when it had in fact been corrupted only by his Christianity" (*The Portable Nietzsche*, trans. W. Kaufmann [New York: Viking, 1954], 572). It is true that Pascal had what was for him an astonishing contemplative experience on the night of Nov. 23, 1654—one that converted him entirely to Jesus Christ. I do not doubt the power of such experiences, but it seems to me self-evident that they are no more the exclusive property of devout Christians than are tears shed in joy. Hindus, Buddhists, Muslims, Jews, along with animists of every description have had these experiences throughout history. Pascal, being highly intelligent and greatly learned, should have known this; that he did not (or chose to disregard it) testifies to the stultifying effect of orthodoxy.

[36] They also avenged themselves against their Roman persecutors: "The Christians threw Maximian's wife into the Orontes, and put to death all his relatives. In Egypt and Palestine they massacred the magistrates who had most strongly opposed Christianity. The widow and daughter of Diocletian, having taken refuge in Thessalonica, were recognized, and their bodies were thrown into the sea." Voltaire, "Christianity," *Philosophical Dictionary*, 137.

[37] Wistrich, *Anti-Semitism*, 19–20.

[38] Augustine (*The City of God*, XVIII, 46):

> Therefore, when they do not believe our Scriptures, their own, which they blindly read, are fulfilled in them, lest perchance any one should say that the Christians have forged these prophecies about Christ which are quoted under the name of the sibyl, or of others, if such there be, who do not belong to the Jewish people. For us, indeed, those suffice which are quoted from the books of our enemies, to whom we

make our acknowledgment, on account of this testimony which, in spite of themselves, they contribute by their possession of these books, while they themselves are dispersed among all nations, wherever the Church of Christ is spread abroad. For a prophecy about this thing was sent before in the Psalms, which they also read, where it is written, "My God, His mercy shall prevent me. My God hath shown me concerning mine enemies, that Thou shalt not slay them, lest they should at last forget Thy law: disperse them in Thy might" [Ps. 69:10–11]. Therefore God has shown the Church in her enemies the Jews the grace of His compassion, since, as saith the apostle, "their offense is the salvation of the Gentiles" [Rom. 11:11]. And therefore He has not slain them, that is, He has not let the knowledge that they are Jews be lost in them, although they have been conquered by the Romans, lest they should forget the law of God, and their testimony should be of no avail in this matter of which we treat. But it was not enough that he should say, "Slay them not, lest they should at last forget Thy law," unless he has also added, "Disperse them"; because if they had only been in their own land with that testimony of the Scriptures, and everywhere, certainly the Church which is everywhere could not have had them as witnesses among all nations to the prophecies which were sent before concerning Christ.

[39] See J. Trachtenberg, *The Devil and the Jews: The Medieval Conception of the Jew and Its Relation to Modern Anti-Semitism* (1943; reprint, Philadelphia: Jewish Publication Society, 1983), 153.

[40] Ibid., 140.

[41] Ibid., 114. The Reformation, by undermining belief in the doctrine of transubstantiation, seems to have rendered host desecration less of a concern. Thus, it was during the schismatic sixteenth century that the persecution of Jews as "sorcerers" came into its own.

[42] The Egyptian paper *Al Akhbar* and the Saudi paper *Al Riyadh* have both published articles purporting to verify the blood libel. The Syrian defense minister Mustafa Tlas has written a book, *The Matzoh of Zion*, charging the Jews with ritual murder. Nazi propaganda on the subject, dating from the 1930s, now appears on Islamist websites. See Kertzer, "Modern Use."

[43] Cited in J. Glover, *Humanity: A Moral History of the Twentieth Century* (New Haven: Yale Univ. Press, 1999), 328.

[44] Ibid., 360–61.

45 D. J. Goldhagen, *Hitler's Willing Executioners: Ordinary Germans and the Holocaust* (New York: Alfred A. Knopf, 1996), 28–48.

46 Kertzer, "Modern Use."

47 It has grown fashionable to assert that the true horror of the Holocaust, apart from its scale, was that it was an expression of *reason*, and that it therefore demonstrates a pathology inherent to the Western Enlightenment tradition. The truth of this assertion is held by many scholars to be self-evident—for no one can deny that technology, bureaucracy, and systematic managerial thinking made the genocidal ambitions of the Third Reich possible. The romantic thesis lurking here is that reason itself has a "shadow side" and is therefore no place to turn for the safeguarding of human happiness. This is a terrible misunderstanding of the situation, however. The Holocaust marked the culmination of German tribalism and two thousand years of Christian fulminating against the Jews. Reason had nothing to do with it. Put a telescope in the hands of a chimpanzee, and if he bashes his neighbor over the head with it, reason's "shadow side" will have been equally revealed. (K. Wilber, *Sex, Ecology, Spirituality* [Boston: Shambhala, 1995], 663–64, makes the same point.)

48 M. Gilbert, *The Holocaust: A History of the Jews of Europe during the Second World War* (New York: Henry Holt, 1985), 22.

49 Ibid.

50 Quoted in G. Wills, "Before the Holocaust," *New York Times Book Review*, Sept. 23, 2001.

51 Quoted in Goldhagen, *Hitler's Willing Executioners*, 106. Of course, Church-mandated anti-Semitism was not confined to Germany. Consider the statement of the Roman Catholic primate of Poland, August Cardinal Hlond, in a 1936 pastoral letter: "There will be the Jewish problem as long as the Jews remain. It is a fact the Jews are fighting against the Catholic Church, persisting in free thinking, and are the vanguard of godlessness, Bolshevism, and subversion. . . . It is a fact that the Jews deceive, levy interest, and are pimps. It is a fact that the religious and ethical influence of the Jewish young people on the Polish young people is a negative one." As J. Carroll, "The Silence," *New Yorker*, April 7, 1997, points out, "Hlond's letter was careful to say that these 'facts' did not justify the murder of Jews, but it is hard to see how such anti-Semitism on the part of the leading Catholic in Poland was unconnected with what followed. Over the decades and centuries of this millennium such sentiments expressed by Christian leaders were not unusual."

[52] G. Lewy, *The Catholic Church and Nazi Germany* (New York: McGraw-Hill, 1964), 282, quoted in Goldhagen, *Hitler's Willing Executioners*, 110.

[53] Cited in L. George, *Crimes of Perception: An Encyclopedia of Heresies and Heretics* (New York: Paragon House, 1995), 211.

[54] Pope John Paul II, *Crossing the Threshold of Hope* (New York: Alfred A. Knopf, 1994), 10. This book really is a breathtaking piece of sophistry, evasion, and narrow-mindedness. It demonstrates my thesis in almost every line, erudite references to Wittgenstein, Feuerbach, and Ricoeur notwithstanding.

[55] M. Aarons and J. Loftus, *Unholy Trinity: The Vatican, the Nazis, and the Swiss Banks*, rev. ed. (New York: St. Martin's Griffin, 1998); G. Sereny, *Into That Darkness: An Examination of Conscience* (New York: Vintage, 1974).

[56] See Sereny, *Into That Darkness*, 318.

[57] See, e.g., Glover, *Humanity*, chap. 40.

4 The Problem with Islam

[1] As we saw in chapter 2, this is a direct consequence of what it means—logically, psychologically, and behaviorally—to believe that our beliefs actually represent the way the world is. The moment you believe that religious (or spiritual, or ethical) propositions say anything at all of substance, you will be obliged to admit that they can be more or less accurate, comprehensive, or useful. Hierarchies of this sort are built into the very structure the world. We will take a closer look at ethics in chapter 6.

[2] R. A. Pape, "The Strategic Logic of Suicide Terrorism," *American Political Science Review* 97, no. 3 (2003): 20–32, has argued that suicidal terrorism is best understood as a strategic means to achieve certain well-defined nationalist goals and should not be considered a consequence of religious ideology. In support of this thesis, he recounts the manner in which Hamas and Islamic Jihad have systematically used suicide bombings to extract concessions from the Israeli government. Pape argues that had these organizations been merely "irrational" or "fanatic," we would not expect to see such a calculated use of violence. Their motivation must be, therefore, primarily nationalistic. Like most commentators on this infernal wastage of human life, Pape seems unable to imagine what it would be like to actually *believe* what millions of Muslims profess to believe. The fact that terrorist groups have demonstrable, short-term goals does not in the least suggest that they are not

primarily motivated by their religious dogmas. Pape claims that "the most important goal that a community can have is the independence of its homeland (population, property, and way of life) from foreign influence or control." But he overlooks the fact that these communities define themselves in *religious* terms. Pape's analysis is particularly inapposite with respect to Al Qaeda. To attribute "territorial" and "nationalistic" motives to Osama bin Laden seems almost willfully obscurantist, since Osama's only apparent concerns are the spread of Islam and the sanctity of Muslim holy sites. Suicide bombing, in the Muslim world at least, is an explicitly religious phenomenon that is inextricable from notions of martyrdom and jihad, predictable on their basis, and sanctified by their logic. It is no more secular an activity than prayer is.

3 B. Lewis, *The Crisis of Islam: Holy War and Unholy Terror* (New York: Modern Library, 2003), 32.

4 M. Ruthven, *Islam in the World*, 2d ed. (Oxford: Oxford Univ. Press, 2000), 7.

5 Some of these hadiths are cited in Lewis, *Crisis of Islam*, 32. Others are drawn from an Internet database: www.usc.edu/dept/MSA/reference/searchhadith.html.

6 Lewis, *Crisis of Islam*, 55.

7 "Idolatry is worse than carnage" (Koran 2:190). The rule of the Mogul emperor Akbar (1556–1605) offers an exception here, but it is merely that Akbar's tolerance of Hinduism was a frank violation of Islamic law.

8 F. Zakaria, *The Future of Freedom: Illiberal Democracy at Home and Abroad* (New York: W. W. Norton, 2003), 126.

9 See A. Dershowitz, *The Case for Israel* (Hoboken, N.J.: John Wiley, 2003), 61.

10 These facts and dates are drawn from R. S. Wistrich, *Anti-Semitism: The Longest Hatred* (New York: Schocken Books, 1991), and Dershowitz, *Case for Israel.*

11 L. Binder, *Islamic Liberalism: A Critique of Development Ideologies* (Chicago: Univ. of Chicago Press, 1988), 129.

12 A. Cowell, "Zeal for Suicide Bombing Reaches British Midland," *New York Times*, May 2, 2003. Consider the case of England: British Muslims have been found fighting with the Taliban, plotting terror attacks in Yemen, attempting to blow up airplanes, and kidnapping and killing Western journalists in Pakistan. Recently, two British citizens volunteered for suicide missions in Israel (one succeeded, one failed).

Terrorist Hunter (New York: HarperCollins, 2003), whose anonymous author has gone undercover to tape the proceedings at Muslim conferences in the United States, depicts a shocking level of intolerance among Muslims living in the West. The author reports that at one conference, held at the Ramada Plaza hotel in suburban Chicago, Arab American children performed skits in which they killed Jews and became martyrs. Sheikh Ikrima Sabri, the grand mufti of Jerusalem and Palestine (appointed by Yasir Arafat), recently announced, "The Jews do not dare to bother me, because they are the most cowardly creatures Allah has ever created. . . . We tell them: In as much as you love life, the Muslim loves death and martyrdom" (ibid., 134). Sabri, who regularly calls for the destruction of America and all infidel nations, and encourages child suicide bombers ("The younger the martyr, the more I respect him"—ibid., 132), spoke these words not in a mosque on the West Bank but at the Twenty-sixth Annual Convention of the Islamic Circle of North America, in Cleveland, Ohio.

[13] Lewis, *Crisis of Islam*, xxviii.

[14] Ruthven, *Islam in the World*, 137.

[15] Yosuf Islam, in his wisdom, had this to say in a written response to those who were shocked by his apparent endorsement of Khomeini's fatwa:

> Under Islamic Law, the ruling regarding blasphemy is quite clear; the person found guilty of it must be put to death. Only under certain circumstances can repentance be accepted. . . . The fact is that as far as the application of Islamic Law and the implementation of full Islamic way of life in Britain is concerned, Muslims realize that there is very little chance of that happening in the near future. But that shouldn't stop us from trying to improve the situation and presenting the Islamic viewpoint wherever and whenever possible. That is the duty of every Muslim and that is what I did.

(See catstevens.com/articles/00013). If even a Western educated ex-hippie was talking this way, what do you think the sentiments were on the streets of Tehran?

[16] K. H. Pollack, "'The Crisis of Islam': Faith and Terrorism in the Muslim World," *New York Times Book Review*, April 6, 2003.

[17] As Thomas Carlyle (1795–1881) wrote, "I must say, it is as toilsome reading as I ever undertook. A wearisome confused jumble, crude, incondite; endless iterations, longwindedness, entanglement . . . insupportable stupidity, in short! Nothing but a sense of duty could carry any European through the Koran!" Cited in Ruthven, *Islam in the World*, 81–82.

[18] Cited in P. Berman, *Terror and Liberalism* (New York: W. W. Norton, 2003), 68.

[19] www.people-press.org.

[20] Christopher Luxenberg (this is a pseudonym), a scholar of ancient Semitic languages, has recently argued that a mistranslation is responsible for furnishing the Muslim paradise with "virgins" (Arabic *hur*, transliterated as "houris"—literally "white ones"). It seems that the passages describing paradise in the Koran were drawn from earlier Christian texts that make frequent use of the Aramaic word *hur*, meaning "white raisins." White raisins, it seems, were a great delicacy in the ancient world. Imagine the look on a young martyr's face when, finding himself in a paradise teeming with his fellow thugs, his seventy houris arrive as a fistful of raisins. See A. Stille, "Scholars Are Quietly Offering New Theories of the Koran," *New York Times*, March 2, 2002.

[21] S. P. Huntington, *The Clash of Civilizations and the Remaking of World Order* (New York: Simon and Schuster, 1996).

[22] E. W. Said, "The Clash of Ignorance," *Nation*, Oct. 4, 2001.

[23] E. W. Said, "Suicidal Ignorance," *CounterPunch*, Nov. 18, 2001.

[24] For an alarming look at the rising political influence of Christianity in the developing world, see P. Jenkins, "The Next Christianity," *Atlantic Monthly*, Oct. 2002, pp. 53–68.

[25] From the United Nations' *Arab Human Development Report 2002*, cited in Lewis, *Crisis of Islam*, 115–17.

[26] See R. D. Kaplan, "The Lawless Frontier," *Atlantic Monthly*, March 2000, pp. 66–80.

[27] S. Atran, "Opinion: Who Wants to Be a Martyr?" *New York Times*, May 5, 2003. Atran also reports that a Pakistani relief worker interviewed nearly 250 aspiring Palestinian suicide bombers and their recruiters and concluded, "None were uneducated, desperately poor, simple-minded or depressed. . . . They all seemed to be entirely normal members of their families." He also cites a 2001 poll conducted by the Palestinian Center for Policy and Survey Research indicating "that Palestinian adults with 12 years or more of education are far more likely to support bomb attacks than those who cannot read."

[28] B. Hoffman, "The Logic of Suicide Terrorism," *Atlantic Monthly*, June 2003, pp. 40–47.

[29] Indeed, this may be happening in Iran. Having truly achieved a Muslim theocracy, the Iranian people now have few illusions that their problems are the result of their insufficient conformity to Islam.

30 Zakaria, *Future of Freedom*, cites a CNN poll (Feb. 2002) conducted across nine Muslim countries. Some 61 percent of those polled said they do not believe that Arabs were responsible for the Sept. 11 attacks. No doubt the 39 percent who thought otherwise represent millions who wish the Arab world would take credit for a job well done.

31 It would be impossible to do justice to the richness of the Muslim imagination in the context of this book. To take only one preposterous example: it seems that many Iraqis believe that the widespread looting that occurred after the fall of Saddam's regime was orchestrated by Americans and Israelis, as part of a Zionist plot. The attacks upon American soldiers were carried out by CIA agents "as part of a covert operation to justify prolonging the U.S. military occupation." Wow! See J. L. Anderson, "Iraq's Bloody Summer," *New Yorker*, Aug. 11, 2003, pp. 43–55.

32 Berman, *Terror and Liberalism*, 153.

33 Also see M. B. Zuckerman, "Graffiti on History's Walls," *U.S. News and World Report*, Nov. 3, 2003, for an account of anti-Semitism in the mainstream European press.

34 Dershowitz, *Case for Israel*, 2.

35 This miraculous ascension (*mi'raj*) is fully described only in the hadith, though it may be alluded to in the Koran (17:1). The likening of the Israelis to the Nazis is especially egregious, given that the Palestinians distinguished themselves as Nazi collaborators during the war years. Their calculated attacks upon Jews in the 1930s and 1940s led to the deaths of hundreds of the thousands of European Jews who would otherwise have been permitted to immigrate by the British. This result does not appear to have been inadvertent. Hajj Amin al-Husseini, the grand mufti of Jerusalem and the leader of the Palestinians throughout the war years, served as an adviser to the Nazis on the Jewish question, was given a personal tour of Auschwitz by Heinrich Himmler, and aspired to open his own death camp for the Jews in Palestine once the Germans had won the war. These activities were well publicized and merely increased his popularity in the Arab world when, as a war criminal sought by the Allies, he was given asylum in Egypt. As recently as 2002, Yasser Arafat, the head of the Palestinian Authority, referred to Husseini as a "hero." See Dershowitz, *Case for Israel*, 56.

36 Berman, *Terror and Liberalism*, 183.

37 Ibid., 206–7.

38 See ibid., 108: "Khomeini whipped up a religious fervor for that kind of mass death—a belief that to die on Khomeini's orders in a human wave

attack was to achieve the highest and most beautiful of destinies. All over Iran young men, encouraged by their mothers and their families, yearned to participate in those human wave attacks—actively yearned for martyrdom. It was a mass movement for suicide. The war was one of the most macabre events that has ever occurred. . . ."

39 Ibid.

40 J. Baudrillard, *The Spirit of Terrorism*, trans. C. Turner (New York: Verso, 2002).

41 It may seem strange to encounter phrases like "our enemies," uttered without apparent self-consciousness, and it is strange for me to write them. But there is no doubt that enemies are what we have (and I leave it for the reader to draw the boundaries of "we" as broadly or narrowly as he or she likes). The liberal fallacy that I will attempt to unravel in the present section is the notion that we *made* these enemies and that we are, therefore, their "moral equivalent." We are not. An analysis of their religious ideology reveals that we are confronted by people who would have put us to sword, had they had the power, long before the World Bank, the International Monetary Fund, and the World Trade Organization were even a gleam in the eye of the first rapacious globalizer.

42 N. Chomsky, *9–11* (New York: Seven Stories Press, 2001), 119.

43 P. Unger, *Living High & Letting Die: Our Illusion of Innocence* (Oxford: Oxford Univ. Press, 1996).

44 A. Roy, *War Talk* (Cambridge, Mass.: South End Press, 2003), 84–85.

45 J. Glover, *Humanity: A Moral History of the Twentieth Century* (New Haven: Yale Univ. Press, 1999), 58.

46 Ibid., 62.

47 Are intentions really the bottom line? What are we to say, for instance, about those Christian missionaries in the New World who baptized Indian infants only to promptly kill them, thereby sending them to heaven? Their intentions were (apparently) good. Were their actions ethical? Yes, within the confines of a deplorably limited worldview. The medieval apothecary who gave his patients quicksilver really was trying to help. He was just mistaken about the role this element played in the human body. Intentions matter, but they are not all that matters.

48 Zakaria, *Future of Freedom*, 138.

49 Ibid., 143.

50 Ibid., 123.

51 Ibid., 150.

52 Robert Kaplan, "Supremacy by Stealth," *Atlantic Monthly*, Jan. 2003, pp.

65–83, has made a strong case that interventions of this sort should be almost entirely *covert* and will, for the foreseeable future, be the responsibility of the United States to carry out.

[53] Glover, *Humanity*, 140.

[54] M. Rees, *Our Final Hour* (New York: Basic Books, 2003), 42.

5 *West of Eden*

[1] "At a 1971 dinner, Reagan told California legislator James Mills that 'everything is in place for the battle of Armageddon and the Second Coming of Christ.' The President has permitted Jerry Falwell to attend National Security Council briefings and author and Armageddon-advocate Hal Lindsey to give a talk on nuclear war with Russia to top Pentagon strategists." Cited in E. Johnson, "Grace Halsell's Prophecy and Politics: Militant Evangelists on the Road to Nuclear War," *Journal of Historical Review* 7, no. 4 (Winter 1986).

[2] See G. Gorenberg, *The End of Days: Fundamentalism and the Struggle for the Temple Mount* (Oxford: Oxford Univ. Press, 2000), for a lengthy analysis.

[3] Ibid., p. 80.

[4] "Justic Roy Moore's Lawless Battle," editorial to *New York Times*, Dec. 17, 2002.

[5] Frank Rich, "Religion for Dummies," *New York Times*, April 23, 2002.

[6] www.gallup.com.

[7] Rich, "Religion." See also F. Clarkson, *Eternal Hostility: The Struggle between Theocracy and Democracy* (Monroe, Maine: Common Courage Press, 1997).

[8] E. Bumiller, "Evangelicals Sway White House on Human Rights Issues Abroad," *New York Times*, Oct. 26, 2003.

[9] C. Mooney, "W.'s Christian Nation," *American Prospect*, June 1, 2003. Also see the website for Americans United for Separation of Church and State (www.au.org).

[10] One of the concerns with giving federal funds to religious organizations is that these organizations are not bound by the same equal employment opportunity regulations that apply to the rest of the nonprofit world. Church groups can ban homosexuals, people who have divorced and remarried, those who have married interracially, etc., and still receive federal funds. They can also find creative ways to use these funds to proselytize. Granting such funds in the first place puts the federal govern-

ment in the position of deciding what is, and what isn't, a genuine religion—a responsibility that seems fraught with problems of its own.

[11] M. Dowd, "Tribulation Worketh Patience," *New York Times*, April 9, 2003.

[12] W. M. Arkin, "The Pentagon Unleashes a Holy Warrior," *Los Angeles Times*, Oct. 16, 2003.

[13] J. Hendren, "Religious Groups Want Outspoken General Punished,"*Los Angeles Times*, Oct. 17, 2003.

[14] G. H. Gallup Jr., *Religion in America 1996* (Princeton: Princeton Religion Research Center, 1996).

[15] Paul Krugman, "Gotta Have Faith," *New York Times*, April 27, 2002.

[16] A. Scalia, "God's Justice and Ours," *First Things*, May 2002, pp. 17–21.

[17] www.gallup.com/poll/releases/pro30519.asp.

[18] Mooney, "W.'s Christian Nation."

[19] See Scalia's dissent to *Daryl Renard Atkins, Petitioner, v. Virginia*, on writ of certiorari to the supreme court of Virginia, June 20, 2002.

[20] See Scalia's dissent to *John Geddes Lawrence and Tyron Garner, Petitioners v. Texas*, on writ of certiorari to the court of appeals of Texas, fourteenth district, June 26, 2003.

[21] Ted Bundy claimed, on the eve of his execution, that violent pornography had inscribed certain terrible ideas indelibly into his head. See R. Shattuck, *Forbidden Knowledge: From Prometheus to Pornography* (New York: St. Martin's Press, 1996), for a discussion of this.

[22] There is a distinction between public and private freedoms that I have glossed over here. Clearly, there are innumerable behaviors that are blameless in private that we ban in most public spaces, simply because they pose a nuisance to others. Cooking food on a public sidewalk, cutting one's hair on a commercial aircraft, or taking one's pet snake to the movies are among the countless examples of private freedoms that do not translate into public virtues.

[23] Happily, the ruling by the Supreme Court in *Lawrence and Garner v. Texas* seems to have rendered these laws unconditional (see www.cnn.com/2003/LAW/06/26/scotus.sodomy).

[24] Viewing the drug problem from the perspective of health care is instructive: our laws against providing addicts with clean needles have increased the spread of AIDS, hepatitis C, and other blood-borne diseases. Since the purity and dosage of illegal drugs remains a matter of guesswork for the user, the rates of poisoning and overdose from drug use are unnecessarily high (as they were for alcohol during Prohibition). Perversely, the criminal prohibition of drugs has actually made it easier for minors to get

them, because the market for them has been driven underground. The laws limiting the medical use of opiate painkillers do little more than keep the terminally ill suffering unnecessarily during their last months of life.

25 L. Carroll, "Fetal Brains Suffer Badly from the Effects of Alcohol," *New York Times*, Nov. 4, 2003.

26 www.drugwarfacts.com.

27 www.rand.org/publications/RB/RB6010/.

28 These events are described in E. Schlosser, *Reefer Madness: Sex, Drugs, and Cheap Labor in the American Black Market* (New York: Houghton Mifflin, 2003).

29 Some 51 percent of all violent offenders are released from jail after serving two years or less, and 76 percent were released after serving four years or less (www.lp.org). At the federal level, the average sentence for a drug offense in the U.S. is $6^1/_4$ years (from the Office of National Drug Control Policy [ONDCP] *Drug Data Summary*, www.whitehousedrugpolicy.gov).

30 And yet, this mountain of imponderables reaches higher still. In many states, a person who has been merely *accused* of a drug crime can have his property seized, and those who informed against him can be rewarded with up to 25 percent of its value. The rest of these spoils go to police departments, which now rely upon such property seizures to meet their budgets. This is precisely the arrangement of incentives that led to this sort of corruption during the Inquisition (if one can even speak of such a process being "corrupted"). Like the heretic, the accused drug offender has no hope but to trade information for a reduced sentence. The person who can't (or won't) implicate others inevitably faces punishments of fantastical severity. Information has grown so valuable, in fact, that a black market for it has emerged. Defendants who have no information to trade can actually buy drug leads from professional informers (and they do not come cheap). The net result of all this is that police departments have learned to target property rather than crime. Property can be seized and forfeited even if a defendant is ultimately found innocent of any criminal offense. One national survey found that 80 percent of property seizures occur without any criminal prosecution whatsoever (www.drugwarfacts.com). Under these enlightened laws, couples in their eighties have permanently lost their homes because a grandchild was caught with marijuana. For more facts of this sort see Schlosser, *Reefer Madness*.

The war on drugs has clearly done much to erode our civil liberties. In particular, the standards for search and seizure, pretrial release, and judicial discretion in sentencing have all been revised in an attempt to make this unwinnable war easier to prosecute. Since drug offenses are covered by local, state, and federal jurisdictions, people can be tried multiple times for the same crime—some have been found not guilty at one level, only to receive life sentences upon subsequent prosecution. On more than one occasion, members of Congress have introduced legislation seeking to apply the death penalty to anyone caught selling drugs. Unsurprisingly, our attempts to eradicate the supply of drugs in other countries have been even more detrimental to the liberties of others. In Latin America, we have become a tireless benefactor of human rights violators. (See, for example, the Human Rights Watch website: www.hrw.org.)

In environmental terms, the war on drugs has been no more auspicious. The aerial spraying of herbicides has hastened the destruction of the rainforest as well as contaminated water supplies, staple crops, and people. The U.S. government has recently sought approval to use a genetically engineered "killer fungus," designed to attack marijuana crops domestically and coca and opium plants abroad. For the moment, some rather obvious environmental concerns have prevented its use. (See www.lindesmith.org.)

[31] From the ONDCP *Drug Data Summary* (March 2003). The war on drugs has also become a great engine of racial inequity, for while blacks constitute only 12 percent of the U.S. population and 13 percent of U.S. drug users, 38 percent of those arrested and 59 percent of those convicted for drug crimes are black. Our drug laws have contributed to the epidemic of fatherlessness in the black community, and this—along with the profits and resultant criminality of the drug trade—has devastated our inner cities. (See www.drugwarfacts.com.)

[32] Ibid.

[33] M. S. Gazzaniga, "Legalizing Drugs: Just Say Yes," *National Review*, July 10, 1995, pp. 26–37, makes a similar estimate. Needless to say, the cost has only grown with time.

[34] W. F. Buckley Jr., "The War on Drugs Is Lost," *National Review*, Feb. 12, 1996.

[35] www.lindesmith.org.

[36] When was the last time someone was killed over an alcohol or tobacco deal gone awry? We can be confident that the same normalcy would be achieved if drugs were regulated by the government. At the inception of the modern "war on drugs," the economist Milton Friedman observed that "legalizing drugs would simultaneously reduce the amount of crime

and raise the quality of law enforcement." He then invited the reader to "conceive of any other measure that would accomplish so much to promote law and order" (Friedman, "Prohibition and Drugs," *Newsweek*, May 1, 1972). What was true then remains true after three decades of pious misrule; the criminality associated with the drug trade is the inescapable consequence of our drug laws themselves.

[37] According to the U.S. government, twelve of the twenty-eight groups that have been officially classed as terrorist organizations finance their activities, in whole or in part, by the drug trade. (See www.theantidrug. com/drugs_terror/terrorgroups.html.)

[38] S. Weinberg, "What Price Glory," *New York Review of Books*, Nov. 6, 2003, pp. 55–60.

[39] All of this folly persists, even though the legalized and regulated sale of drugs would most effectively keep them out of the hands of minors (when was the last time someone was caught selling vodka in a schoolyard?), eradicate organized crime, reduce the annual cost of law enforcement by tens of billions of dollars, raise billions more in new sales taxes, and free hundreds of thousands of police officers for the job of fighting violent crime and terrorism. Against these remarkable benefits stands the fear that the legalization of drugs would lead to an epidemic of drug abuse and addiction. Common sense, as well as comparisons between the United States and places like Holland, reveals this fear to be unfounded. As more than 100 million of the estimated 108 million Americans who have used illegal drugs can attest, addiction is a phenomenon distinct from mere use, and users merely require good information to keep from becoming addicts. Addicts require treatment, of course—for which there are at present insufficient funds.

This is not to deny that a small percentage of people who use drugs (both legal and illegal) have their lives powerfully disrupted by them. We generally think of this problem as having two stages of severity: "abuse" and "addiction." It remains true, however, that most people who use drugs do not abuse them, and many illegal drugs do not readily become sources of addiction even in the hands of abusers (marijuana, LSD, psilocybin, mescaline, etc.). To say that a drug is addictive is to say that people develop both tolerance to it (and therefore require progressively higher doses to achieve the same effect) and withdrawal symptoms upon stoppage. It is not hard to see why well-intentioned people would worry that others might become inadvertent slaves of such biochemistry. While opium and its derivatives (like heroin and morphine) are the classic examples of drugs of this sort, nicotine and alcohol can fall into this category as well (depending on usage). Given our laws, however, all users of illicit drugs—whether dysfunctional or not, addicted or not—are considered criminals and subject to arrest, imprisonment, property seizure, and other punishments by the state.

Our drug policy has created arbitrary and illusory distinctions between biologically active substances, while obscuring valid ones. No one doubts that the use of certain drugs can destroy the lives of certain people. But the same can be said of almost any commodity. People destroy their lives and the lives of their dependents by simply overeating. In 2003 the Centers for Disease Control declared obesity to be the greatest public health problem in the United States, and yet few of us imagine that new criminal laws should be written to control the use of cheeseburgers. Where drugs are a problem, they are a problem whose remedy is better education and better health care, not incarceration. Simply observe the people in public life who are incapable of having a rational discussion on these matters (start with John Ashcroft and work your way down), and you will find that religious faith does much to inform their view of the world.

[40] See, e.g., D. Kahneman and A. Tversky, "On the Reality of Cognitive Illusions," *Psychological Review* 103 (1996): 582–91.

[41] "Misguided Faith on AIDS" (editorial), *New York Times*, Oct. 15, 2003.

[42] N. Kristof, "When Prudery Kills," *New York Times*, Oct. 8, 2003.

[43] Ibid.

[44] Kristof also misinterprets Einstein's famous statement "Science without religion is lame; religion without science is blind," suggesting that Einstein was voicing respect for religious credulity. Science without religion is lame, merely because "science can only be created by those who are thoroughly imbued with the aspiration toward truth and understanding. This source of feeling, however, springs from the sphere of religion." Whereas religion without science is blind because religion has *no access to the truth*—it was, to Einstein's mind, nothing other than this "source of feeling," this striving for something greater that cannot itself be scientifically justified. Faith, therefore, is hunger only; while reason is its food.

Einstein seemed to consider faith nothing more than a eunuch left to guard the harem while the intellect was away solving the problems of the world. By pretending that it could proceed without any epistemic aspirations whatsoever, Einstein robbed religion of the *truth* of its doctrine. In so doing, he also relieved it of its capacity to err. This is not the faith that evangelicals, or any other religious believers, have ever practiced. See Einstein, *Ideas and Opinions* (New York: Wings Books, 1954), 41–49.

6 A Science of Good and Evil

[1] N. Davies, *Europe: A History* (Oxford: Oxford Univ. Press, 1996), 543.

[2] This linkage between happiness and ethics is not a mere endorsement of *utilitarianism*. There may be ethical questions that escape a utilitarian analysis, but they will be questions of *ethics*, or so I will argue, only to the degree that anyone is in a position to suffer on account of them. I have elected to bypass the categories of moral theory that usually frame any discussion of ethics—*utilitarianism* (or *consequentialism*) and *deontology* being the most common. I do not believe that these categories are as conceptually distinct, or as useful, as their omnipresence in the literature suggests.

[3] One could argue that these behaviors do "victimize" others in more subtle ways. If a compelling argument of this sort exists, I am not aware of it. There is undoubtedly something to say about the relationship between such behavior and one's own happiness, but this becomes a matter of *ethics* only when the happiness of others is also at stake.

[4] See M. D. Hauser, "Swappable Minds," in *The Next Fifty Years*, ed. J. Brockman (New York: Vintage, 2002).

[5] B. Russell, *Why I Am Not a Christian*, ed. P. Edwards (New York: Simon and Schuster, 1957), vi.

[6] This observation formed the central strand of Carl Jung's famous study of Job, *Answer to Job*, trans. R. F. C. Hull (Princeton: Princeton Univ. Press, 1958).

[7] The belief that human beings are endowed with freedom of will underwrites both our religious conception of "sin" and our judicial ideal of "retributive justice." This makes free will a problem of more than passing philosophical interest. Without freedom of will, sinners would just be poorly calibrated clockwork, and any notion of justice that emphasized their *punishment* (rather than their rehabilitation or mere containment) would seem deeply incongruous. Happily, we will find that we need no illusions about a person's place in the causal order to hold him accountable for his actions, or to take action ourselves. We can find secure foundations for ethics and the rule of law without succumbing to any obvious cognitive illusions.

Free will is actually more than an illusion (or less) in that it cannot even be rendered coherent *conceptually*, since no one has ever described a manner in which mental and physical events could arise that would attest to its existence. Surely, most illusions are made of sterner stuff than this. If, for instance, a man believes that his dental fillings are receiving radio broadcasts, or that his sister has been replaced by an alien who looks exactly like her, we would have no difficulty specifying what would have to be true of the world for his beliefs to be, likewise, true. Strangely, our notion of "free of will" achieves no such intelligibility. As a concept, it simply has no descriptive, or even logical, moorings. Like some perverse, malodorous rose, however we might attempt to enjoy its beauty up close, it offers up its own contradiction.

The idea of free will is an ancient artifact of philosophy, of course, as well as a subject of occasional, if guilty, interest among scientists—e.g., M. Planck, *Where Is Science Going?* trans. and ed. J. Murphy (1933; reprint, Woodbridge, Conn.: Ox Bow Press, 1981); B. Libet, "Do We Have Free Will?" *Journal of Consciousness Studies* 6, nos. 8–9 (1999): 47–57; S. A. Spence and C. D. Frith, "Towards a Functional Anatomy of Volition," ibid., 11–29; A. L. Roskies, "Yes, But Am I free?" *Nature Neuroscience* 4 (2001): 1161; and D. M. Wegner, *The Illusion of Conscious Will* (Cambridge: MIT Press, 2002). It has long been obvious, however, that any description of the will in terms of causes and effects sets us sliding toward a moral and logical crevasse, for either our wills are determined by prior causes, and we are not responsible for them, or they are the product of chance, and we are not responsible for them. The notion of free will seems particularly suspect once we begin thinking about the brain. If a man's "choice" to shoot the president is determined by a certain pattern of neural activity, and this neural activity is in turn the product of prior causes—perhaps an unfortunate coincidence of an unhappy childhood, bad genes, and cosmic-ray bombardment—what can it possibly mean to say that his will is "free"? Despite the clever exertions of many philosophers who have sought to render free will "compatible" with both deterministic and indeterministic accounts of mind and brain, the project appears to be hopeless. The endurance of free will, as a problem in need of analysis, is attributable to the fact that most of us *feel* that we freely author our own actions and acts of attention (however difficult it may be to make sense of this notion in logical or scientific terms). It is safe to say that no one was ever moved to entertain the existence of free will because it holds great promise as an abstract idea.

In physical terms, every action is clearly reducible to a totality of impersonal events merely propagating their influence: genes are transcribed, neurotransmitters bind to their receptors, muscle fibers contract, and John Doe pulls the trigger on his gun. For our commonsense notions of agency to hold, our actions cannot be merely lawful products of our biology, our conditioning, or anything else that might lead others to predict them—and yet, were our actions to be actually divorced from such a causal network, they would be precisely those for which we could claim no responsibility. It has been fashionable, for several decades now, to speculate about the manner in which the indeterminacy of quantum processes, at the level of the neuron or its constituents, could yield a form of mental life that might stand free of the causal order; but such speculation is entirely oblique to the matter at hand—for an indeterminate world, governed by chance or quantum probabilities, would grant no more autonomy to human agents than would the incessant drawing of lots. In the face of any real independence from prior causes, every gesture would seem to merit the statement "I don't know what came over me." Upon the horns of this dilemma, fanciers of free will can often be heard making shrewd use of philosophical language, in an attempt to render our intuitions about a person's moral responsibility immune to worries about causation. (See Ayer, Chisholm, Strawson, Frankfurt, Dennett, and Watson—all in G. Watson, ed., *Free Will* [Oxford: Oxford Univ. Press, 1982].) Although we can find no room for it in the causal order, the notion of free will is still accorded a remarkable deference in philosophical and scientific literature, even by scientists who believe that the mind is entirely dependent upon the workings of the brain.

What most people overlook is that free will does not even correspond to any *subjective* fact about us. Consequently, even rigorous introspection soon grows as hostile to the idea of free will as the equations of physics have, because apparent acts of volition merely arise, spontaneously (whether caused, uncaused, or probabilistically inclined, it makes no difference), and cannot be traced to a point of origin in the stream of consciousness. A moment or two of serious self-scrutiny and the reader might observe that he no more authors the next thought he thinks than the next thought I write.

[8] We may have the ethical obligation to preserve certain rocks for future generations, but this is an obligation we would have with respect to other people, not with respect to the rocks themselves. The equation of a creature's being conscious with there being "something that it is like to be"

said creature comes from T. Nagel, "What Is It like to Be a Bat," in *Mortal Questions* (Cambridge: Cambridge Univ. Press, 1979).

9 That is, they *felt* no pain, in the phenomenal sense; even Descartes could see that animals avoided certain stimuli—he just didn't think that there was "something that it was like" for them to do so. His error here is based on a kernel of truth: it is conceivable that something could *seem* to be conscious without *being* conscious (i.e., passing the Turing test says nothing about whether or not a physical system *actually is* conscious; it just leaves us feeling, from the outside, that it probably is). Behaviorism amounts to the doctrine that *seeming to be conscious* is all there is to *being* conscious. If even a kernel of truth is to be found lurking here, I have yet to find it.

10 Cited in J. M. Masson and S. McCarthy, *When Elephants Weep: The Emotional Lives of Animals* (New York: Delacorte Press, 1995), 18.

11 The stakes here should be obvious. What is it like to be a chimpanzee? If we knew more about the details of chimpanzee experience, even our most conservative use of them in research might begin to seem unconscionably cruel. Were it possible to trade places with one of these creatures, we might no longer think it ethical to so much as separate a pair of chimpanzee siblings, let alone perform invasive procedures on their bodies for curiosity's sake. It is important to reiterate that there are surely facts of the matter to be found here, whether or not we ever devise methods sufficient to find them. Do pigs led to slaughter feel something akin to terror? Do they feel a terror that no decent man or woman would ever knowingly impose upon another sentient creature? We have, at present, no idea at all. What we do know (or should) is that an answer to this question could have profound implications, given our current practices.

All of this is to say that our sense of compassion and ethical responsibility tracks our sense of a creature's likely phenomenology. Compassion, after all, is a response to suffering—and thus a creature's *capacity* to suffer is paramount. Whether or not a fly is "conscious" is not precisely the point. The question of ethical moment is, What could it possibly be conscious *of*?

Much ink has been spilled over the question of whether or not animals have conscious mental states at all. It is legitimate to ask how and to what degree a given animal's experience differs from our own (Does a chimpanzee attribute states of mind to others? Does a dog recognize himself in a mirror?), but is there really a question about whether any nonhuman animals have conscious experience? I would like to suggest that there is not. It is not that there is sufficient experimental evidence to overcome our doubts on this score; it is just that such doubts are unreasonable. Indeed, no experiment could prove that *other human beings* have conscious experience, were we to assume otherwise as our working hypothesis.

The question of scientific parsimony visits us here. A common misconstrual of parsimony regularly inspires deflationary accounts of animal minds. That we *can* explain the behavior of a dog without resort to notions of consciousness or mental states does not mean that it is easier or more elegant to do so. It isn't. In fact, it places a greater burden upon us to explain *why* a dog brain (cortex and all) is not sufficient for consciousness, while human brains are. Skepticism about chimpanzee consciousness seems an even greater liability in this respect. To be biased on the side of withholding attributions of consciousness to other mammals is not in the least parsimonious in the scientific sense. It actually entails a gratuitous proliferation of theory—in much the same way that solipsism would, if it were ever seriously entertained. How do I know that other human beings are conscious like myself? Philosophers call this the problem of "other minds," and it is generally acknowledged to be one of reason's many cul de sacs, for it has long been observed that this problem, once taken seriously, admits of no satisfactory exit. But need we take it seriously?

Solipsism appears, at first glance, to be as parsimonious a stance as there is, until I attempt to explain why all other people *seem* to have minds, why their behavior and physical structure are more or less identical to my own, and yet I am uniquely conscious—at which time it reveals itself to be the least parsimonious theory of all. There is no argument for the existence of other human minds apart from the fact that to assume otherwise (that is, to take solipsism as a serious hypothesis) is to impose upon oneself the very heavy burden of explaining the (apparently conscious) behavior of zombies. The devil is in the details for the solipsist; his solitude requires a very muscular and inelegant bit of theorizing to be made sense of. Whatever might be said in defense of such a view, it is not in the least "parsimonious."

The same criticism applies to any view that would make the human brain a unique island of mental life. If we withhold conscious emotional states from chimpanzees in the name of "parsimony," we must then explain not only how such states are uniquely realized in our own case but also why so much of what chimps do as an *apparent* expression of emotionality is not what it seems. The neuroscientist is suddenly faced with the task of finding the difference between human and chimpanzee brains that accounts for the respective existence and nonexistence of emotional states; and the ethologist is left to explain why a creature, as *apparently* angry as a chimp in a rage, will lash out at one of his rivals without feeling anything at all. If ever there was an example of a philosophical dogma creating empirical problems where none exist, surely this is one.

[12] For a recent review of the cognitive neuroscience of moral cognition see W. D. Casebeer, "Moral Cognition and Its Neural Constituents," *Nature Reviews Neuroscience* 4 (2003): 840–46. It is clearly too early to draw any strong conclusions from this research.

[13] There is a wide literature on morality and ethics—I use these words interchangeably—but like most writers who have pretensions to "first philosophy," I have not found much use for it here. In considering questions of ethics, I think we should exhaust the resources of common sense before we begin ransacking the armory of philosophies past. In this, my intuitions are vaguely Kantian and therefore lead me to steer as clear of Kant as of any other philosopher. Putting the matter this way—purporting to take "common sense" in hand, where others have gotten mired in technicalities—risks begging many of the questions that certain readers will want to ask. Indeed, one person's common sense is invariably another's candidate for original sin. The manner in which I have circumscribed the domain of ethics is also somewhat idiosyncratic, and consequently my account will fail to catch some of the concerns that people regularly consider to be integral to the subject. This, as far as I can see, is not so much a weakness of my approach as one of its strengths, because I believe that our map of the moral wilderness should be redrawn. The complex interrelationships between morality, law, and politics will also be set aside for the present. While these domains certainly overlap, an analysis of their mutual (and well contested) influence upon one another is beyond the scope of this book.

[14] A circularity is surely lurking here, since only those who have demonstrated the requisite degree of convergence will be deemed "adequate." This circularity is not unique to ethics, however; nor is it a problem. That we generally require people to demonstrate an understanding of current theories before we take their views seriously does not mean that revolutions in our understanding of the world are not possible.

[15] C. Hitchens, "Mommie Dearest," *Slate*, Oct. 20, 2003, slate.msn.com.

[16] R. Rorty, *Hope in Place of Knowledge: The Pragmatics Tradition in*

Philosophy (Taipei: Institute of European and American Studies, Academia Sinica, 1999), 90–91.

17 William James is usually considered the father of pragmatism. Whether he should be viewed as having extended the philosophy of Charles Sanders Peirce, or utterly debauched it, seems to be very much an open question—one that can be persuasively answered either way by consulting James in half his moods. There is no doubt that the great man contradicted himself greatly. As George Santayana said, "The general agreement in America to praise [James] as a marvelous person, and to pass on, is justified by delight at the way he started, without caring where he went." (See his *Persons and Places* [Cambridge: MIT Press, 1963], 401.) For the tenets of pragmatism, I have principally relied on the work of Richard Rorty, who articulates this philosophical position as clearly and consistently as any of its fans or critics could wish.

18 The emphasis on utility, rather than on truth, can be easily caricatured and misunderstood—and has been ever since William James first articulated the principles of pragmatism in a lecture before the Philosophical Union of the University of California in 1898. Far from being the absurdity of wishful thinking that Bertrand Russell lampooned in his *History of Western Philosophy*—where we encounter a wayward pragmatist finding it useful to believe that every man in sight is named Ebenezer Wilkes Smith—when presented in all its subtleties, pragmatism can be made to seem synonymous with every species of good sense. One can easily find oneself careening, in a single hour, through the stages that James sketched for the career of any successful theory: at first it appears ridiculous; then true but trivial; then so important that one is tempted to say that one knew it all along.

19 P. Berman, *Terror and Liberalism* (New York: W. W. Norton, 2003), 171.

20 We should note that realism is an epistemological position, not an ontological one. This is a regular source of confusion in philosophy. It is often assumed, for instance, that realism is opposed to various forms of idealism and subjectivism and, indeed, to certain developments in the physical sciences (like Bohr's interpretation of quantum mechanics) that seem to grant the mind a remarkable role in the governance of creation. But if the moon does not exist unless someone is looking at it, this would still be a realistic truth (in that it would be true, whether or not anyone knew that this is the way the world works). To say that reality has a definite character is not to say that this character must be intelligible to us, or that it might not be perversely shifty—or, indeed, that consciousness and

thought might not play some constitutive role in defining it. If reality changes its colors every time a physicist blinks his eyes, this would still be a *realistic* truth.

21 There is a naïve version of realism that has few defenders today. It is the view of the world that most of us inherit along with ten fingers and ten toes and maintain in innocence of philosophy. Such realism holds that the world is more or less as common sense would have it: tables and chairs really exist in a physical space of three dimensions; grass is green; the sky is blue; everything is made of atoms; and every atom is crammed with particles tinier still. The basic view is that our senses, along with their extensions—telescopes, microscopes, etc.—merely deliver us the facts of the universe as they are. While being an indispensable heuristic for making one's way in the world, this is not the stuff of which current scientific and philosophical theories are made. Nor is it the form of realism that any philosophical realist currently endorses.

Thomas Nagel, an eloquent opponent of pragmatism, offers us, in *The Last Word* (Oxford: Oxford Univ. Press, 1997), 30, three propositions that he feels can be adequately accounted for only by realism:

1. There are many truths about the world that we will never know and have no way of finding out.
2. Some of our beliefs are false and will never be discovered to be so.
3. If a belief is true, it would be true even if no one believed it.

While a pragmatist like Rorty will concede that this manner of speaking is intelligible, he will maintain that it is just that—a manner of *speaking*—and he will shuttle all statements of this kind into his pragmatism by reading words like "true" in a purely discursive sense and then pirouette to his basic thesis: "We can talk like this, of course, but to know the nature of anything is merely to know the history of the way it has been talked about." The pragmatist attempts to conserve our realistic intuitions by conceding that if one is going to play certain language games correctly and use words like "true" so as to be understood, one will, of course, grant one's assent to statements like "There were mountains around before there was anyone to talk about mountains"—but he will never hesitate to add that the "truth" of such a statement is just a matter of our common agreement.

22 J. Habermas, *On the Pragmatics of Communication*, ed. M. Cooke (Cambridge: MIT Press, 1998), 357.

23 To set all the relevant features of the pragmatic construal of knowledge

before us, it will be useful to briefly consider the work of Donald Davidson. Davidson has been very influential in philosophical circles, and his views on mind and meaning now appear to underwrite Rorty's pragmatism. Davidson asserts, in an undated manuscript titled "The Myth of the Subjective," that any view of the world, along with its concepts and truth claims, must be translatable into any other:

> Of course there are contrasts from epoch to epoch, from culture to culture, and person to person of kinds we all recognize and struggle with; but these are contrasts which with sympathy and effort we can explain and understand. Trouble comes when we try to embrace the idea that there might be more comprehensive differences, for this seems (absurdly) to ask us to take up a stance outside our own ways of thought.
>
> In my opinion, we do not understand the idea of such a really foreign scheme. We know what states of mind are like, and how they are correctly identified; they are just those states whose contents can be discovered in well-known ways. If other people or creatures are in states not discoverable by these methods, it cannot be because our methods fail us, but because those states are not correctly called states of mind—they are not beliefs, desires, wishes, or intentions.

Perhaps the first thing a realist will want to say in response to these ideas is that we need not ("absurdly") take a stance outside our own to make sense of the claim that radically different views of the universe might exist. As T. Nagel, *The View from Nowhere* (Oxford: Oxford Univ. Press, 1986), points out, a community of pragmatists with the mental age of nine would simply be *wrong* to think that "truth" is just a matter of justification among themselves, and they would be right to think that other human beings understand facts about the world that they will never be able to translate into their discourse. Who is to say that our own view of the world might not appear similarly delimited from some other vantage point?

Davidson's doctrine of translatability comes bundled with what he calls his "principle of charity": all language users must be endowed with mostly true beliefs, for beliefs can be recognized as *beliefs* only against a background of massive agreement. All interlocutors, therefore, must be deemed by us to be basically rational—for the moment we imagine confronting a mind stocked stem to stern with *false* beliefs, we realize that we would see no basis to call it a "mind" in the first place. Davidson's view here amounts to a curious inversion of Wittgenstein's famous line "If a lion could talk, we would not understand him." For Davidson, if we cannot understand him, *he cannot be talking.*

Davidson's conclusions here appear rather incredible. What if a speaker and an interpreter have mutually intelligible and *false* canons of belief? Whether or not a given community's beliefs about reality are mutually translatable need have nothing to do with whether or not they are *true.* Mutual intelligibility may signify nothing more than homology of error; my errors may be enough like your own to pass for "truth" in your discourse. We need only imagine the communities of gorillas and chimpanzees getting their most precocious, language-trained members together to test this: each might fail to recognize the utterances of the other (perhaps they were taught incompatible forms of sign language) and conclude that the other is not a language user at all. In this case, these ape translators would both be wrong. If, on the other hand, they were to successfully converse and agreed with Rorty that "truth" is just a matter of what prevails in their discourse, they would likewise be wrong—because the men and women watching their interaction would be acquainted with a variety of truths that they could not possibly be made to understand.

According to pragmatism, beliefs serve their purpose in different contexts, and there is simply no cognitive project that corresponds to "knowing how things are" or "knowing what reality is really like." Our ape pragmatists would likely concur, but they might also say that there is no such project as "knowing how to fly to the moon" or "knowing where babies come from" either. Let us postulate that apes are cognitively closed to the facts of rocket design and biology as *we* know them—that is, try as he or she might, no ape scientist will ever have the requisite cognitive abilities to bring the relevant data into view, much less make theoretical sense of them. To this community of pragmatists, such facts simply do not exist. It seems clear that if there could exist worldviews which supersede our own in this way, then what passes for "truth" in our discourse could not be the final measure of what is true.

The only means Rorty has found to resist this slide into ever-widening contexts of knowledge is to follow Davidson in claiming that we could translate *any* language into our own, and therefore incorporate any "truths" that more advanced language users might articulate. Davidson's reasoning is actually circular here, because the only reason why we could translate any language is that *translatability is his criterion for picking out a language in the first place.* This simply begs the question at issue.

Davidson's claims about translatability also seem to rely on a kind of verificationist fallacy: he mistakes the way we pick out language use in the world for what language is in itself. The fact that in order to *ascribe* language to another creature we must first translate his language into our own is simply irrelevant to the question of whether or not this creature is *actually* a language user, has a mind, or is communicating with his own kind. The error here tracks that of behaviorism—which cast a stultifying shadow over the sciences of mind for most of the twentieth century. That we may be constrained to pick out mentality in others by their behavior and verbal utterance does not mean that such outward signs *constitute* what mind is in itself.

According to Rorty and Davidson, there is no language game that human beings could not, in principle, play. The spectrum of possible minds, points of view, "true" descriptions of the world is therefore continuous. All possible languages are commensurable; all cognitive horizons can be ultimately fused. Whether or not this is true is not really the point. The point is that it amounts to a *realistic* claim about the nature of language and cognition.

It seems that there are two possible forms of retort to pragmatism: in the first place we could seek to demonstrate that it is not *pragmatic*, and specifically that it is not as pragmatic as realism. The approach here would be to show that it serves neither our ends of fashioning a coherent picture of the world nor other ends to which we might be purposed. It may be, for instance, that talking about truth and knowledge in terms of human "solidarity," as Rorty does, could ultimately subvert the very solidarity at issue. While I believe that a pragmatic case against pragmatism can be made, I have not made it here (B. Williams, in "Auto-da-Fé," *New York Review of Books*, April 28, 1983, has taken a stab at it). Instead, I have attempted to show that pragmatism is covertly realistic, arguing that in the act of distancing himself from the sins of realism, the pragmatist commits them with both hands. The pragmatist seems to be tacitly saying that he has surveyed the breadth and depth of all possible acts of cognition (not just his own, and not just those that are human) and found both that all knowledge is discursive and that all spheres of discourse can be potentially fused. Pragmatism, therefore, amounts to the assertion that any epistemic context wider than our own can be ruled out in principle. While I find these claims incredible, the more important point is that a pragmatist can believe otherwise only as a realist.

As a final note, I would like to point out that both pragmatic and realistic objections to pragmatism can be made to converge. Let us first reduce pragmatism and realism to their core theses (P and R respectively):

P: All statements about the world are "true" only by virtue of being justified in a sphere of discourse.

R: Certain statements about the world are true, whether or not they can be justified—and many justified statements happen to be false.

There appear to be two routes over the precipice for the pragmatist—and both can be reached when we press the question "What if P seems wrong to everybody and R seems right?" After all, the pragmatist must admit the possibility that we might live in a world where P will fail to be justified (that is, pragmatism itself may prove to be unpragmatic), which raises the question of whether or not P applies to itself. If P applies to itself, and is not justified, then it would seem that pragmatism self-destructs the moment it loses its subscribers. The pragmatist cannot resist this line by saying that P does *not* apply to itself, for then he will have falsified P and endorsed R; nor can he say that it is a necessary truth that P will always be justified.

Another logical peril emerges for the pragmatist the moment R becomes justified. According to P, if R is justified, it is "true"—but R cannot remain true by virtue of being justified. If the pragmatist attempts to resist the revaluation of "true" that R itself urges upon us, by saying that R cannot be *really* true (in the sense that it corresponds to reality as it is), this would be tantamount to saying that P itself is true realistically. Hence, he will fall into contradiction with his thesis once again. This is a rock and a hard place that the pragmatist cannot even be intelligibly accused of standing between—for they are, after all, the *same* place. It is, therefore, upon the very rock of realism—or beneath it—that we should seek the pragmatist out.

[24] This is often called, erroneously, the "naturalistic fallacy." The naturalistic fallacy, due to G. E. Moore, is a fallacy of another sort. Moore claimed that our judgments of goodness cannot be reduced to other properties like happiness. He would undoubtedly argue that I have committed the naturalistic fallacy in defining ethics in terms of human happiness. Moore felt that his "open question argument" was decisive here: it would seem, for instance, that we can always coherently ask of any state of happiness, "Is this form of happiness itself *good*?" The fact that the question still makes sense suggests that happiness and goodness cannot be the same. I would argue, however, that what we are really asking in such a case is "Is this form of happiness conducive to (or obstructive of) some

higher happiness?" This question is also coherent, and keeps our notion of what is good linked to the experience of sentient beings.

25 S. Pinker, *The Blank Slate* (New York: Viking, 2002), 53–54.

26 J. Glover, *Humanity: A Moral History of the Twentieth Century* (New Haven: Yale Univ. Press, 1999), 24.

27 Cited in O. Friedrich, *The End of the World: A History* (New York: Coward, McCann & Geoghegan, 1982), 61.

28 The role of Christian dogma in turning sexual neurosis into a principle of cultural oppression need hardly be elaborated upon. Perhaps the most shocking disclosures in recent years (coming amid thousands of reports about pedophile priests in the United States) were those that surrounded a group of nuns that ran orphanages throughout Ireland during the 1950s and 1960s. The incongruously named Sisters of Mercy tortured children as young as eleven months (flogging and scalding them, as well as subjecting them to astonishing acts of psychological cruelty) for "the sins of their parents" (i.e., the sin of their own illegitimacy). In the service of ancient ideas about female sexuality, original sin, virgin births, etc., thousands of these infants were forcibly removed from the care of their unwed mothers and sent overseas for adoption.

29 Reports of honor killings have been steadily trickling out of Muslim countries for years. For a recent example, see N. Banerjee, "Rape (and Silence about It) Haunts Baghdad," *New York Times*, July 16, 2003. The UNICEF Web site posts the following statistics:

> In 1997, some 300 women were estimated to have been killed in the name of "honour" in one province of Pakistan alone. According to 1999 estimates, more than two-thirds of all murders in Gaza strip and West bank were most likely "honour" killings. In Jordan there are an average of 23 such murders per year.
>
> Thirty-six "honour" crimes were reported in Lebanon between 1996 and 1998, mainly in small cities and villages. Reports indicate that offenders are often under 18 and that in their communities they are sometimes treated as heroes. In Yemen as many as 400 "honour" killings took place in 1997. In Egypt there were 52 reported "honour" crimes in 1997.

30 In the Buddhist tradition, which has approached the cultivation of these states most systematically, *love* and *compassion* are cultivated alongside *equanimity* and *sympathetic joy* (that is, joy in the happiness of others). Each state is believed to balance the others.

[31] It seems reasonably clear that not all people are equally endowed with ethical intelligence. In particular, not all people are equally adept at discerning the link between their intentions toward others and their own happiness. While it may seem undemocratic to posit a hierarchy of moral knowledge, we know that knowledge cannot be equally distributed in the world. This is not to say that one must master a wide body of facts to be moral. Morality may be more like chess than like medicine—there may be very few facts to understand, but it can still be remarkably difficult to use what one has learned impeccably. To assert that there should be no "experts" in morals—as both Kantians and anti-Kantians tend to do—is, on my account, rather like saying that there should be no experts in chess, perhaps adducing as one's evidence that every party to our discourse can plainly see how to move the pieces. We need no experts to tell us how the matter stands; nor do we need experts to tell us that cruelty is wrong. But we do need experts to tell us what the best move is from any given position; and there is little doubt that we will need experts to tell us that loving all people, without distinction, makes one happier than feeling preferential love for one's intimates (if this is indeed the case).

Why should we think that living a profoundly ethical life would be any more common an attainment than playing brilliant chess? Why should penetrating insight into the logical relations among one's ethical beliefs be any easier to come by than penetrating insight into any other logical framework? As in any field, some cherished intuitions may prove irreconcilable with some others, and the search for coherence will force itself upon us as a practical necessity. Not everyone can play championship chess, and not everyone can figure out how to live so as to be as happy as possible. We can offer heuristics for playing winning chess, of course (secure the middle of the board, keep good pawn structure, etc.); and we can offer heuristics for bringing ethical truths to light (Kant's categorical imperative, Rawls' "original position," etc.). The fact that not every last one of us sees the point of them does not cast doubt upon their usefulness. There is no doubt that the relations among our ethical precepts and intuitions admit of deeper insights, requiring greater and greater intellectual capacities on the part of all of us to comprehend and, comprehending, to be inspired to practice. Here, I think, the greatest difference among persons is to be found (along with the greatest difference between the ethical and the epistemic spheres), since any insight into ethical normativity must lay claim to our emotions in order to become effective. Once he has understood that π is the ratio of a circle's circumference to its diameter, not even the most libertine geometer will feel tempted to compute a circle's area using another measure. When a person sees that it is generally wrong to lie, however, this normative ground, once conquered, must be secured by *feeling*. He must *feel* that lying is beneath him—that it is tending to lead him away from happiness—and such a conversion of moral sentiments seems to require more than mere conceptual understanding. But then, so do certain kinds of reasoning. See A. Damasio, *Descartes' Error: Emotion, Reason, and the Human Brain* (New York: Avon Books, 1994).

Put this way, it is easy to see that two people who both have learned that lying is not conducive to happiness may differ considerably in the depth to which they feel this proposition to be true, and therefore in the degree to which they feel obliged to conform to it in their actions. Instances of discrepancy between belief and action in the moral sphere are legion: it is one thing to think it "wrong" that people are starving elsewhere in the world; it is another to find this as intolerable as one would if these people were one's friends. There may, in fact, be no ethical justification for all of us fortunate people to carry on with our business while other people starve (see P. Unger, *Living High & Letting Die: Our Illusion of Innocence* [Oxford: Oxford Univ. Press, 1996]). It may be that a clear view of the matter—that is, a clear view of the dynamics of our own happiness—would oblige us to work tirelessly to alleviate the hunger of every last stranger as though it were our own. On this account, how could one go to the movies and remain ethical? One couldn't. One would simply be taking a vacation from one's ethics.

32 *60 Minutes*, Sept. 26, 2002.

33 That these men are being held indefinitely, without access to legal counsel, should be genuinely troubling to us, however. See R. Dworkin, "Terror and the Attack on Civil Liberties," *New York Review of Books*, Nov. 6, 2003, pp. 37–41, for a fine analysis of the legal and ethical issues here.

34 It seems to me that we can stop this inquisitorial slide by recourse to the "perfect weapon" argument presented in chapter 4. There is a difference, after all, between intending to inflict suffering on an innocent person and inflicting it by accident. To include a suspected terrorist's family among the instruments of torture would be a flagrant violation of this principle.

35 Quoted in Glover, *Humanity*, 55.

36 I suspect that if our media did not censor the more disturbing images of war, our moral sentiments would receive a correction on two fronts: first, we would be more motivated by the horrors visited upon us by our ene-

mies: seeing Daniel Pearl decapitated, for instance, would have surely provoked a level of national outrage that did not arise in the absence of such imagery. Second, if we did not conceal the horrible reality of collateral damage from ourselves, we would be far less likely to support the dropping of "dumb" bombs, or even "smart" ones. While our newspapers and newscasts would be horrible to look at, I believe we would feel both greater urgency and greater restraint in our war on terrorism.

[37] See J. D. Greene et al., "An fMRI Investigation of Emotional Engagement in Moral Judgment," *Science* 293 (Sept. 14, 2001): 2105–8; and J. D. Greene, "From Neural 'Is' to Moral 'Ought': What Are the Moral Implications of Neuroscientific Moral Psychology?" *Nature Reviews Neuroscience* 4 (2003): 846–49.

[38] For an illuminating account of the use of "coercion" by U.S. and Israeli interrogators, see M. Bowden, "The Dark Art of Interrogation," *Atlantic Monthly*, March 2003, pp. 51–77.

[39] Many flavors of pacifism can be found in the philosophical literature. I am considering here what is often called "absolute" pacifism—that is, the belief that violence is *never* morally acceptable, whether in self-defense or on behalf of others. This is the sort of pacifism that Gandhi practiced, and it is the only form that seems to carry with it pretensions of moral impregnability.

[40] Am I saying that overt opposition to a wrong is the ethical standard? Yes, when the stakes are high, I think that it is. One can always make the argument that covert resistance in particularly dangerous situations— where open opposition would be to forfeit one's life—is the best possible course. Those remarkable men and women who hid Jews in their basements or ferried them to safety during World War II provide the textbook example of this. Surely they did more good by living and helping others in secret than by openly protesting the Nazis and dying on principle. But this was their situation only because so few people were willing to offer open opposition in the first place. If more had, there would have been Nazis hiding in basements, writing journals to the God that had forsaken them, not innocent little girls bound for Auschwitz. Thus, as a categorical imperative, confrontation with evil seems the best imperative we've got. What form this confrontation takes, of course, is open to debate. But simply making room for human evil, or sidestepping it, doesn't seem an ethically auspicious option.

[41] G. Orwell, "Reflections on Gandhi," in *The Oxford Book of Essays*, ed. J. Gross (Oxford: Oxford Univ. Press, 1949), 506.

7 Experiments in Consciousness

1 I am not suggesting that thoughts themselves are not equivalent to certain states of the brain. In conventional terms, however, there is a rather large difference between taking a drug and taking on a new idea. That both have the power to alter our perception is one of the more fascinating facts about the human mind.

2 While this literature is too wide to cite here, numerous examples of such texts can be found in my bibliography.

3 What happens after death is surely a mystery, as is the relationship between consciousness and the physical world, but there is no longer any doubt whether the character of our minds is dependent upon the functioning of our brains—and dependent in ways that are profoundly counterintuitive. Consider one of the common features of the near-death experience: the nearly dying seem regularly to encounter their loved ones who have gone before them into the next world. See A. Kellehear, *Experiences Near Death: Beyond Medicine and Religion* (Oxford: Oxford Univ. Press, 1996). We know, however, that recognizing a person's face requires an intact fusiform cortex, primarily in the right hemisphere. Damage to this area of the brain definitely robs the mind of its powers of facial recognition (among other things), a condition we call prosopagnosia. People with this condition have nothing wrong with their primary vision. They can see color and shape perfectly well. They can recognize almost everything in their environment, but they cannot distinguish between the faces of even their closest friends and family members. Are we to imagine in such cases that a person possesses an intact soul, somewhere behind the mind, that retains his ability to recognize his loved ones? It would seem so. Indeed, unless the soul retains all of the normal cognitive and perceptual capacities of the healthy brain, heaven would be populated by beings suffering from all manner of neurological deficit. But then, what are we to think of the condition of the neurologically impaired while alive? Does a person suffering from aphasia have a soul that can speak, read, and think flawlessly? Does a person whose motor skills have been degraded by cerebellar ataxia have a soul with preserved hand-eye coordination? This is rather like believing that inside every wrecked car lurks a new car just waiting to get out.

The implausibility of a soul whose powers are independent of the brain only increases once we recognize that even normal brains can be placed somewhere on a continuum of pathology. I know my soul speaks

English, because that is the language that comes out of me whenever I speak or write. I used to know a fair amount of French as well. It seems that I've forgotten most of it, though, since my attempts at communication while in France provoke little more than amusement and consternation in the natives. We know, however, that the difference between my remembering and not remembering something is a matter of physical differences in the neural circuits in my brain—specifically in the synaptic connections that are responsible for information encoding, information retrieval, or both. My loss of French, therefore, can be considered a form of neurological impairment. And any Frenchman who found his linguistic ability suddenly degraded to the level of my own would rush straight to the hospital. Would his soul retain his linguistic ability in any case? Has my soul retained its memory of how to conjugate the verb *bruire*? Where does this notion of soul-brain independence end? A native speaker of one of the Bantu languages would find that the functioning of my language cortex leaves even more to be desired. Given that I was never exposed to Bantu sounds as a child, it is almost certain that I would find it difficult in the extreme, if not impossible, to distinguish between them, much less reproduce them in a way that would satisfy a native speaker. But perhaps my soul has mastered the Bantu languages as well. There are only five hundred of them.

4 Whether the angle of approach is through the study of priming effects and visual masking, change blindness (D. J. Simons et al., "Evidence for Preserved Representations in Change Blindness," *Consciousness and Cognition* 11, no. 1 [2002]: 78–97), visual extinction and visuospatial neglect (G. Rees et al., "Neural Correlates of Consciousness in Humans," *Nature Reviews Neuroscience* 3 [April 2002]: 261–70), binocular rivalry and other bistable percepts (R. Blake and N. K. Logothetis, "Visual Competition," *Nature Reviews Neuroscience* 3, no. 1 [2002]: 13–21; N. K. Logothetis, "Vision: A Window on Consciousness," *Scientific American Special Edition* 12, no. 1 [2002] 18–25), or blind-sight (L. Weiskrantz, "Prime-sight and Blindsight," *Consciousness and Cognition* 11, no. 4 [2002]: 568–81), the signature of conscious perception is always the same: the subject (be he man or monkey) simply tells us, by word or deed, whether or not the character of his experience has changed.

5 Why isn't general anesthesia a way of ruling it out? Bathe the brain in the requisite chemicals, and people lose consciousness—end of story. The problem, however, is that we do not know that consciousness itself is truly interrupted during anesthesia. The problem with conflating

consciousness with reportability is that we cannot distinguish the genuine cessation of consciousness from a mere failure of memory. What was it like to be asleep last night? You may feel that it was like nothing at all—you were "unconscious." But what about the dreams you don't remember? You were surely conscious while having them. Indeed, you may have been conscious throughout all the stages of sleep. We cannot rule out this possibility through subjective report alone.

6 Nevertheless, these are exactly the sorts of equivalences that scientists and philosophers working on "the self" are apt to draw. A conference was recently held at the New York Academy of Sciences entitled "The Self: From Soul to Brain," and while much of interest was said about the brain, not a single presenter defined the self in such a way as to distinguish it from truly global concepts like "the human mind" or "personhood." The feeling that we call "I" was left entirely untouched.

7 Certain philosophers, while they clearly have not transcended the subject/object divide as a matter of stable experience, *conceptually* repudiate it in their thinking. Sartre, for instance, saw that the subject could be nothing more than another object in the field of consciousness and, as such, was "contemporaneous with the World":

> The World has not created *me*; the *me* has not created the World. These are two objects for absolute, impersonal consciousness, and it is by virtue of this consciousness that they are connected. This absolute consciousness, when it is purified of the *I*, no longer has anything of the *subject*. . . . It is quite simply a first condition and absolute source of existence. And the relation of interdependence established by this absolute consciousness between *me* and the World is sufficient for the me to appear as "endangered" before the World, for the *me* (indirectly and through the intermediary states) to draw the whole of its content from the World. No more is needed in the way of a philosophical foundation for an ethics and a politics which are absolutely positive.
>
> J. P. Sartre, *The Transcendence of the Ego: An Existentialist Theory of Consciousness*, trans. F. Williams and R. Kirkpatrick (New York: Hill and Wang, 1937), 105–6.

Maurice Merleau-Ponty makes a similar point, even while confining himself to subject/object language: "The world is inseparable from the subject, but from a subject which is nothing but a project of the world, and the subject is inseparable from the world, but from a world which the subject itself projects." Cited in F. Varela at al., *The Embodied Mind: Cognitive Science and Human Experience* (Cambridge: MIT Press, 1991), 4.

[8] This is not to say that infants are mystics. Nevertheless, a process of increasing individuation clearly occurs from birth onward. See K. Wilber, *Sex, Ecology, Spirituality* (Boston: Shambhala, 1995), for a criticism of the false equation between what he calls the *pre-rational* and the *trans-rational*. As Wilber points out, there is no reason to romanticize childhood in spiritual terms. Indeed, if our children appear to inhabit the kingdom of heaven, why stop with them? We might as well direct our envy at our primate cousins, for they—when they are not too overcome by the pleasures of cannibalism, gang rape, and infanticide to seem so— are the most gleeful children of all.

[9] Thus, a man like Heidegger, who was an abject admirer of Hitler, can nevertheless be commended to our attention, with scarcely a hint of shame, as one of the giants of European thought. Schopenhauer, who was undoubtedly a clever fellow, hurled a seamstress down a flight of stairs, injuring her permanently (he was, we are told, annoyed by the sound of her voice). Other eminent thinkers could also be singled out—Wittgenstein was a manifestly tortured soul and an enthusiastic practitioner of corporal punishment when in the company of unruly little girls—but, and this is the astonishing fact, not a single Western thinker can be named who rivals the great philosopher-mystics of the East. There are those who feel no embarrassment at reaching as far back as Plotinus for an example of a mystic reared in an Eastern corner of the West. But Plotinus, by his own admission, enjoyed only an occasional glimpse of the plenum that he so eloquently described. In the context of one of the Eastern schools of contemplative practice, he would have been acknowledged for nothing more than having set out toward the goal in earnest.

The situation appears to have been somewhat different in the ancient world. Greek philosophers spoke frequently of the state of *eudaimonia*— the objective state of happiness that was thought to attend the good life— but their efforts to reach it were not very sophisticated. The closest thing to an Eastern mysticism to be found among the ancient Greeks was skepticism, in the tradition of Pyrrho of Elis (ca. 365–270 BC)—but Pyrrho's teachings amounted to disavowal of philosophy altogether. Happiness has since been relegated to the ontological backwater of moral philosophy, and the ideal of the philosopher as sage is not even a distant memory.

The teachings of Pyrrho, which have survived in the writings of the second-century physician Sextus Empiricus, enunciate what is clearly a spiritual discipline, not at all unlike the dialectic of Madhyamika in Mahayana Buddhism. The Skeptic (with a capital S) is not merely a philosopher who failed in his office—having sought to gather true beliefs about the world and found his basket empty at the end of the day—he is the person who has found the peace (Greek *ataraxia*) to which such a failure can lead.

Skepticism, in Pyrrho's sense, is not the dogmatic assertion that nothing at all can be known. It is the acknowledgment that whatever we know at present is simply the way things *seem*, and the Skeptic refuses to take another step into the twilight of metaphysical views. He knows that he does not know anything other than appearances—and the fact that this seems to be a truth about the nature of experience is, likewise, nothing more than the way things appear to him at present. As Sextus says, "the Skeptic continues to search," studiously withholding judgment (Greek *epoché*). He does not even judge that this is a position that should be maintained—rather, every belief on offer seems to invite its own contradiction, and the Skeptic has merely taken note of the unsatisfactoriness of the situation thus far. The man is befuddled, and he is happy to stay that way.

This position has rarely been accorded the respect that it deserves in the West, for it has been widely doubted whether it can be honestly maintained by any means short of administering repeated blows to one's head. It is also generally conflated (as in B. Russell, *A History of Western Philosophy* [New York: Simon and Schuster, 1945]) with the more dogmatic mistrust of knowledge evinced by Arcesilaus, Carneades, and the other regents of Plato's Academy during its two-hundred-year flirtation with the refusal of all dogmas—having decided, in opposition to obvious contradictions in its tradition, to take its inspiration from Socrates in only his skeptical moods. Academic skepticism appears to have been a more strident critique of the knowledge of others—and therefore a declaration of the "truth" that no one knows anything at all—though it is true that in conversation, Pyrrho's suspension of belief would have amounted to much the same thing. Consequently, most philosophers have not recognized Pyrrho's innovation to be the empirical turn toward profundity that it genuinely was. It is said that Pyrrho acquired his discipline from a naked ascetic (Greek *gymnosophist*) he met while on Alexander's campaign to the borders of India. He is also reported to have been quite a saintly figure, presumably as a consequence of the peace he acquired in the absence of opinions. It should be noted, however, that the ataraxia which Sextus describes in his *Outlines of Pyrrhonism* was not "enlightenment" in the Eastern sense—rather, it seems to have amounted to little more than a condition of not suffering as much as ordinary men. Nevertheless, ataraxia was a realizable spiritual goal supported by sound reasoning and, as such, represents an empirical advance over the aims of mere philosophy.

10 There is more to Diamond's thesis than this, but it essentially boils down to the unequal geographical distribution of animals and foodstuffs that can be readily domesticated.

11 At least on paper. Nevertheless, what is so remarkably barren about the Western philosophical tradition is that while the occasional lucky man in his most muscular moments of inquiry may have won a brief, experiential insight into the nondual nature of consciousness—someone like Schelling, for instance, or Rousseau while he was lolling in a boat on Lake Geneva—philosophers in the East have spent millennia articulating and integrating such insights into distinct methods of contemplative practice: rendering them both reproducible and verifiable by consensus.

12 My debt to a variety of contemplative traditions that have their origin in India will be obvious to many readers. The esoteric teachings of Buddhism (e.g., the Dzogchen teachings of the Vajrayana) and Hinduism (e.g., the teachings of Advaita Vedanta), as well as many years spent practicing various techniques of meditation, have done much to determine my view of our spiritual possibilities. While these traditions do not offer a unified perspective on the nature of the mind or the principles of spiritual life, they undoubtedly represent the most committed effort human beings have made to understand these things through introspection. Buddhism, in particular, has grown remarkably sophisticated. No other tradition has developed so many methods by which the human mind can be fashioned into a tool capable of transforming itself. Attentive readers will have noticed that I have been very hard on religions of faith—Judaism, Christianity, Islam, and even Hinduism—and have not said much that is derogatory of Buddhism. This is not an accident. While Buddhism has also been a source of ignorance and occasional violence, it is not a religion of faith, or a religion at all, in the Western sense. There are millions of Buddhists who do not seem to know this, and they can be found in temples throughout Southeast Asia, and even the West, praying to Buddha as though he were a numinous incarnation of Santa Claus. This distortion of the tradition notwithstanding, it remains true that the esoteric teachings of Buddhism offer the most complete methodology we

have for discovering the intrinsic freedom of consciousness, unencumbered by any dogma. It is no exaggeration to say that meetings between the Dalai Lama and Christian ecclesiastics to mutually honor their religious traditions are like meetings between physicists from Cambridge and the Bushmen of the Kalahari to mutually honor their respective understandings of the physical universe. This is not to say that Tibetan Buddhists are not saddled with certain dogmas (so are physicists) or that the Bushmen could not have formed some conception of the atom. Any person familiar with both literatures will know that the Bible does not contain a discernible fraction of the precise spiritual instructions that can be found in the Buddhist canon. Though there is much in Buddhism that I do not pretend to understand—as well as much that seems deeply implausible—it would be intellectually dishonest not to acknowledge its preeminence as a system of spiritual instruction.

As for the many distinguished contemplatives who have graced the sordid history of Christianity—Meister Eckhart, Saint John of the Cross, Saint Teresa of Avila, Saint Seraphim of Sarov, the venerable Desert Fathers, et al.—these were certainly extraordinary men and women: but their mystical insights, for the most part, remained shackled to the dualism of church doctrine, and accordingly failed to fly. Where they do take to the air, with a boost from Neoplatonism and other heterodox views, it is in defiance of the very tradition they might have epitomized (had it been wise enough to transcend its own literary conceits), and therefore they serve as hallowed exceptions that prove the rule—mystical Christianity was dead the day Saul set out for Damascus.

Contemplatives within the other Semitic traditions have had their mystical impulses similarly constrained. Sufism (itself influenced by Buddhism, Hinduism, Zoroastrianism, and Christian monasticism) has generally been considered a form of heresy in the Muslim world—as the terrible deaths of Al-Hallaj (854–922) and other distinguished Sufis attest. Where its doctrine has remained mindful of the Koran, Sufism is wedded to an indissoluble dualism; similarly, Jewish Kabbalists (whose teachings bear the influence of Christian Gnosticism, Sufism, and Neoplatonism) do not seem to have considered a truly nondual mysticism a possibility. See G. Scholem, *Kabbalah* (New York: Dorsette Press, 1974).

There is no denying the mystical talents of many Jewish, Christian, and Muslim contemplatives. Every religious tradition, no matter how wayward its beliefs, is likely to have produced a handful of men and women who profoundly realized the inherent freedom of consciousness.

As consciousness already *is* free of subject and object duality, the emergence of an Eckhart or a Rumi is no surprise at all. The existence of such spiritual luminaries, however, suggests nothing about the adequacy of the Bible and the Koran as contemplative manuals. I trust that some lucky man has been enlightened while being run over by a train or flung from the bow of a pirate ship. Does this mean that such mishaps constitute adequate spiritual instruction? While I do not deny that every tradition, East and West, is likely to have produced a few mystics whose insights breached the gilded prison of their faith, the failures of faith-based religion are so conspicuous, its historical degradation so great, its intolerance so of this world, that I think it is time we stopped making excuses for it.

The New Age has offered little progress in this regard, because it has made spiritual life seem generally synonymous with the forfeiture of brain cells. Most of the beliefs and practices that have been designated as "spiritual," in this New Age or in any other, have arisen and thrive in a perfect vacuum of critical intelligence. Indeed, many New Age ideas are so ridiculous as to produce terror in otherwise dispassionate men. In response to the absurdities that are arrayed, each year, at events like the Whole Life Expo, scientists and other rational people have found new reason to criticize and discard all spiritual claims and their evidence. And so it is that every man who concerns himself with the disposition of the planets before the disposition of his ideas simply heaps more fuel upon the dark fires of cynicism.

But there have been other sources of cynicism. Inevitably, spiritual practice must be taught by those who are expert in it, and those who profess to be experts—to be genuine gurus—are not always as selfless as they claim. As a consequence of their antics, many educated people now believe that a guru is simply a man who, while professing his love for all beings, secretly longs to rule an ashram populated exclusively by beautiful young women. This stereotype is not without its exemplars—and while the occasional yogi of renown may lick a leper's wounds with apparent enthusiasm, many display far more ordinary longings.

I know a group of veteran spiritual seekers who, after searching for a teacher among the caves and dells of the Himalayas for many months, finally discovered a Hindu yogi who seemed qualified to lead them into the ethers. He was as thin as Jesus, as limber as an orangutan, and wore his hair matted, down to his knees. They promptly brought this prodigy to America to instruct them in the ways of spiritual devotion. After a suitable period of acculturation, our acetic—who was, incidentally, also admired for his physical beauty and for the manner in which he played the drum—decided that sex with the prettiest of his patrons' wives would suit his pedagogical purposes admirably. These relations were commenced at once, and endured for some time by a man whose devotion to wife and guru, it must be said, was now being sorely tested. His wife, if I am not mistaken, was an enthusiastic participant in this "tantric" exercise, for her guru was both "fully enlightened" and as dashing a swain as Lord Krishna. Gradually, this saintly man further refined his spiritual requirements, as well as his appetites. The day soon dawned when he would eat nothing for breakfast but a pint of Häagen-Dazs vanilla ice cream topped with cashews. We might well imagine that the meditations of a cuckold, wandering the frozen-food aisles of a supermarket in search of an enlightened man's enlightened repast, were anything but devotional. This guru was soon sent back to India with his drum.

[13] Padmasambhava, *Self-liberation through Seeing with Naked Awareness*, trans. J. M. Reynolds (New York: Station Hill Press, 1989), 12.

[14] Padmasambhava was an eighth-century mystic who is generally credited with having brought the teachings of Buddhism (particularly those of Tanta and Dzogchen) from India to Tibet.

[15] No doubt, many students of Christian, Muslim, and Jewish esoterica will claim that my literal reading of their scriptures betrays my ignorance of their spiritual import. To be sure, occult, alchemical, and conventionally mystical interpretations of various passages in the Bible and the Koran are as old as the texts themselves, but the problem with such hermeneutical efforts—whether it be the highly dubious theory of *gematria* (the translation of the Hebrew letters of the Torah into their numerical equivalents so that numerologists can work their interpretive magic upon the text) or the glib symbol seeking of popular scholars like Joseph Campbell—is that they are perfectly unconstrained by the contents of the texts themselves. One can interpret every text in such a way as to yield almost any mystical or occult instruction.

A case in point: I have selected another book at random, this time from the cookbook aisle of a bookstore. The book is *A Taste of Hawaii: New Cooking from the Crossroads of the Pacific*. Therein I have discovered an as yet uncelebrated mystical treatise. While it appears to be a recipe for *wok-seared fish and shrimp cakes with ogo-tomato relish*, we need only study its list of ingredients to know that we are in the presence of an unrivaled spiritual intelligence:

snapper filet, cubed
3 teaspoons chopped scallions
salt and freshly ground black pepper
a dash of cayenne pepper
2 teaspoons chopped fresh ginger
1 teaspoon minced garlic
8 shrimp, peeled, deveined, and cubed
$1/2$ cup heavy cream; 2 eggs, lightly beaten
3 teaspoons rice wine; 2 cups bread crumbs
3 tablespoons vegetable oil; $2^1/2$ cups ogo tomato relish

The *snapper filet*, of course, is the individual himself—you and I—
awash in the sea of existence. But here we find it cubed, which is to say
that our situation must be remedied in all three dimensions of body,
mind, and spirit.

Three teaspoons of chopped scallions further partakes of the cubic
symmetry, suggesting that that which we need add to each level of our
being by way of antidote comes likewise in equal proportions. The import
of the passage is clear: the body, mind, and spirit need to be tended to with
the same care.

Salt and freshly ground black pepper: here we have the perennial
invocation of opposites—the white and the black aspects of our nature.
Both good and evil must be understood if we would fulfill the recipe for
spiritual life. Nothing, after all, can be excluded from the human experience (this seems to be a Tantric text). What is more, salt and pepper come
to us in the form of grains, which is to say that our good and bad qualities are born of the tiniest actions. Thus, we are not good or evil in general, but only by virtue of innumerable moments, which color the stream
of our being by force of repetition.

A dash of cayenne pepper: clearly, being of such robust color and flavor,
this signifies the spiritual influence of an enlightened adept. What shall we
make of the ambiguity of its measurement? How large is a dash? Here we
must rely upon the wisdom of the universe at large. The teacher himself
will know precisely what we need by way of instruction. And it is at just
this point in the text that the ingredients that bespeak the heat of spiritual
endeavor are added to the list—for after a dash of cayenne pepper, we find
two teaspoons of chopped fresh ginger and *one teaspoon of minced garlic*.
These form an isosceles trinity of sorts, signifying the two sides of our spiritual nature (male and female) united with the object meditation.

Next comes *eight shrimp*—peeled, deveined, and cubed. The eight shrimp, of course, represent the eight worldly concerns that every spiritual aspirant must decry: fame and shame; loss and gain; pleasure and pain; praise and blame. Each needs to be deveined, peeled, and cubed—that is, purged of its power to entrance us and incorporated on the path of practice.

That such metaphorical acrobatics can be performed on almost any text—and that they are therefore meaningless—should be obvious. Here we have scripture as Rorschach blot: wherein the occultist can find his magical principles perfectly reflected; the conventional mystic can find his recipe for transcendence; and the totalitarian dogmatist can hear God telling him to suppress the intelligence and creativity of others. This is not to say that no author has ever couched spiritual or mystical information in allegory or ever produced a text that requires a strenuous hermeneutical effort to be made sense of. If you pick up a copy of *Finnegans Wake*, for instance, and imagine that you have found therein allusions to various cosmogonic myths and alchemical schemes, chances are that you have, because Joyce put them there. But to dredge scripture in this manner and discover the occasional pearl is little more than a literary game.

16 For a recent scholarly treatment of the phenomenology of Buddhist meditation that is compatible with my usage here, see B. A. Wallace, "Intersubjectivity in Indo-Tibetan Buddhism," *Journal of Consciousness Studies* 8, nos. 5–7 (2001): 209–30. For extensive discussion of meditation by neuroscientists, see J. H. Austin, *Zen and the Brain* (Cambridge: MIT Press, 1998), and C. deCharms, *Two Views of Mind: Abhidharma and Brain Science* (Ithaca, N.Y.: Snow Lion Publications, 1998).

17 I believe this metaphor comes from Sri Nisargadatta Maharaj, but I have forgotten where in his many discourses I read it.

18 It is often said that a person cannot learn these things from reading a book. In the general case, this is undoubtedly true. I would add that one is by no means guaranteed to recognize the intrinsic nonduality of consciousness simply by having an eminent meditation master point it out. The conditions have to be just right: the teacher has to be really delivering the goods, leaving no conceptual doubt as to what is to be recognized; and the student has to be endowed with sufficient concentration of mind to follow his instructions and notice what there is to notice. In this sense, meditation is undoubtedly an acquired skill.

19 The recognition of the nonduality of consciousness is not susceptible to

a linguistically oriented analysis. While it is perfectly natural that men who knew only their thoughts would attempt to reduce everything to language, the efforts of Wittgenstein and his imitators in philosophy do not cut deeply enough to shed any light upon this terrain. Perhaps an intuition of these things could be read into Wittgenstein's celebrated statement "What we cannot speak about we must pass over in silence." But the true mystery, whereof we cannot speak, can nevertheless be recognized.

20 Meditation has, in fact, been the subject of scientific study for many years. See J. Andresen, "Meditation Meets Behavioral Medicine: The Story of Experimental Research on Meditation," *Journal of Consciousness Studies* 7, nos. 11–12 (2000): 17–73, for an exhaustive review. Much of this research has employed EEG and physiological measures and, in so doing, has not attempted to localize changes in brain function. Most studies that have utilized modern techniques of neuroimaging have not studied meditation relative to the self-sense per se. See A. B. Newberg et al., "The Measurement of Regional Cerebral Blood Flow during the Complex Cognitive Task of Meditation: A Preliminary SPECT Study," *Psychiatry Research: Neuroimaging Section* 106 (2000 and 2001): 113–22, for the results of a SPECT study. To my knowledge, only one group has begun working with meditators who are producing the specific, subjective effect of losing their sense of self; a preliminary report on these studies can be found in D. Goleman, *Destructive Emotions: A Scientific Dialogue with the Dalai Lama* (New York: Bantam, 2003).

21 F. Varela, "Neurophenomenology," *Journal of Consciousness Studies* 3, no. 4 (1996): 330–49, makes this point with regard to the scientific validity of "subjective" data: "The line of separation—between rigor and lack of it—is not to be drawn between first and third person accounts, but determined rather by whether there is a clear methodological ground leading to a communal validation and shared knowledge."

22 I would like to briefly address the concern that the experience of nonduality brought on by meditation is entirely private, and therefore not amenable to independent verification. Are we obliged merely to take a meditator's word for it? And if so, is this a problem?

Those who would demand an independent measure of mental events should first consider two things: (1) many features of human experience are irretrievably private and, as a consequence, self-report remains our only guide to their existence: depression, anger, joy, visual and auditory hallucinations, dreams, and even pain are among the innumerable "first-person" facts that can be finally verified only by self-report; (2) in those cases where independent measures of internal states *do* exist, they exist only by virtue of their reliable correlation with self-report. Even fear, which is now dependably linked to a variety of physiological and behavioral measures—increased startle response, rising cortisol, increased skin conductance, etc.—cannot be taken off the gold standard of self-report. Imagine what would happen if subjective ratings of fear ever broke free of such "independent" measures: if, say, 50 percent of subjects claimed to feel no fear when their cortisol levels rose and to feel terror when they fell. These measures would cease to be of any use at all in the study of fear. It is important that we not lose sight of the cash value that physiological and behavioral variables have in the study of mental events: *they are only as good as the subjects say they are.* (I do not mean to suggest that people are subjectively incorrigible, or that every mental event is best studied by recourse to self-report. When the topic under consideration is how things *seem* to the subject, however, self-report will be our only compass.)

[23] Indeed, the future looks rather like the past in this respect. We may live to see the technological perfection of all the visionary strands of traditional mysticism: shamanism (Siberian or South American), Gnosticism, Kabbalah, Hermetism and its magical Renaissance spawn (Hermeticism), and all the other byzantine paths whereby man has sought the Other in every guise of its conception. But all these approaches to spirituality are born of a longing for esoteric knowledge and a desire to excavate the visionary strata of the mind—in dreams, or trance, or psychedelic swoon—in search of the sacred. While I have no doubt that remarkable experiences are lying in wait for the initiate down each of these byways, the fact that consciousness is always the prior context and condition of every visionary experience is a great clarifying truth—and one which brands all such excursions as fundamentally unnecessary. That consciousness is not improved—not made emptier of self, or more mysterious, transcendental, etc.—by the pyrotechnics of esotericism is a fact, which contemplatives of every persuasion could confirm in their own experience.

The modern version of the visionary impulse, perhaps best exemplified in the exquisite ravings of Terence McKenna, is the equation of spiritual transcendence with *information* of a transcendental kind. Thus, any experience (most effectively invoked with the aid of psychedelic drugs) in which the mind is flooded by paradoxical disclosures—visions of other realms, ethereal beings, the grammatology of alien intelligences, etc.—is considered to be an improvement upon ordinary consciousness. What such a romance of the subtle overlooks, however, is the sublimity of consciousness itself, prior to subject/object perception. That subtle disclosures are captivating to the intellect (whether or not they are "true"), there can be no doubt. But their impermanence—any vision, having arisen, is destined to pass away—proves that such phenomena are not the basis for permanent transformation.

I do not mean to suggest, however, that these "interior" landscapes should remain unexplored. Increasingly subtle appearances hold intrinsic interest for anyone who would acquire more knowledge about the body, the mind, or the universe at large. I am simply saying that to seek *freedom* amid any continuum of possible disclosures seems a mistake, one that only the nondual schools of mysticism have adequately criticized. What is more, the fascination with such esoterica is largely responsible for the infantilism and mere credulity that attends most expressions of spirituality in the West. Either we find mere belief, wedded to the hideous presumption of its own sufficiency, or we are met by the frenzied search for novelty—psychic experience, prophecies of doom or splendor, and a thousand errant convictions about the personality of God. But the fact remains that whatever changes occur in the stream of our experience—whether a vision of Jesus appears to each of us, or the totality of human knowledge can one day be downloaded directly onto our synapses—in spiritual terms we will be consciousness first, and only, and already free of "I." It does not seem too soon for us to realize this.

²⁴ Whether mysticism entails the transcendence of all concepts is surely an open question. The claim here is merely that the concepts that underwrite our dualistic perception of the world are left aside by mystics.

Bibliography

Aarons, M., and J. Loftus. *Unholy Trinity: The Vatican, the Nazis, and the Swiss Banks.* Rev. ed. New York: St. Martin's Griffin, 1998.

Abraham, R., T. McKenna, and R. Sheldrake. *Trialogues at the Edge of the West: Chaos, Creativity, and the Resacralization of the World.* Santa Fe: Bear Publishing, 1992.

Adolphs, R., D. Tranel, and A. R. Damasio. "The Human Amygdala in Social Judgment." *Nature* 393 (June 4, 1998): 470–74.

Ahmad, Z., L. M. Balsamo, B. C. Sachs, B. Xu, and W. D. Gaillard. "Auditory Comprehension of Language in Young Children: Neural Networks Identified with fMRI." *Neurology* 60 (2003): 1598–605.

Albert, D. Z. *Quantum Mechanics and Experience.* Cambridge: Harvard Univ. Press, 1992.

Allman, J. M. *Evolving Brains.* New York: Scientific American Library, 1999.

Anderson, J. R. "The New Theoretical Framework." In *The Adaptive Character of Thought.* Hillsdale, N.J.: Erlbaum, 1990.

Andresen, J. "Meditation Meets Behavioral Medicine: The Story of Experimental Research on Meditation." *Journal of Consciousness Studies* 7, nos. 11–12 (2000): 17–73.

Anonymous. *Terrorist Hunter.* New York: HarperCollins, 2003.

Anscombe, G. E. M. "The First Person." In *Self-knowledge,* ed. Q. Cassam. Oxford: Oxford Univ. Press, 1975.

Appleyard, B. *Understanding the Present: Science and the Soul of Modern Man.* New York: Doubleday, 1992.

Armstrong, K. *A History of God.* New York: Alfred A. Knopf, 1994.

Astavakra. *The Ashtavakra Gita.* Translated by Thomas Byrom. Boston: Shambhala, 1990.

Augustine, Saint. *The City of God.* Translated by M. Dods. Chicago: Univ. of Chicago Press, 1952.

———. *Confessions.* Translated by J. G. Pilkington. Great Britain: Folio Society, 1993.

Austin, J. H. *Zen and the Brain: Toward an Understanding of Meditation and Consciousness.* Cambridge: MIT Press, 1998.

Austin, J. L. *Sense and Sensibilia.* London: Oxford Univ. Press, 1962.

Ayer, A. J. *Wittgenstein.* New York: Random House, 1985.

Bacovcin, H., trans. *The Way of a Pilgrim and A Pilgrim Continues His Way.* New York: Doubleday, 1978.

Baddeley, A. "The Fractionation of Working Memory." *Proceedings of the National Academy of Sciences U.S.A.* 93 (1996): 13468–72.

Baier, A. C. *Moral Prejudices: Essays on Ethics.* Cambridge: Harvard Univ. Press, 1994.

Baker, L. R. *Saving Belief: A Critique of Physicalism.* Princeton: Princeton Univ. Press, 1987.

Bankei. *The Unborn: The Life and Teaching of Zen Master Bankei (1622–1693).* Translated by N. Waddell. San Francisco: North Point Press, 1984.

Barnstone, W., ed. *The Other Bible: Jewish Pseudepigrapha, Christian Apocrypha, Gnostic Scriptures, Kabbalah, Dead Sea Scrolls.* San Francisco: Harper San Francisco, 1984.

Barrett, W., and H. D. Aiken., eds. *Philosophy in the 20th Century.* 4 vols. New York: Random House, 1962.

Baudrillard, J. *The Spirit of Terrorism.* Translated by C. Turner. New York: Verso, 2002.

Baumgartner, P., and S. Payr, eds. *Speaking Minds: Interviews with Twenty Eminent Cognitive Scientists.* Princeton: Princeton Univ. Press, 1995.

Bechara, A., H. Damasio, D. Tranel, and A. R. Damasio. "Deciding Advantageously before Knowing the Advantageous Strategy." *Science* 275 (1997): 1293–95.

Becker, E. *The Denial of Death.* New York: Free Press, 1973.

Beedle, A. S. "A Philosopher Looks at Neuroscience." *Journal of Neuroscience Research* 55 (1999): 141–46.

Beloff, J. "Minds and Machines: A Radical Dualist Perspective." *Journal of Consciousness Studies* 1, no. 1 (1994): 32–37.

Bennet, J. "In Israeli Hospital, Bomber Tells of Trying to Kill Israelis." *New York Times,* June 8, 2002.

Bennett, J. "How Is Cognitive Ethology Possible?" In *Cognitive Ethology: The Minds of Other Animals,* ed. C. A. Ristau. Hillsdale, N.J.: Erlbaum, 1991.

Benson, H., with M. Stark. *Timeless Healing: The Power and Biology of Belief.* New York: Charles Scribner, 1996.

Bergson, H. *Time and Free Will: An Essay on the Immediate Data of Consciousness.* Translated by F. L. Pogson. 1910; reprint, London: George Allen & Unwin, 1971.

Berkow, R., ed. *The Merck Manual of Diagnosis and Therapy.* 16th ed. Rahway, N.J.: Merck Research Laboratories, 1992.

Berman, P. "The Philosopher of Islamic Terror." *New York Times Magazine,* March 23, 2003.

————. *Terror and Liberalism*. New York: W. W. Norton, 2003.

Beyerstein, B. L. "Neuropathology and the Legacy of Spiritual Possession." *Skeptical Inquirer* 12, no. 3 (1998): 248–61.

Binder, L. *Islamic Liberalism: A Critique of Development Ideologies*. Chicago: Univ. of Chicago Press, 1988.

Blake, R., and N. K. Logothetis. "Visual Competition." *Nature Reviews Neuroscience* 3, no. 1 (2002): 13–21.

Blakemore, C., and S. Jennett, eds. *The Oxford Companion to the Body*. Oxford: Oxford Univ. Press, 2001.

Block, N. "Troubles with Functionalism." In *The Nature of Mind*, ed. D. Rosenthal. Oxford: Oxford Univ. Press, 1991.

————. "The Mind as the Software of the Brain." In *An Invitation to Cognitive Science: Thinking*, ed. E. E. Smith and D. N. Osherson. Cambridge: MIT Press, 1995.

Block, N., O. Flanagan, and G. Güzeldere, eds. *The Nature of Consciousness: Philosophical Debates*. Cambridge: MIT Press, 1997.

Bloom, H. *Omens of the Millennium: The Gnosis of Angels, Dreams, and Resurrection*. New York: Riverhead Books, 1996.

————, ed. *The Book of J*. Translated by D. Rosenberg. New York: Vintage, 1990.

Bobrow, R. S. "Paranormal Phenomena in the Medical Literature: Sufficient Smoke to Warrant a Search for Fire." *Medical Hypotheses* 60 (2003): 864–68.

Bogen J. E. "Mental Duality in the Intact Brain." *Bulletin of Clinical Neuroscience* 51 (1986): 3–29.

————. "On the Neuropsychology of Consiousness: Parts I and II." *Consciousness and Cognition* 4 (1995): 52–62, 137–58.

Bohm, D., and B. J. Hiley. *The Undivided Universe*. London: Routledge, 1993.

Bok, S. *Lying: Moral Choice in Public and Private Life*. New York: Vintage, 1978.

Bouveresse, J. *Wittgenstein Reads Freud: The Myth of the Unconscious*. Translated by C. Cosman. Princeton: Princeton Univ. Press, 1995.

Bowden, M. "The Dark Art of Interrogation." *Atlantic Monthly*, March 2003, pp. 51–77.

Bowker, J., ed. *The Oxford Dictionary of World Religions*. Oxford: Oxford Univ. Press, 1997.

————. *What Muslims Believe*. Oxford: Oneworld, 1998.

Boyer, P. *When Time Shall Be No More: Prophecy Belief in Modern American Culture*. Cambridge: Harvard Univ. Press, 1992.

Braun, S. *The Science of Happiness: Unlocking the Mysteries of Mood*. New York: John Wiley, 2000.

Briggs, R. *Witches and Neighbors: The Social and Cultural Context of European Witchcraft*. New York: Viking, 1996.

Brisick, W., ed. *Crystal Cave: A Compendium of Teachings by Masters of the Practice Lineage*. Translated by E. P. Kunsang. Katmandu: Rangjung Yeshe Publications, 1990.

Brockman, J., ed. *The Next Fifty Years: Science in the First Half of the Twenty-first Century*. New York: Vintage, 2002.

———, ed. *The Third Culture*. New York: Simon and Schuster, 1995.

Buber, M., ed. *Ecstatic Confessions*. Translated by E. Cameron. New York: Harper and Row, 1985.

———. *I and Thou*. Translated by W. Kaufmann. New York: Charles Scribner, 1970.

Buckley, W. F., Jr. "The War on Drugs Is Lost." *National Review*, Feb. 12, 1996.

———. "Abolish Drug Laws?: 400 Readers Give Their Views." *National Review*, July 1, 1996.

Buddhaghosa. *The Path of Purification*. Translated by Bhikkhu Nanamoli. Kandy, Sri Lanka: Buddhist Publication Society, 1975.

Burt, A. M. *Textbook of Neuroanatomy*. Philadelphia: W. B. Saunders, 1993.

Campbell, A. "Cartesian Dualism and the Concept of Medical Placebos." *Journal of Consciousness Studies* 1, no 2 (1994): 230–33.

Campbell, J. *The Hero with a Thousand Faces*. Princeton: Princeton Univ. Press, 1949.

Canetti, E. *Crowds and Power*. Translated by C. Stewart. New York: Farrar, Straus and Giroux, 1962.

Carroll, J. "The Silence." *New Yorker*, April 7, 1997.

———. *Constantine's Sword: The Church and the Jews*. Boston: Houghton Mifflin, 2001.

Casebeer, W. D. "Moral Cognition and Its Neural Constituents." *Nature Reviews Neuroscience* 4 (2003): 840–46.

Chalmers, D. J. *The Conscious Mind: In Search of a Fundamental Theory*. Oxford: Oxford Univ. Press, 1996.

Cheney, D. L., and R. M. Seyfarth. *How Monkeys See the World: Inside the Mind of Another Species*. Chicago: Univ. of Chicago Press, 1990.

Chisholm, R. M. "On the Observability of the Self." *Philosophy and Phenomenological Research* 30 (1969): 7–21.

Chomsky, N. *9-11*. New York: Seven Stories Press, 2001.

Chuang Tzu. *Basic Writings*. Translated by B. Watson. New York: Columbia Univ. Press, 1964.

Churchland, P. M. *Scientific Realism and the Plasticity of Mind*. Cambridge: Cambridge Univ. Press, 1979.

———. *Matter and Consciousness*. Cambridge: MIT Press, 1988.

———. "Knowing Qualia: A Reply to Jackson." In *The Nature of Consciousness: Philosophical Debates*, ed. N. Block, O. Flanagan, and G. Güzeldere. Cambridge: MIT Press, 1997.

Churchland, P. S., and P. M. Churchland. "Neural Worlds and Real Worlds." *Nature Reviews Neuroscience* 3 (2002): 903–7.

Cialdini, R. B. *Influence: The Psychology of Persuasion*. New York: Quill, 1993.

Cohen, J. D., and K. I. Blum. "Reward and Decision." *Neuron* 36, no. 2 (2002): 193–98.

Collins, L., and D. Lapierre. *Freedom at Midnight*. New York: Simon and Schuster, 1975.

Conway, M. A. "Repression Revisited." *Nature* 410 (March 15, 2001): 319–20.

Conze, E. *A Short History of Buddhism*. Oxford: Oneworld, 1980.

———, trans. and ed. *Buddhist Texts through the Ages*. Boston: Shambhala, 1990.

Copleston, F. *A History of Philosophy*. 9 vols. New York: Image, 1960–77.

Corballis, M. C. "Sperry and the Age of Aquarius: Science, Values, and the Split Brain." *Neuropsychologia* 36 (1998): 1083–87.

Crick, F. *The Astonishing Hypothesis: The Scientific Search for the Soul*. New York: Charles Scribner, 1994.

Crick, F., and C. Koch. "Consciousness and Neuroscience." *Cerebral Cortex* 8 (1998): 97–107.

———. "The Unconscious Humunculus." In *The Neural Correlates of Consciousness*, ed. T. Metzinger. Cambridge: MIT Press, 1999.

———. "The Problem of Consciousness." *Scientific American Special Edition* 12, no. 1 (2002): 10–17.

Dahlbom, B., ed. *Dennett and His Critics*. Oxford: Blackwell, 1993.

Damasio, A. *Descartes' Error: Emotion, Reason, and the Human Brain*. New York: Avon Books, 1994.

———. "How the Brain Creates the Mind." *Scientific American Special Edition* 12, no. 1 (2002): 4–9.

———. *Looking for Spinoza: Joy, Sorrow, and the Feeling Brain*. New York: Harcourt, 2003.

Daprati, E., N. Franck, N. Georgieff, J. Proust, E. Pacherie, J. Dalery, M. Jeannerod. "Looking for the Agent: An Investigation into Consciousness and Self-consciousness in Schizophrenic Patients." *Cognition* 65 (1997): 71–86.

Davidson, D. "A Coherence Theory of Truth and Knowledge." Undated MS.

———. "A Nice Derangement of Epitaphs." Undated MS.

———. "The Myth of the Subjective." Undated MS.

———. "Actions, Reasons, and Causes." In *Essays on Actions and Events*. Oxford: Oxford Univ. Press, 1980.

———. "Paradoxes of Irrationality." In *Philosophical Essays on Freud*, ed. R. Wollheim and J. Hopkins. Cambridge: Cambridge Univ. Press, 1982.

———. *Inquiries into Truth and Interpretation*. Oxford: Clarendon Press, 1984.

———. "Deception and Division." In *The Multiple Self*, ed. J. Elster. Cambridge: Cambridge Univ. Press, 1985.

———. "Knowing One's Own Mind." *Proceedings and Addresses of the American Philosophical Association* 60 (1987): 441–58.

———. "Who Is Fooled?" In *Self-Deception and Paradoxes of Rationality*, ed. J. P. Dupuy. Stanford: CSLI Publications, 1998.

Davies, N. *Europe: A History*. Oxford: Oxford Univ. Press, 1996.

Davies, P. *Are We Alone?: Philosophical Implications of the Discovery of Extraterrestrial Life*. New York: Basic Books, 1995.

Davies, P., and J. Gribbin. *The Matter Myth*. New York: Simon and Schuster, 1992.

Davies, P., and J. R. Brown, eds. *The Ghost in the Atom*. Cambridge: Cambridge Univ. Press, 1986.

Davies, R. R., J. H. Xuereb, and J. R. Hodges. "The Human Perirhinal Cortex in Semantic Memory: An in Vivo and Postmortem Volumetric Magnetic Resonance Imaging Study in Semantic Dementia, Alzheimer's Disease and Matched Controls." *Neuropathology and Applied Neurobiology* 28, no. 2 (April 2002): 167–68 [abstract].

Davis, M. H., and I. S. Johnsrude. "Hierarchical Processing in Spoken Language Comprehension." *Journal of Neuroscience* 23 (2003): 3423–31.

Davis, P. J., and R. Hersh. *The Mathematical Experience*. Boston: Houghton Mifflin, 1981.

Dawkins, R. *Climbing Mount Improbable*. New York: W. W. Norton, 1996.

Dawood, N. J., trans. *The Koran*. New York: Viking, 1956.

de Quincey, C. "Consciousness All the Way Down?" *Journal of Consciousness Studies* 1, no. 2 (1994): 217–29.

———. "Conceiving the 'Inconceivable'?" *Journal of Consciousness Studies* 7, no. 4 (2000): 67–81.

deCharms, C. *Two Views of Mind: Abhidharma and Brain Science*. Ithaca, N.Y.: Snow Lion Publications, 1998.

Delacour, J. "An Introduction to the Biology of Consciousness." *Neuropsychologia* 33 (1995): 1061–74.

Denes, G., and M. Signorini. "Door But Not Four and 4 a Category Specific Transcoding Deficit in a Pure Acalculic Patient." *Cortex* 37, no. 2 (2001): 267–77.

Dennett, D. C. "Intentional System in Cognitive Ethology: The 'Panglossian Paradigm' Defended." *Behavioral and Brain Sciences* 6 (1983): 343–90.

———. *Elbow Room: The Varieties of Free Will Worth Wanting*. Cambridge: MIT Press, 1984.

———. *Consciousness Explained*. Boston: Little, Brown, 1991.

———. *Darwin's Dangerous Idea: Evolution and the Meanings of Life*. New York: Simon and Schuster, 1995.

———. "Facing Backwards on the Problem of Consciousness." *Journal of Consciousness Studies* 3, no. 1 (1996): 4–6.

———. "It's Not a Bug, It's a Feature." *Journal of Consciousness Studies* 7, no. 4 (2000): 25–27.

Dershowitz, A. *The Case for Israel*. Hoboken, N.J.: John Wiley, 2003.

Descartes, R. *Discourse and Method and Meditations*. Translated by L. J. Lafleur. Indianapolis: Library of Liberal Arts, 1960.

Deutsch, D. *The Fabric of Reality*. New York: Penguin, 1997.

Dewey, J. *Reconstruction in Philosophy*. 1920; reprint, Boston: Beacon Press, 1957.

Diamond, J. *Guns, Germs, and Steel: The Fates of Human Societies.* New York: W. W. Norton, 1997.

———. "The Last Americans: Environmental Collapse and the End of Civilization." *Harper's,* June 2003, pp. 43–51.

Didion, J. "Mr. Bush and the Divine." *New York Review of Books,* Nov. 6, 2003, pp. 81–86.

Dobbie-Bateman, A. F. *The Spiritual Instructions of St. Seraphim of Sarov.* Clearlake: Dawn Horse Press, 1973.

Doherty, C., ed. *What the World Thinks in 2002.* Washington, D.C.: Pew Research Center for the People & the Press, 2002.

Doty, R. W. "The Five Mysteries of the Mind, and Their Consequences." *Neuropsychologia* 36 (1998): 1069–76.

Du Pasquier, R. *Unveiling Islam.* Translated by T. J. Winter. Cambridge: Islamic Texts Society, 1992.

Dudjom Rinpoche. *The Nyingma School of Tibetan Buddhism, Its Fundamentals and History.* Translated by G. Dorje and M. Kapstein. 2 vols. Boston: Wisdom Publications, 1991.

Dupuy, J. P. 1989. "Common Knowledge, Common Sense." *Theory and Decision,* 27 (1989): 37–62.

———, ed. *Self-Deception and Paradoxes of Rationality.* Stanford: CSLI Publications, 1998.

Durant, W. *The Age of Faith.* 1950; reprint, Norwalk, Conn.: Easton Press, 1992.

Dworkin, R. "Terror & the Attack on Civil Liberties." *New York Review of Books,* Nov. 6, 2003, pp. 37–41.

Dyson, F. *Imagined Worlds.* Cambridge: Harvard Univ. Press, 1997.

Eccles, J. C. *How the Self Controls Its Brain.* Berlin: Springer-Verlag, 1994.

Edelman, G. M., and G. Tononi. *A Universe of Consciousness.* New York: Basic Books, 2000.

Edwards, P. *Reincarnation: A Critical Examination.* Amherst: Prometheus Books, 1996.

———, ed. *The Encyclopedia of Philosophy.* 8 vols. New York: Collier Macmillan, 1967.

Einstein, A. *Ideas and Opinions.* New York: Wings Books, 1954.

———. *Out of My Later Years.* New York: Wings Books, 1956.

———. *Einstein On Peace.* Edited by O. Nathan and H. Norden. New York: Avenel Books, 1960.

———. *Relativity: The Special and the General Theory.* New York: Crown, 1961.

Fain, G. L. *Molecular and Cellular Physiology of Neurons.* Cambridge: Harvard Univ. Press, 1999.

Farah, C. E. *Islam.* Hauppauge, N.Y.: Barron's Educational Services, 2000.

Feigl, H. *The "Mental" and the "Physical."* Minneapolis: Univ. of Minnesota Press, 1958.

Feinberg, T. E. *Altered Egos: How the Brain Creates the Self.* Oxford: Oxford Univ. Press, 2001.

Feldman, D. H., and L. T. Goldsmith. *Nature's Gambit: Child Prodigies and the Development of Human Potential.* New York: Basic Books, 1986.

Feldman, F. *Confrontations with the Reaper: A Philosophical Study of the Nature and Value of Death.* Oxford: Oxford Univ. Press, 1992.

Feser, E. "Can Phenomenal Qualities Exist Unperceived?" *Journal of Consciousness Studies* 5, no. 4 (1998): 405–14.

Feynman, R. *The Character of Physical Law.* New York: Modern Library, 1965.

———. *Six Easy Pieces.* New York: Addison-Wesley, 1995.

———. *The Meaning of It All: Thoughts of a Citizen Scientist.* Reading, Mass.: Addison-Wesley, 1998.

Fingarette, H. *Self-Deception.* Berkeley: Univ. of California Press, 2000.

Flanagan, O. *Consciousness Reconsidered.* Cambridge: MIT Press, 1992.

———. "Consciousness as a Pragmatist Views It." In *The Cambridge Companion to William James,* ed. R. A. Putnam. Cambridge: Cambridge Univ. Press. 1997.

Fletcher, P. C., F. Happé, U. Frith, S. C. Baker, R. J. Dolan, R. S. J. Fackowiak, and C. D. Frith. "Other Mind in the Brain: A Functional Imaging Study of 'Theory of Mind' in Story Comprehension." *Cognition* 57 (1995): 109–28.

Flew, A., ed. *Readings in the Philosophical Problems of Parapsychology.* Buffalo: Prometheus Books, 1987.

Fodor, J. *The Mind Doesn't Work That Way.* Cambridge: MIT Press, 2000.

Fodor, J. A., and Z. W. Pylyshyn. "Systematicity of Cognitive Representation." Excerpt from "Connectionism and Cognitive Architecture." In *Connections and Symbols,* ed. S. Pinker and J. Mehler. Cambridge: MIT Press, 1988.

Føllesdal, D. "What Computers Cannot Do: Two Strategies." In *Transcendental Philosophy and Everyday Experience,* ed. T. Rockmore and V. Zeman. Atlantic Highlands, N.J.: Humanities Press, 1997.

Forman, R. K. C. "Mysticism, Language, and the *Via Negativa.*" *Journal of Consciousness Studies* 1, no. 1 (1994): 38–49.

Freeman, W. J. "Self, Awareness of Self, and the Illusion of Control." *Behavioral and Brain Sciences* 20 (1997): 112–13.

———. "Three Centuries of Category Errors in Studies of the Neural Basis of Consciousness and Intentionality." *Neural Networks* 10 (1997): 1175–83.

Freud, S. *The Major Works of Sigmund Freud.* Chicago: Univ. of Chicago Press, 1952.

Friedman, M. "Prohibition and Drugs." *Newsweek,* May 1, 1972.

Friedrich, O. *The End of the World: A History.* New York: Coward, McCann & Geoghegan, 1982.

———. *The Kingdom of Auschwitz.* New York: Harper Perennial, 1994.

Frith, C. D. "Attention to Action and Awareness of Other Minds." *Consciousness and Cognition* 11 (2002): 481–87.

Frith, C. D., and U. Frith. 1999. "Interacting Minds—A Biological Basis." *Science's Compass* 286 (1999): 1692–95.

Fuller, G. E. *The Future of Political Islam.* New York: Palgrave Macmillan, 2003.

Fuster, J. M. *Cortex and Mind: Unifying Cognition.* Oxford: Oxford Univ. Press, 2002.

Gallup, G. H., Jr. *Religion in America 1996.* Princeton: Princeton Religion Research Center, 1996.

Gallup, G. H., Jr., and R. Bezilla. *The Role of the Bible in American Society.* Princeton: Princeton Religion Research Center, 1990.

Garab Dorje. *The Golden Letters: The Three Statements of Garab Dorje the First Teacher of Dzogchen together with a Commentary by Dza Patrul Rinpoche.* Translated and edited by J. Reynolds. Ithaca, N.Y.: Snow Lion Publications, 1996.

Gardner, M. *The New Ambidextrous Universe: Symmetry and Asymmetry from Mirror Reflections to Superstrings.* New York: W. H. Freeman, 1990.

———. *The New Age: Notes of a Fringe-Watcher.* New York: Prometheus Books, 1991.

———. *Relativity Simply Explained.* New York: Dover, 1996.

Gazzaniga, M.S. "Legalizing Drugs: Just Say Yes." *National Review,* July 10, 1995.

———. "The Split Brain Revisited." *Scientific American Special Edition* 12, no. 1 (2002): 26–37.

———, ed. *The New Cognitive Neurosciences.* 2d ed. Cambridge: MIT Press, 2000.

Gazzaniga, M. S., J. E. Bogen, and R. W. Sperry. "Some Functional Effects of Sectioning the Cerebral Commissures in Man." *Proceedings of the National Academy of Sciences* 48 (1962): 1765–69.

Gazzaniga, M. S., R. B. Ivry, and G. R. Mangun. *Cognitive Neuroscience: The Biology of the Mind.* New York: W. W. Norton, 1998.

Gentner, D., and A. B. Markman. "Structure Mapping in Analogy and Similarity." *American Psychologist* 52 (1997): 45–56.

George, L. *Crimes of Perception: An Encyclopedia of Heresies and Heretics.* New York: Paragon House, 1995.

Gigerenzer, G. "On Narrow Norms and Vague Heuristics: A Reply to Kahneman and Tversky." *Psychological Review* 103 (1996): 592–96.

Gilbert, D. T. "How Mental Systems Believe." *American Psychologist* 46 2 (1991): 107–19.

Gilbert, D. T., et al. "Unbelieving the Unbelievable: Some Problems in the Rejection of False Information." *Journal of Personality and Social Psychology* 59 (1990): 601–13.

Gilbert, M. *The Holocaust: A History of the Jews of Europe during the Second World War.* New York: Henry Holt, 1985.

Gilovich, T. *How We Know What Isn't So.* New York: Free Press, 1991.

Giovagnoli, A. R., A. Erbetta, and O. Bugiani. "Preserved Semantic Access in Global

Amnesia and Hippocampal Damage." *Clinical Neuropsychology* 15 (2001): 508–15 [abstract].

Gleick, J. *Isaac Newton.* New York: Pantheon Books, 2003.

Glenny, M. "Why the Balkans Are So Violent." *New York Review of Books,* Sept. 19, 1996, pp. 34–39.

Glimcher, P. W. "Decisions, Decisions, Decisions: Choosing a Biological Science of Choice." *Neuron* 36, no. 2 (2002): 323–32.

Glover, J. *Humanity: A Moral History of the Twentieth Century.* New Haven: Yale Univ. Press, 1999.

Glynn, I. *An Anatomy of Thought: The Origin and Machinery of the Mind.* Oxford: Oxford Univ. Press, 1999.

Goel, V., B. Gold, S. Kapur, and S. Houle. "The Seats of Reason? An Imaging Study of Deductive and Inductive Reasoning." *Neuroreport* 8 (March 24, 1997): 1305–10.

Goel, V., and R. J. Dolan. "Explaining Modulation of Reasoning by Belief." *Cognition* 87, no. 1 (2003): B11–22.

Goenka, S. N. *The Art of Living: Vipassana Meditation as Taught by S. N. Goenka.* Edited by W. Hart. New York: Harper and Row, 1987.

Goffman, E. *Interaction Ritual: Essays on Face to Face Behavior.* New York: Pantheon Books, 1967.

Gold, J. I., and M. N. Shadlen. "Representation of a Perceptual Decision in Developing Oculomotor Commands." *Nature* 404 (March 23, 2000): 390–94.

———. "Banburismus and the Brain: Decoding the Relationship between Sensory Stimuli, Decisions, and Reward." *Neuron* 36, no. 2 (2002): 299–308.

Goldberg, E. *The Executive Brain: Frontal Lobes and the Civilized Mind.* Oxford: Oxford Univ. Press, 2001.

Goldberg, J. "Letter from Cairo: Behind Mubarak." *New Yorker,* Oct. 8, 2001, pp. 48–55.

Goldhagen, D. J. *Hitler's Willing Executioners: Ordinary Germans and the Holocaust.* New York: Alfred A. Knopf, 1996.

Goleman, D. *Destructive Emotions: A Scientific Dialogue with the Dalai Lama.* New York: Bantam Books, 2003.

Goodenough, E. R. "Depth Psychology: Wish Projection." In *Toward a Mature Faith.* Lanham, Md.: Univ. Press of America, 1955.

———. "A Historian of Religion Tries to Define Religion." *Zygon* 2 (1967): 7–22.

Gorenberg, G. *The End of Days: Fundamentalism and the Struggle for the Temple Mount.* Oxford: Oxford Univ. Press, 2000.

Gould, S. J. "Nonoverlapping Magisteria." *Natural History,* March 1997.

Gourevitch, P. "Letter from Korea: Alone in the Dark." *New Yorker,* Sept. 8, 2003, pp. 55–75.

Govinda, A. Lama. *A Living Buddhism for the West.* Translated by M. Walshe. Boston: Shambhala, 1989.

Graham, G., and G. L. Stephens, eds. *Philosophical Psychopathology.* Cambridge: MIT Press, 1994.

Green, D. *Gold in the Crucible: Teresa of Avila and the Western Mystical Tradition.* Longmead, Eng.: Element Books, 1989.

Greene, J. D. "From Neural 'Is' to Moral 'Ought': What Are the Moral Implications of Neuroscientific Moral Psychology?" *Nature Reviews Neuroscience* 4 (2003): 846–49.

Greene, J. D., et al. "An fMRI Investigation of Emotional Engagement in Moral Judgment." *Science* 293 (Sept. 14, 2001): 2105–8.

Gregory, R. L., ed. *The Oxford Companion to the Mind.* Oxford: Oxford Univ. Press, 1987.

Griffin, D. R. *Animal Minds.* Chicago: Univ. of Chicago Press, 1992.

————. "Panexperientialist Physicalism and the Mind-Body Problem." *Journal of Consciousness Studies* 4, no. 3 (1997): 248–68.

Griffiths, P. J. *On Being Mindless: Buddhist Meditation and the Mind-Body Problem.* La Salle, Ill.: Open Court, 1986.

Guttenplan, S., ed. *A Companion to the Philosophy of Mind.* Oxford: Blackwell, 1994.

Haack, S. "Science, Scientism, and Anti-Science in the Age of Preposterism." *Skeptical Inquirer* 21, no. 6 (1997): 37–42.

Habermas, J. *The Philosophical Discourse of Modernity.* Translated by F. Lawrence. Cambridge: MIT Press, 1990.

————. *The Past as Future.* Translated and edited by M. Pensky. Lincoln: Univ. of Nebraska Press, 1994.

————. *On the Pragmatics of Communication.* Edited by M. Cooke. Cambridge: MIT Press, 1998.

Hadamard, J. *The Mathematician's Mind: The Psychology of Invention in the Mathematical Field.* Princeton: Princeton Univ. Press, 1945.

Hagen, S. *How the World Can Be the Way It Is.* Wheaton, Ill.: Quest Books, 1995.

Haggard, P. "The Psychology of Action." *British Journal of Psychology* 92 (2001): 113–28.

Haggard, P., and E. Magno. "Localizing Awareness of Action with Transcortical Magnetic Stimulation." *Experimental Brain Research* 127 (1999): 102–7.

Haggard, P., and M. Eimer. "On the Relation between Brain Potentials and the Awareness of Voluntary Movements." *Experimental Brain Research* 126 (1999): 128–33.

Hall, M. P. *The Secret Teachings of All Ages.* Los Angeles: Philosophical Research Society, 1977.

Hameroff, S. R. "Quantum Coherence in Microtubules: A Neural Basis for Emergent Consciousness?" *Journal of Consciousness Studies* 1, no. 1 (1994): 91–118.

Hameroff, S., A. W. Kaszniak, and A. C. Scott, eds. *Toward a Science of Consciousness: The First Tucson Discussions and Debates.* Cambridge: MIT Press, 1996.

Hardcastle, V. G. "The Naturalists versus the Skeptics: The Debate over a Scientific Understanding of Consciousness." *Journal of Mind and Behavior* 14, no. 1 (1993): 27–50.

————. "Psychology's Binding Problem and Possible Neurobiological Solutions." *Journal of Consciousness Studies* 1, no. 1 (1994): 66–90.

Hardcastle, V. G., and O. Flanagan. "Multiplex vs. Multiple Selves: Distinguishing Dissociative Disorders." *Monist* 82 (1999): 645–57.

Harding, D. E. *On Having No Head: Zen and the Re-discovery of the Obvious*. London: Arkana, 1961.

Harman, G. "Rationality." In *An Invitation to Cognitive Science: Thinking*, ed. E. E. Smith and D. N. Osherson. Cambridge: MIT Press, 1995.

Harman, W. "The Scientific Exploration of Consciousness: Towards an Adequate Epistemology." *Journal of Consciousness Studies* 1, no. 1 (1994): 140–48.

Hart, J., R. Sloan Berndt, and A. Caramazza. "Category-Specific Naming Deficit following Cerebral Infarction." *Nature* 316 (Aug. 1, 1985): 439–40.

Haught, J. A. *Holy Hatred: Religious Conflicts of the '90s*. Amherst: Prometheus Books, 1995.

Hauser, M. D. *Wild Minds: What Animals Really Think*. New York: Henry Holt, 2001.

————. "Swappable Minds." In *The Next Fifty Years*, ed. J. Brockman. New York: Vintage, 2002.

Hauser, M. D., N. Chomsky, and W. Tecumseh Fitch. "The Faculty of Language: What Is It, Who Has It, and How Did It Evolve?" *Science* 298 (2002): 1569–79.

Hawking, S., and R. Penrose. *The Nature of Space and Time*. Princeton: Princeton Univ. Press. 1996.

Hegel, G. W. F. *The Phenomenology of Mind*. Translated by J. B. Baillie. New York: Harper and Row, 1967.

Heisenberg, W. *Physics and Philosophy: The Revolution in Modern Science*. New York: Harper and Row, 1958.

Hill, F. *A Delusion of Satan: The Full Story of the Salem Witch Trials*. New York: Doubleday, 1995.

Hille, B. *Ionic Channels of Excitable Membranes*. 2d ed. Sunderland, Mass.: Sinauer Associates, 1992.

Hitchens, C. "Mommie Dearest." *Slate*, Oct. 20, 2003. http://slate.msn.com.

Hobbes, T. *Leviathan*.1651; reprint, Chicago: Univ. of Chicago Press, 1952.

Hobson, J. A. *The Chemistry of Conscious States*. Boston: Little, Brown, 1994.

Hoffman, B. "The Logic of Suicide Terrorism." *Atlantic Monthly*, June 2003, pp. 40–47.

Hoffmann, R. J., trans. *Porphyry's Against the Christians*. Amherst: Prometheus Books, 1994.

Hofstadter, D. R. *The Tumult of Inner Voices or What Is the Meaning of the Word "I"?*. Cedar City, Utah: Grace A. Tanner Lecture in Human Values, 1982.

Hofstadter, D. R., and D. C. Dennett. *The Mind's I: Fantasies and Reflections on Self and Soul*. New York: Bantam Books, 1981.

Holton, G. *Einstein, History, and Other Passions: The Rebellion against Science at the End of the Twentieth Century*. Reading, Mass.: Addison-Wesley, 1996.

Holyoak, K. J. "Problem Solving." In *An Invitation to Cognitive Science: Thinking*, eds. E. E. Smith and D. N. Osherson. Cambridge: MIT Press, 1995.

Holyoak, K. J., and J. E. Hummel. "Toward an Understanding of Analogy within a Biological Symbol System." In *The Analogical Mind: Perspectives from Cognitive Science*, ed. D. Gentner, K. J. Holyoak, and B. N. Kokinov. Cambridge: MIT Press, 2001.

Holyoak, K. J., and P. C. Cheng. "Pragmatic Reasoning with a Point of View." *Thinking and Reasoning* 1 (1995): 289–313.

Honderich, T., ed. *The Oxford Companion to Philosophy*. Oxford: Oxford Univ. Press, 1995.

Hopkins, J. *Emptiness Yoga: The Tibetan Middle Way*. Ithaca, N.Y.: Snow Lion Publications, 1987.

Horgan, J. *The End of Science: Facing the Limits of Knowledge in the Twilight of the Scientific Age*. Reading, Mass.: Helix Books, 1996.

———. *The Undiscovered Mind: How the Human Brain Defies Replication, Medication, and Explanation*. New York: Free Press, 1999.

———. *Rational Mysticism: Dispatches from the Border between Science and Spirituality*. Boston: Houghton Mifflin, 2003.

Horner, I. B., trans. *Milinda's Questions*. 2 vols. Oxford: Pali Text Society, 1990.

Howard, M. "What's in a Name? How to Fight Terrorism." *Foreign Affairs* 81, no. 1 (2002): 8–13.

Hume, D. *The Philosophical Works of David Hume*. 4 vols. 1854; reprint, Bristol, Eng: Thoemmes Press, 1996.

Humphrey, N. "How to Solve the Mind-Body Problem." *Journal of Consciousness Studies* 7, no. 4 (2000): 5–20.

Huntington, S. P. *The Clash of Civilizations and the Remaking of World Order*. New York: Simon and Schuster, 1996.

Huxley, A. *The Perennial Philosophy*. New York: Harper and Row, 1944.

Ignatieff, M. "Why Are We in Iraq? (And Liberia? And Afghanistan?)." *New York Times Magazine*, Sept. 7, 2003.

Inge, W. R. *The Philosophy of Plotinus*. 2 vols. 1929; reprint, Westport, Conn.: Wood Press, 1968.

Jackson, F. "What Mary Didn't Know." In *The Nature of Consciousness: Philosophical Debates*, ed. N. Block, O. Flanagan, and G. Güzeldere. Cambridge: MIT Press, 1997.

Jackson, R. R., ed. and trans. *Is Enlightenment Possible?: Dharmakirti and rGyal tshab rje on Knowledge, Rebirth, No-Self and Liberation*. Ithaca, N.Y.: Snow Lion Publications, 1993.

James, W. *The Principles of Psychology*. 2 vols. 1890; reprint, New York: Dover, 1950.

———. *The Will to Believe*. 1897; reprint, New York: Longmans, Green, 1919.

———. *Essays in Radical Empiricism*. 1912; reprint, Lincoln: Univ. of Nebraska Press.

———. *The Writings of William James: A Comprehensive Edition*. Edited by J. J. McDermott. Chicago: Univ. of Chicago Press, 1997.

Jeannerod, M. "To Act or Not to Act: Perspectives on the Representation of Actions." *Quarterly Journal of Experimental Psychology* 52A, no. 1 (1999): 1–29.

———. 2001. "Neural Simulation of Action: A Unifying Mechanism for Motor Cognition." *NeuroImage* 14 (2001): S103–S109.

Jenkins, P. "The Next Christianity." *Atlantic Monthly*, Oct. 2002, pp. 53–68.

John Paul II (pope). *Crossing the Threshold of Hope*. New York: Alfred A. Knopf, 1994.

Johnson, E. "Grace Halsell's Prophecy and Politics: Militant Evangelists on the Road to Nuclear War." *Journal of Historical Review* 7, no. 4 (Winter 1986).

Johnson, P. *A History of Christianity*. New York: Simon and Schuster, 1976.

Johnson-Laird, P. N., and R. M. J. Byrne. *Deduction*. Hillsdale, N.J.: Erlbaum, 1991.

Jung, C. G. *Answer to Job*. Translated by R. F. C. Hull. Princeton: Princeton Univ. Press, 1958.

Kafatos, M., and R. Nadeau. *The Conscious Universe*. New York: Springer-Verlag, 1990.

Kahneman, D., and A. Tversky. "On the Reality of Cognitive Illusions." *Psychological Review* 103 (1996): 582–91.

Kaku, M. *Hyperspace*. Oxford: Oxford Univ. Press, 1994.

Kalat, J. W. *Biological Psychology*. 6th ed. Pacific Grove, Calif.: Brooks/Cole Publishing, 1998.

Kandel, E. R., et al. *Principles of Neural Science*. 4th ed. New York: McGraw-Hill, 2000.

Kant, I. *The Critique of Pure Reason*. Translated by T. K. Abbott. Chicago: Univ. of Chicago Press, 1952.

Kaplan, R. D. *The Ends of the Earth: A Journey at the Dawn of the 21st Century*. New York: Random House, 1996.

———. "Was Democracy Just a Moment?" *Atlantic Monthly*, Dec. 1997, pp. 55–80.

———. "The Lawless Frontier." *Atlantic Monthly*, March 2000, pp. 66–80.

———. "Looking the World in the Eye." *Atlantic Monthly*, May 2001, pp. 68–82.

———. "The World in 2005." *Atlantic Monthly*, March 2002, pp. 54–56.

———. "Supremacy by Stealth." *Atlantic Monthly*, Jan. 2003, pp. 65–83.

Kaufmann, W. *Existentialism from Dostoevsky to Sartre*. New York: New American Library, 1956.

———. *Critique of Religion and Philosophy*. Princeton: Princeton Univ. Press, 1958.

———. *Nietzsche: Philosopher, Psychologist, Anti-Christ*. Princeton: Princeton Univ. Press, 1974.

Kellehear, A. *Experiences near Death: Beyond Medicine and Religion*. Oxford: Oxford Univ. Press, 1996.

Keller, B. "The Thinkable." *New York Times Magazine*, May 4, 2003.

Kennedy, P. *Preparing for the Twenty-first Century*. New York: Vintage, 1993.

Kershaw, I. *Hitler, 1889–1936: Hubris*. New York: W. W. Norton, 1998.

Kertzer, J. I. "The Modern Use of Ancient Lies." *New York Times,* May 9, 2002.

Kim, J. "Epiphenomenal and Supervenient Causation." In *The Nature of Mind,* ed. D. Rosenthal. Oxford: Oxford Univ. Press, 1991.

———. "The Myth of Nonreductive Materialism." In *Supervenience and Mind.* Cambridge: Cambridge Univ. Press, 1993.

———. *Mind in a Physical World: An Essay on the Mind-Body Problem and Mental Causation.* Cambridge: MIT Press, 1998.

Kircher, T. T. J., C. Senior, M. L. Phillips, P. J. Benson, E. T. Bullmore, M. Brammer, A. Simmons, S. C. R. Williams, M. Bartels, and A. S. David. "Towards a Functional Neuroanatomy of Self Processing: Effects of Faces and Words." *Cognitive Brain Research* 10 (2000): 133–44.

Kircher, T. T. J., C. Senior, M. L. Phillips, S. Rabe-Hesketh, P. J. Benson, E. T. Bullmore, M. Brammer, A. Simmons, M. Bartels, and A. S. David. "Recognizing One's Own Face." *Cognition* 78 (2001): B1–B15.

Klagge, J. C. "Wittgenstein and Neuroscience." *Synthese* 78 (1989): 319–43.

Klein, E. *Conversations with the Sphinx: Paradoxes in Physics.* Translated by D. Le Vay. London: Souvenir Press, 1996.

Korsgaard, C. M. *The Sources of Normativity.* Cambridge: Cambridge Univ. Press, 1996.

Krakauer, J. *Under the Banner of Heaven: A Story of Violent Faith.* New York: Doubleday, 2003.

Kripke, S. "From *Naming and Necessity.*" In *The Nature of Mind,* ed. D. Rosenthal. Oxford: Oxford Univ. Press, 1991.

Krishnamurti, J., and D. Bohm. *The Ending of Time.* San Francisco: Harper San Francisco, 1985.

Kristof, N. "When Prudery Kills." *New York Times,* Oct. 8, 2003.

Krugman, P. "'Some Crazy Guy.'" *New York Times,* June 13, 2003.

Kuhn, T. S. *The Structure of Scientific Revolutions.* 1962; reprint, Chicago: Univ. of Chicago Press, 1970.

Kurzweil, R. *The Age of Spiritual Machines.* New York: Penguin, 1999.

Lahav, R. "The Conscious and the Non-conscious: Philosophical Implications of Neuropsychology." In *Mindscapes: Philosophy, Science, and the Mind,* ed. M. Carrier and P. K. Machamer. Pittsburgh: Univ. of Pittsburgh Press, 1997.

Lanier, J. "Death: The Skeleton Key of Consciousness Studies?" *Journal of Consciousness Studies* 4, no. 2 (1997): 181–85.

Lazare, D. "False Testament: Archeology Refutes the Bible's Claim to History." *Harper's,* March 2002, pp. 39–47.

Lehrer, K. *Self Trust.* Oxford: Oxford Univ. Press, 1997.

Lelyveld, J. "All Suicide Bombers Are Not Alike." *New York Times Magazine,* Oct. 28, 2001.

Leslie, J. *The End of the World: The Science and Ethics of Human Extinction.* London: Routledge, 1996.

Levi, P. *The Drowned and the Saved.* New York: Vintage, 1989.

Levine, J. "On Leaving Out What It's Like." In *The Nature of Consciousness: Philosophical Debates,* ed. N. Block, O. Flanagan, and G. Güzeldere. Cambridge: MIT Press, 1997.

Levy, L. W. *Blasphemy.* Chapel Hill: Univ. of North Carolina Press, 1993.

Lewis, B. "The Roots of Muslim Rage." *Atlantic Monthly,* March 1990, pp. 47–60.

———. "The Revolt of Islam." *New Yorker,* Nov. 19, 2001, pp. 50–63.

———. *The Crisis of Islam: Holy War and Unholy Terror.* New York: Modern Library, 2003.

Lewis, D. "Mad Pain and Martian Pain." In *The Nature of Mind,* ed. D. Rosenthal. Oxford: Oxford Univ. Press, 1991.

———. "What Experience Teaches." In *The Nature of Consciousness: Philosophical Debates,* ed. N. Block, O. Flanagan, and G. Güzeldere. Cambridge: MIT Press, 1997.

Lewontin, R. C. "The Evolution of Cognition: Questions We Will Never Answer." In *Invitation to Cognitive Science.* Vol. 4, *Methods, Models, and Conceptual Issues,* ed. D. Scarborough and S. Sternberg. Cambridge: MIT Press, 1998.

———. *It Ain't Necessarily So: The Dream of the Human Genome and Other Illusions.* New York: New York Review Books, 2000.

Libet, B. "A Testable Field Theory of Mind-Brain Interaction." *Journal of Consciousness Studies* 1, no. 1 (1994): 119–26.

———. "Do We Have Free Will?" *Journal of Consciousness Studies* 6, nos. 8–9 (1999): 47–57.

———. "'Consciousness, Free Action and the Brain': Commentary on John Searle's Article." *Journal of Consciousness Studies* 8, no. 8 (2001): 59–65.

———. "The Timing of Mental Events: Libet's Experimental Findings and Their Implications." *Consciousness and Cognition* 11 (2002): 291–99.

Lockwood, M. *Mind, Brain & the Quantum: The Compound "I."* Oxford: Blackwell, 1989.

———. "Unsensed Phenomenal Qualities: A Defense." *Journal of Consciousness Studies* 5, no. 4 (1998): 415–18.

Logothetis, N. K. "Vision: A Window on Consciousness." *Scientific American Special Edition* 12, no. 1 (2002): 18–25.

Logothetis, N. K., et al. "Neurophysiological Investigation of the Basis of the fMRI Signal." *Nature* 412 (July 12, 2001): 150–57.

Longchenpa. *Kindly Bent to Ease Us.* 3 vols. Translated by H. V. Guenther. Berkeley, Calif.: Dharma Publishing, 1975.

———. *The Four-Themed Precious Garland.* Translated by A. Berzin. Dharmsala: Library of Tibetan Works and Archives, 1978.

———. *Buddha Mind: An Anthology of Longchen Rabjam's Writings on Dzogpa Chenpo.* Translated by Tulku Thondup Rinpoche, edited by H. Talbott. Ithaca, N.Y.: Snow Lion Publications, 1989.

Luria, A. R. *The Mind of a Mnemonist.* Translated by L. Solotaroff. 1968; reprint, Cambridge: Harvard Univ. Press, 1987.

Lyon, J., and P. Corner. *Altered Fates: Gene Therapy and the Retooling of Human Life*. New York: W. W. Norton, 1995.

Lyons, F., J. R. Hanley, and J. Kay. "Anomia for Common Names and Geographical Names with Preserved Retrieval of Names of People: A Semantic Memory Disorder." *Cortex* 38, no. 1 (2002): 23–35 [abstract].

MacIntyre, A. *The Unconscious: A Conceptual Analysis*. Bristol, Eng.: Thoemmes Press, 1958.

Mackay, C. *Extraordinary Popular Delusions and the Madness of Crowds*. 1841; reprint, New York: Barnes & Noble, 1993.

Maguire, E. A., R. S. J. Frackowiak, and C. D. Frith. "Recalling Routes around London: Activation of the Right Hippocampus in Taxi Drivers." *Journal of Neuroscience* 17 (1997): 7103–10.

Maguire, E. A., C. D. Frith, and R. G. Morris. "The Functional Neuroanatomy of Comprehension and Memory: The Importance of Prior Knowledge." *Brain* 122 (1999): 1839–50.

Maha Boowa Nanasampanno. *Straight from the Heart: Thirteen Talks on the Practice of Meditation*. Translated by Thanissaro Bhikkhu. Bangkok: P. Sumphan Panich, 1987.

———. 1988. *Things as They Are*. Translated by Thanissaro Bhikkhu. Bangkok: P. Samphan Panich, 1988.

Mahasi Sayadaw. *Buddhist Meditation and Its Forty Subjects*. Translated by U Pe Thin. N.p.: Buddha Sasana Council Press, 1957.

———. *Thoughts on the Dhamma*. Kandy, Sri Lanka: Buddhist Publication Society, 1983.

———. *The Progress of Insight*. Translated by Nyanaponika Thera. Kandy, Sri Lanka: Buddhist Publication Society, 1985.

Malachowski, A., ed. *Reading Rorty*. Oxford: Blackwell, 1990.

Manchester, W. *A World Lit Only by Fire: The Medieval Mind and the Renaissance*. Boston: Little, Brown, 1992.

Margulis, L., and D. Sagan. *Slanted Truths: Essays on Gaia, Symbiosis, and Evolution*. New York: Springer-Verlag, 1997.

Marks, C. E. *Commissurotomy, Consciousness, and the Unity of Mind*. Montgomery, Vt.: Bradford Books, 1980.

Marr, D. "Understanding Complex Information-Processing Systems." In *Vision*. New York: W. H. Freeman, 1982.

Martin, J. H. *Neuroanatomy: Text and Atlas*. Stamford, Conn.: Appleton and Lange, 1996.

Masson, J. M. *My Father's Guru*. Reading, Mass.: Addison-Wesley, 1993.

Masson, J. M., and S. McCarthy. *When Elephants Weep: The Emotional Lives of Animals*. New York: Delacorte Press, 1995.

Mates, B., ed. and trans. *The Skeptic Way: Sextus Empiricus's Outlines of Pyrrhonism*. Oxford: Oxford Univ. Press, 1996.

McCormick, P. J., ed. *Star Making: Realism, Anti-realism, and Irrealism.* Cambridge: MIT Press, 1996.

McGinn, C. "Consciousness and Space." *Journal of Consciousness Studies* 2, no. 3 (1995): 220–30.

———. "Can We Solve the Mind-Body Problem?" In *The Nature of Consciousness: Philosophical Debates,* ed. N. Block, O. Flanagan, and G. Güzeldere. Cambridge: MIT Press, 1997.

———. *The Mysterious Flame: Conscious Minds in a Material World.* New York: Basic Books, 1999.

McKenna, T. *The Archaic Revival.* San Francisco: Harper San Francisco, 1991.

———. *Food of the Gods: The Search for the Original Tree of Knowledge.* New York: Bantam Books, 1992.

———. *True Hallucinations.* San Francisco: Harper San Francisco, 1993.

Medin, D. L. "Concepts and Conceptual Structure." *American Psychologist* 44 (1989): 1469–81.

Mele, A. R. "Real Self-Deception." *Behavioral and Brain Sciences* 20 (1997): 91–102.

———. "Understanding and Explaining Real Self-Deception." *Behavioral and Brain Sciences* 20 (1997): 127–36.

———. *Self-Deception Unmasked.* Princeton: Princeton Univ. Press, 2001.

Melton, J. G., ed. *American Religious Creeds.* 3 vols. New York: Triumph Books, 1991.

Menand, L. *The Metaphysical Club: The Story of Ideas in America.* New York: Farrar, Straus and Giroux, 2001.

Merikle, P. M., and M. Daneman. "Conscious vs. Unconscious Perception." In *The New Cognitive Neurosciences.* 2d ed. Edited by M. S. Gazzaniga. Cambridge: MIT Press, 2000.

Metzger, B. M., and M. D. Coogan., eds. *The Oxford Companion to the Bible.* Oxford: Oxford Univ. Press, 1993.

Miller, W. I. *Humiliation: And Other Essays on Honor, Social Discomfort, and Violence.* Ithaca: Cornell Univ. Press, 1993.

———. *The Anatomy of Disgust.* Cambridge: Harvard Univ. Press, 1997.

Minsky, M. *The Society of Mind.* New York: Simon and Schuster, 1985.

———. "Consciousness Is a Big Suitcase." 1998 Interview. www.edge.org/3rd_culture/minsky/index.html

Mischel, W. *Introduction to Personality.* 6th ed. Orlando: Harcourt Brace College Publishers, 1999.

Mishra, P. "The Other Face of Fanaticism." *New York Times Magazine,* Feb. 2, 2003.

Mitchell, S. *The Gospel according to Jesus.* New York: HarperCollins, 1991.

Monk, R. *Ludwig Wittgenstein: The Duty of Genius.* New York: Viking Penguin, 1990.

———. *Bertrand Russell: The Spirit of Solitude, 1872–1921.* New York: Free Press, 1996.

Montaigne. *The Complete Works of Montaigne.* Translated by D. M. Frame. Stanford: Stanford Univ. Press, 1943.

Murphy, J. P. *Pragmatism: From Peirce to Davidson.* Boulder, Colo.: Westview Press, 1990.

Murphy, M. P., and L. A. J. O'Neill, eds. *What Is Life? The Next Fifty Years: Speculations on the Future of Biology.* Cambridge: Cambridge Univ. Press, 1995.

Murti, T. *The Central Philosophy of Buddhism.* London: Allen and Unwin, 1974.

Naess, A. *A Skeptical Dialogue on Induction.* Assen, Netherlands: Vangorcum, 1984.

Nagarjuna. *Nagarjuna's Seventy Stanzas: A Buddhist Psychology of Emptiness.* Translated by D. R. Comito. Ithaca, N.Y.: Snow Lion Publications, 1987.

———. *The Fundamental Wisdom of the Middle Way: Nagarjuna's Mulamadhyamakakarika.* Edited and Translated by J. L. Garfield. Oxford: Oxford Univ. Press, 1995.

Nagel, T. *Mortal Questions.* Cambridge: Cambridge Univ. Press, 1979.

———. *The View from Nowhere.* Oxford: Oxford Univ. Press, 1986.

———. *What Does It All Mean?: A Very Short Introduction to Philosophy.* Oxford: Oxford Univ. Press, 1987.

———. *Other Minds.* Oxford: Oxford Univ. Press, 1995.

———. *The Last Word.* Oxford: Oxford Univ. Press, 1997.

Nahmias, E. A. "Verbal Reports on the Contents of Consciousness: Reconsidering Introspectionist Methodology." *Psyche,* Oct. 2002.

Naipaul, V. S. *Among the Believers: An Islamic Journey.* New York: Vintage, 1981.

———. *India: A Million Mutinies Now.* New York: Viking, 1990.

Namgyal, T. T. *Mahamudra: The Quintessence of Mind and Meditation.* Translated by L. P. Lhalungpa. Boston: Shambhala, 1986.

Nanamoli Thera, ed. *Selected Buddhist Texts.* Vol. 1. Kandy, Sri Lanka: Buddhist Publication Society, 1958.

———, trans. *Mindfulness of Breathing.* Kandy, Sri Lanka: Buddhist Publication Society, 1982.

Nanamoli, Bhikkhu, trans. *The Middle Length Discourses of the Buddha: A New Translation of the Majjhima Nikaya.* Edited by Bhikkhu Bodhi. Boston: Wisdom Publications, 1995.

Narada Maha Thera. *The Buddha and His Teachings.* Kandy, Sri Lanka: Buddhist Publication Society, 1973.

Newberg, A. B. "The Neuropsychology of Religious and Spiritual Experience." *Journal of Consciousness Studies* 7, nos. 11–12 (2000): 251–66.

Newberg, A. B., A. Alavi, M. Baime, M. Pourdehnad, J. Santanna, and E. d'Aquili. "The Measurement of Regional Cerebral Blood Flow during the Complex Cognitive Task of Meditation: A Preliminary SPECT Study." *Psychiatry Research: Neuroimaging Section* 106 (2001): 113–22.

Nichols, M. J., and W. T. Newsome. "The Neurobiology of Cognition." *Nature* 402 (1999): SUPP, C35–C38.

Niemeier, M., J. Douglas Crawford, and D. B. Tweed. "A Bayesian Approach to Change Blindness." *Annals of the New York Academy of Sciences* 956 (2002): 474–75. [abstract]

Nietzsche, F. *The Portable Nietzsche*. Translated by W. Kaufmann. New York: Viking, 1954.

———. *Thus Spoke Zarathustra*. Translated by W. Kaufmann. New York: Penguin Books, 1954.

———. *Beyond Good and Evil*. Translated by W. Kaufmann. New York: Vintage Books, 1966.

———. *On the Genealogy of Morals* and *Ecce Homo*. Translated by W. Kaufmann. New York: Vintage Books, 1967.

———. *The Birth of Tragedy*. New York: Dover, 1995.

Nikhilananda, Swami, trans. *The Bhagavad Gita*. New York: Ramakrishna-Vivekananda Center, 1979.

Nisargadatta Maharaj. *I Am That*. Translated by M. Frydman, edited by S. S. Dikshit. Durham, N.C.: Acorn Press, 1973.

———. *Prior to Consciousness*. Edited by J. Dunn. Durham, N.C.: Acorn Press, 1985.

———. *The Nectar of the Lord's Feet*. Edited by R. Powell. Great Britain: Element Books, 1987.

———. *The Ultimate Medicine*. Edited by R. Powell. San Diego: Blue Dove Press, 1994.

Niznik, J., and J. T. Sanders, eds. *Debating the State of Philosophy: Habermas, Rorty, and Kolakowski*. Westport, Conn.: Praeger, 1996.

Norbu, N. *The Small Golden Key*. Translated by L. Anderson. New York: Jewel Publishing House, 1977.

———. *The Crystal and the Way of Light*. Edited by J. Shane. New York: Routledge and Kegan Paul, 1986.

———. *The Cycle of Day and Night*. Translated by J. M. Reynolds. New York: Station Hill Press, 1987.

———. *Dzogchen: The Self-Perfected State*. Translated by J. Shane. London: Arkana, 1989.

———. *Dream Yoga and the Practice of Natural Light*. Edited by M. Katz. Ithaca, N.Y.: Snow Lion Publications, 1992.

Norbu, T. *Magic Dance*. New York: Jewel Publishing House, 1981.

———. *White Sail*. Boston: Shambhala, 1992.

Nørretranders, T. *The User Illusion: Cutting Consciousness Down to Size*. New York: Viking, 1998.

Nozick, R. *Philosophical Explanations*. Cambridge: Harvard Univ. Press, 1981.

Nuland, S. B. *How We Die: Reflections on Life's Final Chapter*. New York: Alfred A. Knopf, 1994.

Nyanaponika Thera. *The Heart of Buddhist Meditation*. York Beach, Maine: Samuel Weiser, 1962.

———. *The Vision of Dhamma*. Edited by Bhikkhu Bodhi. York Beach, Maine: Samuel Weiser, 1986.

———, ed. *The Three Basic Facts of Existence*. Kandy, Sri Lanka: Buddhist Publication Society, 1974.

———, ed. *The Road to Inner Freedom: A Survey of the Buddha's Teachings*. Kandy, Sri Lanka: Buddhist Publication Society, 1982.

Nyanatiloka. *Fundamentals of Buddhism*. Bauddha Sahitya Sabha, 1949.

———. *The Buddha's Path to Deliverance*. Kandy, Sri Lanka: Buddhist Publication Society, 1952.

———, trans. and ed. *The Word of the Buddha*. Santa Barbara: J. F. Rowny Press, 1959.

Nyoshul Khenpo Rinpoche. *Natural Great Perfection*. Translated by Surya Das. Ithaca, N.Y.: Snow Lion Publications, 1995.

O'Brien, C. C. *On the Eve of Millennium: The Future of Democracy through an Age of Unreason*. New York: Free Press, 1994.

Ojemann, G., J. Ojemann, E. Lettich, and M. Berger. "Cortical Language Localization in Left, Dominant Hemisphere: An Electrical Stimulation Mapping Investigation in 117 Patients." *Journal of Neurosurgery* 71, no. 3 (1989): 316–26.

Oltmanns, T. F., J. M Neale, and G. C. Davison. *Case Studies in Abnormal Psychology*. New York: John Wiley, 1999.

Ornstein, R. *The Right Mind*. New York: Harcourt Brace, 1997.

Orwell, G. "Reflections on Gandhi." In *The Oxford Book of Essays*, ed. J. Gross. Oxford: Oxford Univ. Press, 1991.

Osherson, D. N. "Probability Judgment." In *An Invitation to Cognitive Science: Thinking*, ed. E. E. Smith and D. N. Osherson. Cambridge: MIT Press, 1995.

Osherson. D.N., D. Perani, S. Cappa, T. Schnur, F. Grassi, and F. Fazio. "Distinct Brain Loci in Deductive versus Probabilistic Reasoning." *Neuropsychologia* 36 (1998): 369–76.

Osserman, R. *Poetry of the Universe: A Mathematical Explanation of the Cosmos*. New York: Doubleday, 1995.

Ott, H. *Martin Heidegger: A Political Life*. New York: HarperCollins, 1993.

Ott, J. *Pharmacotheon: Entheogenic Drugs, Their Plant Sources and History*. Kennewick, Wash.: Natural Products Company, 1993.

Padmasambhava. *Self-liberation through Seeing with Naked Awareness*. Translated by J. M. Reynolds. New York: Station Hill Press, 1989.

———. *Dakini Teachings: Padmasambhava's Oral Instructions to Lady Tsogyal*. Translated by E. P. Kunsang. Boston: Shambhala, 1990.

———. *Advice from the Lotus-Born*. Translated by E. P. Kunsang. Boudhanath: Rangjung Yeshe Publications, 1994.

———. *The Light of Wisdom with Commentary by Jamgon Kongtrul the Great*. Translated by E. P. Kunsang. Boston: Shambhala, 1995.

Pape, R. A. "The Strategic Logic of Suicide Terrorism." *American Political Science Review* 97, no. 3 (2003): 20–32.

Pascal, B. *Pensées*.Translated by A. J. Krailsheimer. New York: Penguin Books, 1966.

Patrul Rinpoche. *The Heart Treasure of the Enlightened Ones with Commentary by Dilgo Khyentse*. Boston: Shambhala, 1992.

———. *Kunzang Lama'i Shelung: The Words of My Perfect Teacher*. San Francisco: HarperCollins, 1994.

Pelikan, J. *Jesus through the Centuries*. New York: Harper and Row, 1987.

Peng, K., and R. E. Nisbett. "Culture, Dialectics, and Reasoning about Contradiction." *American Psychologist* 54 (1999): 741–54.

Pennisi, E. "Are Our Primate Cousins 'Conscious'?" *Science* 284 (1999): 2073–76.

Penrose, R. *The Emperor's New Mind*. Oxford: Oxford Univ. Press, 1989.

———. "Mechanisms, Microtubules, and the Mind." *Journal of Consciousness Studies* 1, no. 2 (1994): 241–49.

———. *The Large, the Small and the Human Mind*. Cambridge: Cambridge Univ. Press, 1997.

Perry, J. *A Dialogue on Personal Identity and Immortality*. Indianapolis: Hackett, 1978.

———. *Knowledge, Possibility, and Consciousness*. Cambridge: MIT Press, 2001.

———, ed. *Personal Identity*. Berkeley: Univ. of California Press, 1975.

Peters, E. *Inquisition*. New York: Free Press, 1988.

Pinchbeck, D. *Breaking Open the Head*. New York: Broadway Books, 2002.

Pipes, D. *Militant Islam Reaches America*. New York: W. W. Norton, 2002.

Planck, M. *Where Is Science Going?* Translated and edited by J. Murphy. 1933; reprint, Woodbridge, Conn.: Ox Bow Press, 1981.

Plato. *The Complete Works*. Edited by J. M. Cooper. Indianapolis: Hackett, 1997.

Pollack, K. H. "'The Crisis of Islam': Faith and Terrorism in the Muslim World." *New York Times Book Review*, April 6, 2003.

Popper, K. R. *The Logic of Scientific Discovery*. 1959; reprint, London: Routledge, 1995.

———. *Objective Knowledge*. 1972; reprint, Oxford: Clarendon Press, 1995.

Popper, K. R., and J. C. Eccles. *The Self and Its Brain*. 1977; reprint, London: Routledge, 1993.

Posner, R. A. *The Problematics of Moral and Legal Theory*. Cambridge: Harvard Univ. Press, 1999.

Poundstone, W. *Labyrinths of Reason: Paradox, Puzzles, and the Frailty of Knowledge*. New York: Anchor Press, 1988.

———. *Prisoner's Dilemma*. New York: Doubleday, 1992.

Price, A. F., and W. Mou-Lam., trans. *The Diamond Sutra and the Sutra of Hui-Neng*. Boston: Shambhala, 1990.

Prinz, J. "Functionalism, Dualism and Consciousness." In *Philosophy and the Neurosciences*, ed. W. Bechtel, P. Mandik, J. Mundale, and R. S. Stufflebeam. Oxford: Blackwell, 2001.

Pryse-Phillips, W. *The Oxford Companion to Clinical Neurology*. Oxford: Oxford Univ. Press, 2003.

Putnam, R. A., ed. *The Cambridge Companion to William James*. New York: Cambridge Univ. Press, 1997.

Quattrone, G. A., and A. Tversky. "Self-Deception and the Voter's Illusion." In *The Multiple Self*, ed. J. Elster. Cambridge: Cambridge Univ. Press, 1985.

Quine, W. V. *From a Logical Point of View*. 1953; reprint, Cambridge: Harvard Univ. Press, 1994.

Quine, W. V. *Pursuit of Truth*. Cambridge: Harvard Univ. Press, 1990.

Radin, D. *The Conscious Universe: The Scientific Truth of Psychic Phenomena*. New York: HarperCollins, 1997.

Ramachandran, V. S., and S. Blakeslee. *Phantoms in the Brain*. New York: William Morrow, 1998.

Ramachandran, V. S., and W. Hirstein. "Three Laws of Qualia: What Neurology Tells Us about the Biological Functions of Consciousness."*Journal of Consciousness Studies* 4, nos. 5–6 (1997): 429–57.

Ramana Maharshi. *Talks with Sri Ramana*. Tiruvannamalai: Sri Ramanasramam, 1955.

———. *The Collected Works of Ramana Maharshi*. Edited by A. Osborne. York Beach, Maine: Samuel Weiser, 1972.

———. *Self-enquiry*. Translated by T. M. P. Mahadevan. Tiruvannamalai: Sri Ramanasramam, 1981.

Reber, A. S. "The Cognitive Unconscious: An Evolutionary Perspective." *Consciousness and Cognition* 1 (1992): 93–133.

Rees, G., G. Kreiman, and C. Koch. "Neural Correlates of Consciousness in Humans." *Nature Reviews Neuroscience* 3 (2002): 261–70.

Rees, M. *Our Final Hour*. New York: Basic Books, 2003.

Rhodes, R. *Deadly Feasts: Tracking the Secrets of a Terrifying New Plague*. New York: Simon and Schuster, 1997.

Rips, L. "Deduction and Cognition." In *An Invitation to Cognitive Science: Thinking*, ed. E. E. Smith and D. N. Osherson. Cambridge: MIT Press, 1995.

Rorty, R. *The Consequences of Pragmatism*. Minneapolis: Univ. of Minnesota Press, 1982.

———. *Objectivity, Relativism, and Truth: Philosophical Papers*. Vol. 1. Cambridge: Cambridge Univ. Press, 1991

———. "Universality and Truth." 1994 MS.

———. *Hope in Place of Knowledge: The Pragmatics Tradition in Philosophy*. Taipei: Institute of European and American Studies, Academia Sinica, 1999.

Rosenbaum, R. *Explaining Hitler*. New York: Basic Books, 1998.

Rosenthal, D. *The Nature of Mind*. Oxford: Oxford Univ. Press, 1991.

Roskies, A. L. "Yes, But Am I Free?" *Nature Neuroscience* 4 (2001): 1161.

Roy, A. *War Talk*. Cambridge, Mass.: South End Press, 2003.

Rumelhart, D. E. "Schemata: The Building Blocks of Cognition." In *Theoretical Issues in Reading Comprehension*, ed. R. J. Spiro, B. C. Bruce, and W. F. Brewer. Hillsdale, N.J.: Erlbaum, 1980.

———. "The Architecture of Mind: A Connectionist Approach." In *Foundations of Cognitive Science*, ed. M. I. Posner. Cambridge: MIT Press, 1989.

Russell, B. *The Problems of Philosophy*. 1912; reprint, Indianapolis: Hackett, 1990.

———. *Religion and Science*. 1935; reprint, Oxford: Oxford Univ. Press, 1997.

———. *A History of Western Philosophy*. New York: Simon and Schuster, 1945.

———. *Why I Am Not a Christian*. Edited by P. Edwards. New York: Simon and Schuster, 1957.

Russell, J. "At Two with Nature: Agency and the Development of Self-World Dualism." In *The Body and The Self*, ed. J. L. Bermudez, A. Marcel, and N. Eilan. Cambridge: MIT Press, 1995.

Ruthven, M. *Islam in the World*. 2d ed. Oxford: Oxford Univ. Press, 2000.

Ryle, G. *The Concept of Mind*. 1949; reprint, Chicago: Univ. of Chicago Press, 1984.

Sacks, O. *The Man Who Mistook His Wife for a Hat*. New York: Harper Perennial, 1970.

———. *An Anthropologist on Mars: Seven Paradoxical Tales*. New York: Vintage, 1995.

Saddhatissa, H., trans. *The Sutta-Nipata*. London: Curzon Press, 1985.

Sagan, C. *The Demon Haunted World: Science as a Candle in the Dark*. New York: Random House, 1995.

Sagan, C., and A. Druyan. *Shadows of Forgotten Ancestors*. New York: Random House, 1992.

Said, E. W. "The Clash of Ignorance." *Nation*, Oct. 4, 2001.

———. "Suicidal Ignorance." *CounterPunch*, Nov. 18, 2001.

———. "An Unacceptable Helplessness." *Al-Ahram*, Jan. 16–22, 2003.

———. "A Monumental Hypocricy." *CounterPunch*, Feb. 15, 2003.

Santayana, G. *Skepticism and Animal Faith: Introduction to a System of Philosophy*. New York: Dover, 1923.

———. *Persons and Places*. Cambridge: MIT Press, 1963.

Sartre, J. P. *The Transcendence of the Ego: An Existentialist Theory of Consciousness*. Translated by F. Williams and R. Kirkpatrick. New York: Hill and Wang, 1937.

———. *Being and Nothingness*. Translated by H. E. Barnes. 1956; reprint, New York: Gramercy Books, 1994.

Saxe, R., and N. Kanwisher. "People Thinking about Thinking People: The Role of the Temporo-parietal Junction in 'Theory of Mind.'" *NeuoImage* 19 (2003): 1835–42.

Scalia, A. "God's Justice and Ours." *First Things*, May 2002, pp. 17–21.

Schell, J. *The Fate of the Earth*. New York: Alfred A. Knopf, 1982.

———. *The Unfinished Twentieth Century*. London: Verso, 2001.

Schilpp, P. A., ed. *The Philosophy of Bertrand Russell*. La Salle, Ill.: Open Court, 1944.

———, ed. *Albert Einstein: Philosopher-Scientist*. London: Cambridge Univ. Press, 1949.

Schlosser, E. *Reefer Madness: Sex, Drugs, and Cheap Labor in the American Black Market*. Boston: Houghton Mifflin, 2003.

Schneewind, J. B. "What Has Moral Philosophy Done for Us . . . Lately?" Undated MS.

Scholem, G. *Kabbalah*. New York: Dorsette Press, 1974.

Schooler, J. W., and J. Melcher. "The Ineffability of Insight." In *The Creative Cognition Approach*, ed. S. M. Smith, T. B. Ward, and R. A. Finke. Cambridge: MIT Press, 1995.

Schopenhauer, A. *Essays and Aphorisms*. Edited and translated by R. J. Hollingdale. London: Penguin Books, 1970.

Schrödinger, E. *My View of the World*. Translated by C. Hastings. Woodbridge, Conn.: Ox Bow Press, 1961.

———. *What Is Life, Mind and Matter and Autobiographical Sketches*. Cambridge: Cambridge Univ. Press, 1967.

Searle, J. R. *The Rediscovery of the Mind*. Cambridge: MIT Press, 1992.

———. *The Construction of Social Reality*. New York: Free Press, 1995.

———. "Consciousness and the Philosophers." *New York Review of Books*, March 6, 1997, pp. 43–50.

———. *The Mystery of Consciousness*. New York: New York Review Books, 1997.

———. "Consciousness." *Annual Review of Neuroscience* 23 (2000): 557–78.

———. "Further Reply to Libet." *Journal of Consciousness Studies* 8, no. 8 (2001): 63–65.

———. "Free Will as a Problem in Neurobiology." 2001 MS.

Sereny, G. *Into That Darkness: An Examination of Conscience*. New York: Vintage, 1974.

Shabkar, Lama. *Flight of the Garuda*. Translated E. P. Kunsang. Katmandu: Rangjung Yeshe Publications, 1986.

———. *The Life of Shabkar*. Translated by Matthieu Ricard. Albany: State Univ. of New York Press, 1994.

Shafir, E., and A. Tversky. "Decision Making." In *An Invitation to Cognitive Science: Thinking*, ed. E. E. Smith and D. N. Osherson. Cambridge: MIT Press, 1995.

Shankaracharya. *The Crest-Jewel of Discrimination*. Translated by Swami Prabhavananda and C. Isherwood. Hollywood, Calif.: Vedanta Press, 1947.

———. *Self-knowledge*. Translated and edited by Swami Nikhilananda. Mylapore, Madras: Sri Ramakrishna Math, 1987.

Shattuck, R. *Forbidden Knowledge: From Prometheus to Pornography*. New York: St. Martin's Press, 1996.

Sheldrake, R. *Seven Experiments That Could Change the World*. New York: Riverhead Books, 1995.

———. *The Sense of Being Stared At, and Other Aspects of the Extended Mind*. New York: Crown, 2003.

Sheldrake, R., T. McKenna, and R. Abraham. *The Evolutionary Mind: Trialogues at the Edge of the Unthinkable.* Santa Cruz, Calif.: Trialogue Press, 1998.

Shoemaker, S. "Self-reference and Self-awareness." *Journal of Philosophy* 65 (1968): 555–67.

———. "Functionalism and Qualia." In *The Nature of Mind*, ed. D. Rosenthal. Oxford: Oxford Univ. Press, 1991.

Simon, H. A. "What Is 'Explanation' of Behavior?" *Psychological Science* 3 (1992): 150–61.

Simons, D. J., C. F. Chabris, T. Schnur, D. T. Levin. "Evidence for Preserved Representations in Change Blindness." *Consciousness and Cognition* 11 (2002): 78–97.

Singer, P. *Writings on an Ethical Life.* New York: Ecco Press, 2000.

Singer, W. "Striving for Coherence." *Nature* 397 (Feb. 4, 1999): 391–93.

Sluga, H. "'Whose House Is That?': Wittgenstein on the Self." In *The Cambridge Companion to Wittgenstein*, ed. H. Sluga and D. G. Stern. Cambridge: Cambridge Univ. Press, 1996.

Smith, D. W. "The Structure of (Self-) Consciousness." *Topoi* 5 (1986): 149–56.

Smith, E. E. "Concepts and Categorization." In *An Invitation to Cognitive Science: Thinking*, ed. E. E. Smith and D. N. Osherson. Cambridge: MIT Press, 1995.

Smith, G. H. *Atheism: The Case against God.* Buffalo: Prometheus Books, 1979.

Spence, S. A., and C. D. Frith. "Towards a Functional Anatomy of Volition." *Journal of Consciousness Studies* 6, no. 8–9 (1999): 11–29.

Sperry, R. W. "Cerebral Organization and Behavior." *Science* 133 (1961): 1749–57.

———. "A Powerful Paradigm Made Stronger." *Neuropsychologia* 36 (1998): 1063–68.

Sperry, R. W., D. Zaidel, and D. Zaidel. "Self Recognition and Social Awareness in the Deconnected Minor Hemisphere." *Neuropsychologia* 17 (1979): 153–66.

Squire, L. R., and E. R. Kandel. *Memory: From Mind to Molecules.* New York: Scientific American Library, 2000.

Squires, E. J. "Quantum Theory and the Need for Consciousness." *Journal of Consciousness Studies* 1, no. 2 (1994): 201–4.

Stanovich, K. E., and R. F. West. "Individual Differences in Rational Thought." *Journal of Experimental Psychology: General* 127 (1998): 161–88.

Stcherbatsky, T. *The Buddhist Conception of Nirvana.* Delhi: Motilal Banarsidas, 1968.

Stevenson, I. *Twenty Cases Suggestive of Reincarnation.* Charlottesville: Univ. Press of Virginia, 1974.

———. *Unlearned Language: New Studies in Xenoglossy.* Charlottesville: Univ. Press of Virginia, 1984.

———. *Where Reincarnation and Biology Intersect.* Westport, Conn.: Praeger, 1997.

Storr, A. *Feet of Clay: Saints, Sinners, and Madmen: A Study of Gurus.* New York: Free Press, 1996.

Stroud, B. *The Significance of Philosophical Scepticism.* Oxford: Clarendon Press, 1984.

Swain, J. *The Pleasures of the Torture Chamber*. New York: Dorset Press, 1931.

Swinburne, R. *The Existence of God*. Oxford: Clarendon Press, 1979.

Tarnas, R. *The Passion of the Western Mind*. New York: Harmony Books, 1991.

Taylor, E. *William James on Consciousness beyond the Margin*. Princeton: Princeton Univ. Press, 1996.

Teilhard de Chardin, P. *Toward the Future*. Translated by R. Hague. New York: Harcourt Brace Jovanovich, 1973.

Tenzin Gyatzo (Dalai Lama). *The Buddha Nature: Death and Eternal Soul in Buddhism*. Woodside, Calif.: Bluestar Communications, 1996.

———. *Sleeping, Dreaming, and Dying: An Exploration of Consciousness with the Dalai Lama*. Edited by F. J. Varela. Boston: Wisdom Publications, 1997.

Thompson-Schill, S. L., G. K. Aguirre, M. D'Esposito, and M. J. Farah. "A Neural Basis for Category and Modality Specificity of Semantic Knowledge." *Neuropsychologia* 37 (1999): 671–76.

Thorne, K. S. *Black Holes and Time Warps: Einstein's Outrageous Legacy*. New York: W. W. Norton, 1994.

Tillich, P. *Dynamics of Faith*. New York: Harper and Row, 1957.

———. *A History of Christian Thought*. New York: Simon and Schuster, 1967.

Tipler, F. *The Physics of Immortality*. New York: Doubleday, 1994.

Tononi, G., and G. M. Edelman. "Consciousness and Complexity." *Science's Compass* 282 (Dec. 4, 1998): 1846–51.

Trachtenberg, J. *The Devil and the Jews: The Medieval Conception of the Jew and Its Relation to Modern Anti-Semitism*. Philadelphia: Jewish Publication Society, 1943.

Trevena, J. A., and J. Miller. "Cortical Movement Preparation before and after a Conscious Decision to Move." *Consciousness and Cognition* 11 (2002): 162–90.

Tsele Natsok Rangdrol. *The Lamp of Mahamudra*. Translated by E. P. Kunsang. Boston: Shambhala, 1989.

———. *The Mirror of Mindfulness: The Cycle of the Four Bardos*. Translated by E. P. Kunsang. Boston: Shambhala, 1989.

———. *The Circle of the Sun*. Translated by E. P. Kunsang. Hong Kong: Rangjung Yeshe Publications, 1990.

———. *Empowerment and the Path of Liberation*. Translated by E. P. Kunsang. Hong Kong: Rangjung Yeshe Publications, 1993.

———. *The Heart of the Matter*. Translated by E. P. Kunsang. Hong Kong: Rangjung Yeshe Publications, 1996.

Tuan, Y. *Segmented Worlds and Self: Group Life and Individual Consciousness*. Minneapolis: Univ. of Minnesota Press, 1982.

Tversky, A. "Features of Similarity." *Psychological Review* 84 (1977): 327–52.

Tye, M. *Ten Problems of Consciousness: A Representational Theory of the Phenomenal Mind*. Cambridge: MIT Press, 1995.

U Ba Khin. *The Essentials of Buddha Dhamma in Meditative Practice*. Kandy, Sri Lanka. Buddhist Publication Society, 1981.

U Pandita, Sayadaw. *In This Very Life: The Liberation Teachings of the Buddha.* Translated by U Aggacitta, edited by K. Wheeler. Boston: Wisdom Publications, 1992.

Unger, P. *Living High & Letting Die: Our Illusion of Innocence.* Oxford: Oxford Univ. Press, 1996.

Urgyen Rinpoche, Tulku. *Vajra Heart.* Translated by E. P. Kunsang. Katmandu: Rangjung Yeshe Publications, 1988.

———. *Repeating the Words of the Buddha.* Translated by E. P. Kunsang. Katmandu: Rangjung Yeshe Publications, 1992.

———. *Rainbow Painting.* Translated by E. P. Kunsang. Boudhanath, Nepal: Rangjung Yeshe Publications, 1995.

———. *As It Is.* Translated by E. P. Kunsang. Boudhanath, Nepal: Rangjung Yeshe Publications, 1999.

Van Gulick, R. "Understanding the Phenomenal Mind: Are We All Just Armadillos? Part I: Phenomenal Knowledge and Explanatory Gaps." In *The Nature of Consciousness: Philosophical Debates,* ed. N. Block, O. Flanagan, and G. Güzeldere. Cambridge: MIT Press, 1997.

Varela, F. "Neurophenomenology." *Journal of Consciousness Studies* 3, no. 4 (1996): 330–49.

Varela, F., E. Thompson, and E. Rosch. *The Embodied Mind: Cognitive Science and Human Experience.* Cambridge: MIT Press, 1991.

Vermes, G. *The Religion of Jesus the Jew.* Minneapolis: Fortress Press, 1993.

Vogeley, K., M. Kurthen, P. Falkai, and W. Maier. "Essential Functions of the Human Self Model Are Implemented in the Prefrontal Cortex." *Consciousness and Cognition* 8 (1999): 343–63.

Vogeley, K., P. Bussfeld, A. Newen, S. Herrmann, F. Happe, P. Falkai, W. Maier, N. J. Shah, G. R. Fink, and K. Zilles. "Mind Reading: Neural Mechanisms of Theory of Mind and Self-perspective." *NeuroImage* 14 (2001): 170–81.

Voltaire. *Philosophical Dictionary.* Edited and Translated by T. Besterman. London: Penguin Books, 1972.

Wallace, B. A. *Choosing Reality: A Contemplative View of Physics and the Mind.* Boston: New Science Library, 1989.

———. "Intersubjectivity in Indo-Tibetan Buddhism." *Journal of Consciousness Studies* 8, nos. 5–7 (2001): 209–30.

Walshe, M., trans. *The Long Discourses of the Buddha: A Translation of the Digha Nikaya.* Boston: Wisdom Publications, 1987.

Wansbrough, H. *The New Jerusalem Bible.* New York: Doubleday, 1990.

Washington, P. *Madame Blavatsky's Baboon: A History of the Mystics, Mediums, and Misfits Who Brought Spiritualism to America.* New York: Schocken Books, 1993.

Watson, G., ed. *Free Will.* Oxford: Oxford Univ. Press, 1982.

Watts, A. "Psychedelics and Religious Experience." *California Law Review* 56, no. 1 (1968): 74–85.

Weber, M. *The Sociology of Religion*. 1922; reprint, Boston: Beacon Press, 1991.

Weil, S. *Waiting for God*. New York: Harper and Row, 1973.

Weinberg, S. "What Price Glory." *New York Review of Books*, Nov. 6, 2003, pp. 55–60.

Weiskrantz, L. "Prime-sight and Blindsight." *Consciousness and Cognition* 11 (2002): 568–81.

Whitebread, C. H. "The History of the Non-medical Use of Drugs in the United States." *Journal of Cognitive Liberties* 1, no. 3 (2000): 29–64.

Whitehead, A. N. *Religion in the Making*. 1926; reprint, New York: Fordham Univ. Press, 1996.

Wiesel, E. *Night*. Translated by S. Rodway. New York: Bantam Books, 1960.

Wigner, E. "The Unreasonable Effectiveness of Mathematics in the Natural Sciences." *Communications in Pure and Applied Mathematics* 13, no. 1 (1960).

Wilber, K. *Sex, Ecology, Spirituality*. Boston: Shambhala, 1995.

Wills, G. "Before the Holocaust." *New York Times Book Review*, Sept. 23, 2001.

———. "With God on His Side." *New York Times Magazine*, March 30, 2003.

Wilson, A. N. *Jesus: A Life*. New York: W. W. Norton, 1992.

———. *Paul: The Mind of the Apostle*. New York: W. W. Norton, 1997.

Wilson, E. O. *In Search of Nature*. Washington, D.C.: Island Press, 1996.

Wistrich, R. S. *Anti-Semitism: The Longest Hatred*. New York: Schocken Books, 1991.

Wittgenstein, L. *Tractatus Logico-Philosophicus*. Translated by D. F. Pears and B. F. McGuinness. London: Routledge, 1922 .

———. *Philosophical Investigations*. Translated by G. E. M. Anscombe. Englewood Cliffs, N.J.: Prentice-Hall, 1953.

———. *On Certainty*. Edited by G. E. M. Anscombe and G. H. von Wright, translated by D. Paul and G. E. M. Anscombe. New York: Harper and Row, 1969.

Wrangham, R., and D. Peterson. *Demonic Males: Apes and the Origins of Human Violence*. New York: Houghton Mifflin, 1996.

Wright, R. *The Moral Animal: The New Science of Evolutionary Psychology*. New York: Pantheon Books, 1994.

Wu, M., and P. W. Cheng. "Why Causation Need Not Follow from Statistical Association: Boundary Conditions for the Evaluation of Generative and Preventative Causal Powers." *Psychological Science* 10 (1999): 92–97.

Wyman, D. S. *The Abandonment of the Jews: America and the Holocaust, 1941–1945*. New York: Pantheon Books, 1984.

Yakovlev, A. N. *A Century of Violence in Soviet Russia*. New Haven: Yale Univ. Press, 2002.

Zakaria, F. *The Future of Freedom: Illiberal Democracy at Home and Abroad*. New York: W. W. Norton, 2003.

Zuckerman, M. B. "Graffiti on History's Walls." *U.S. News and World Report*, Nov. 3, 2003.

Acknowledgments

I BEGAN writing this book on September 12, 2001. Many friends read and commented on a long essay that I produced in those first weeks of collective grief and stupefaction, and that text became the basis for this book. I am very grateful for this early feedback. I am also indebted to those colleagues and advisers who patiently awaited my return to scientific research (and to my senses). Several of them generously reviewed two chapters on the brain that did not find a place in the finished book. Their comments were much appreciated. One friend slogged through the text at every stage of its composition, found an agent for me, and helped craft the book proposal. She knows who to call should she ever require an organ transplant. My stepfather also read the entire manuscript, while under considerable time pressure, and gave very useful notes.

My agent and my editor both played an indispensable role in getting the book into its present form and on to the far side of a printer's press. My editor's assistant was a pleasure to work with throughout the entire process of writing and revisions. My copy editor at Norton performed a veritable exorcism upon the text, armed with nothing but a red pencil.

In writing this book, as in all else, I am especially indebted to my mother and to my fiancée. Both showed a level of dedication to the project that no theory of genetic or conjugal self-interest can explain. Their wise and timely interventions spared the good people at Norton abundant horror. While they are in no way responsible for the inadequacies of the book, it would be a far lesser book without them.

Index